D0444132

Ballard Branch

GRIZZLIES, GALES
—— AND ——
GIANT SALMON

NO LONGER PROPERTY OF
SEATTLE PUBLIC LIBRARY

GRIZZLIES, GALES
— AND —
GIANT SALMON

Life at a Rivers Inlet Fishing Lodge

PAT ARDLEY

HARBOUR PUBLISHING

For
Casey and Jess
Our Hearts Beat as One

Copyright © 2018 Pat Ardley
1 2 3 4 5 — 22 21 20 19 18

All rights reserved. No part of this publication may be reproduced, stored in a retrieval system or transmitted, in any form or by any means, without prior permission of the publisher or, in the case of photocopying or other reprographic copying, a licence from Access Copyright, www.accesscopyright.ca, 1-800-893-5777, info@accesscopyright.ca.

Harbour Publishing Co. Ltd.
P.O. Box 219, Madeira Park, BC, V0N 2H0
www.harbourpublishing.com

Project editor Peter A. Robson
Cover design by Setareh Ashraf
Text design by Mary White
Map by Roger Handling
Cover and interior photos courtesy of the author
Excerpt from "Dream #2" by Ken Tobias reprinted with permission of Ken Tobias
Printed and bound in Canada
Printed on forest-friendly paper certified by the Forest Stewardship Council

Harbour Publishing acknowledges the support of the Canada Council for the Arts, which last year invested $153 million to bring the arts to Canadians throughout the country. We also gratefully acknowledge financial support from the Government of Canada and from the Province of British Columbia through the BC Arts Council and the Book Publishing Tax Credit.

Canada Council   Conseil des arts
for the Arts   du Canada

BRITISH COLUMBIA
ARTS COUNCIL
An agency of the Province of British Columbia

 Canada

Library and Archives Canada Cataloguing in Publication

Ardley, Pat, author
    Grizzlies, gales and giant salmon : life at a Rivers Inlet fishing lodge / Pat Ardley.

Issued in print and electronic formats.
ISBN 978-1-55017-831-9 (softcover).—ISBN 978-1-55017-832-6 (HTML)

    1. Ardley, Pat. 2. Rivers Lodge (Rivers Inlet, B.C.). 3. Fishing lodges—British Columbia—Rivers Inlet. 4. Autobiographies. I. Title.

SH572.B8A73 2018   799.17'56097111   C2017-906451-7
                                                      C2017-906452-5

Contents

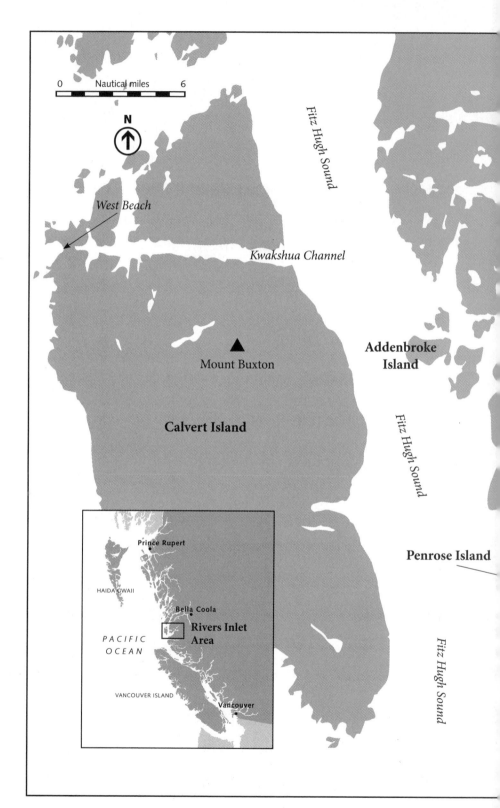

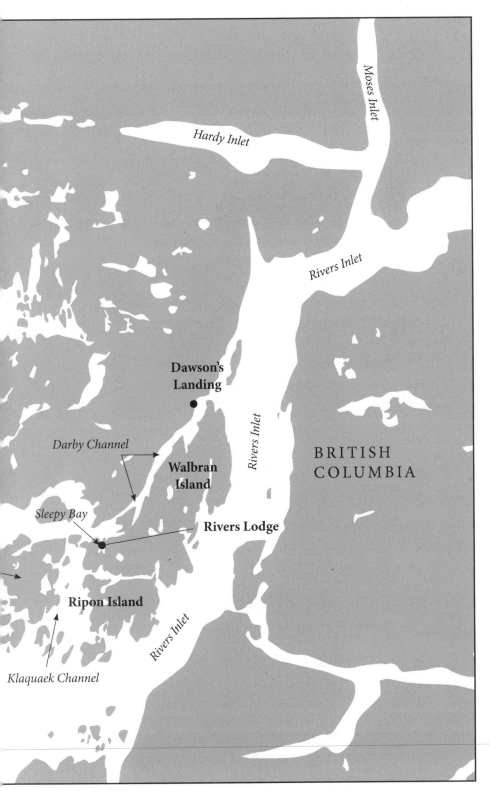

Moses Inlet

Hardy Inlet

Rivers Inlet

Dawson's Landing

Rivers Inlet

Darby Channel

Walbran Island

BRITISH COLUMBIA

Sleepy Bay

Rivers Lodge

Ripon Island

Rivers Inlet

Klaquaek Channel

I have a feeling that my boat
has struck, down there in the depths,
against a great thing.
                      And nothing
happens! Nothing . . . Silence . . . Waves . . .

—Nothing happens? Or has everything happened,
and are we standing now, quietly, in the new life?

                      —Juan Ramón Jiménez, "Oceans"

Preface

"You are living every man's dream!"

I can't tell you how many times I have heard that line in the last forty years. I would be standing with my husband, George, and a few of the guests at our isolated fishing lodge tucked in amongst the tree-covered islands at the mouth of Rivers Inlet on the Central Coast of BC. Guests would wax poetic about how wonderful our lodge is, how great the staff is, how amazing the food is, and how beautiful and wild the country is. Their eyes would light up as they told story after story of exciting adventures out on the boat, catching fish, watching whales, seeing a bald eagle pluck a salmon out of the water and struggle to reach shore. They would turn to George and tell him how lucky he is, what an amazing life he is living, how they would love to trade places with him. I was all but invisible. If there was a woman in the group, at this point she would no doubt turn to me and ask, "So, what do you do all winter? Aren't you bored the whole time?"

How could I be? I was living in the wilderness with the man people called "Hurricane" Ardley! Together he and I had built a world-class fishing resort in the middle of the remote and wild British Columbia coast. This is my side of the story!

Prologue

When he walked in, I barely looked at him but I did notice that he had a moustache and was wearing an old army jacket and a casual shirt with khaki pants. Another fellow at the table said, "George Ardley, I'd like you to meet a dear friend." George gave a curt nod in my direction, reached for a glass of beer and knocked it back. We were at the pub in the Ritz Hotel in downtown Vancouver, with a group of friends who often went there after work for a beer or two—or ten. The place was dark and smelled of stale beer and old cigarette smoke. It was 1972, and I was twenty years old. I was with my friend Janice Cruickshank who worked nearby at Placer Development, where the company had recently installed a brand new computer system that took up an entire floor. I had just arrived from Winnipeg and was staying with her until I found my own place and got my feet on the ground.

A few nights later, Janice invited all of her Vancouver friends to her parents' hotel room on Denman Street for a cocktail party. Her parents were visiting from Regina, and Janice wanted them to meet her new friends as well as see old ones who had also grown up in Regina but had recently moved to Vancouver. I was having a lovely time catching up with childhood friends that I hadn't seen since I was thirteen and moved to Winnipeg, when our host, Mrs. Cruickshank, greeted someone at the door and ushered George into the room. She tried to take his jacket to hang it up but he said, "This? This old thing doesn't need to be hung up," rolled the army jacket in a ball and tossed it behind an armchair. Well, really! I could see the look on proper Mrs. Cruickshank's face was one of distaste. I thought, "Oh my, a rebel, a renegade!" No one had ever done such a thing to Mrs. Cruickshank, the socialite wife of Judge Cruickshank. I was intrigued.

I learned from a mutual friend that George had grown up in Lake Cowichan on Vancouver Island. His parents used to own a grocery store and a café there, but now owned *The Lake News* newspaper, which kept them very busy. George often went back to Lake Cowichan to help with the artwork in the paper. He had gone to the University of British Columbia to become a dentist but then decided he preferred drawing and became a draftsman instead.

Over the next few weeks, George's friend urged him several times to take me out on a date. Of course George ignored the suggestion because someone was trying to tell him what to do. But then one day, while our group was drinking beer and discussing the car rally being organized by George's baseball team that coming weekend, George, who didn't own a car, turned to me and asked if I would like to do the race with him. I owned a car but didn't have enough money to pay for gas. "Sure," I said. "If you fill my gas tank."

I was the driver and George was the navigator as we followed the clues from checkpoint to checkpoint. It was total chaos with one hundred people bombing around the country roads just outside of Vancouver, performing silly challenges at each stop to score rally points. George and I popped balloons between us, played catch with fresh eggs and exchanged seats without getting out of the car, which was quite a feat in my little canary yellow Toyota. At one point I looked over at George and he looked back at me and I saw clear blue, kind, honest eyes that had a sparkle of humour in them. I knew I had found a keeper.

PART ONE

Lighthouse Keeping

Settling in at Addenbroke Lighthouse

"Are *you* going to the lighthouse with George?" George's mother anxiously demanded of me.

His mother was a formidable slip of a woman to whom I would have to prove myself many times before I would be considered part of the family. Her imperious voice brought a sudden hush to those who had gathered to celebrate his mom and dad's thirtieth wedding anniversary. The crowd parted like the Red Sea, and I was left to stand looking straight across at George's mom on the other side of the kitchen. We were gathered at the Vancouver home of George's sister, Marilyn, and her husband, Phil. It was my first time meeting his parents. The silence became palpable as everyone inhaled and waited for my answer.

"Yes," I said. "I am going too." Little did I know that I should have been the one who was concerned about heading into the wilderness with George.

George had been fascinated with lighthouses since an early age when his family travelled to Vancouver from Vancouver Island, passing a lighthouse just outside of the Nanaimo ferry terminal. Then years later he hiked the West Coast Trail on the wild, west side of Vancouver Island with his little brother, Jeff, from the Big Brothers organization. He renewed his fascination while speaking with the lightkeepers at the Pachena Point Lighthouse. Not long after, he saw a lighthouse-keeping job listed in the newspaper and decided to apply. It was a few months after our car-rally date that the government called to tell him they had a posting for him. At twenty-seven, George was quite happy at his architectural draftsman job but was looking for adventure. We both thought it would be fun. This turned out to be quite an understatement.

We were scheduled to leave in early April of 1973 for the Addenbroke Island Lighthouse, some three hundred miles north of Vancouver, to become junior lighthouse keepers. I arranged for a friend to use my car while we were away, and George made arrangements to sublet his apartment. There were a number of going-away parties for us, and we said goodbye to our friends with lots of music, dancing and delightful toasts. We actually said goodbye several times, as with most things governmental our travel schedule moved more slowly than planned. By the third going-away party, George was treated to an enormous, beautifully decorated cake in the face. At that point our friends may have been thinking that we would never leave.

We booked into a motel in downtown Vancouver and were there for two weeks before we finally watched our belongings being lifted onto the freshly painted Coast Guard ship that would deliver them and us to the lighthouse. We climbed on board at 10 AM but in typical fashion we didn't actually leave until about 1:30 PM. The ship zigzagged around the harbour as the crew set their new compass so we wouldn't get lost if we ran into fog on the way. We finally departed from Vancouver and headed out past Lighthouse Park then turned northwest out of Burrard Inlet.

Immediately the ship began to roll, and it didn't stop rolling for the next four days. I sat nervously holding onto a container that was strapped to the deck as I kept my eyes on the distant horizon. We left Vancouver behind and with it, all of my conscious experience with civilization, friends and family, stores full of wondrous things, and cars—all things that I would never again take for granted.

We travelled up the Strait of Georgia and passed miles and miles of shore that rose up into stunningly beautiful snow-capped mountains, miles and miles of tree-covered islands and very little else. No more cities, no towns, no crowds of people—no people! Really, no people! Except for the eight men running the ship, we were already in wilderness.

I knew nothing about coastal wilderness. My elementary school years were spent on the wide-open spaces of the Prairies, and my high school years were spent shopping with friends, eating in fancy restaurants and partying. George would be better equipped since he inherited his dad's love of tinkering with wood and motors and his aptitude for fixing anything and everything.

The West Coast of BC is so rugged with jagged rocky slopes and heavily timbered mountains, occasionally broken only by water tumbling down, that there are very few places with enough open and accessible land to settle a town or village. We cruised quickly up the Inside Passage, manoeuvring through islands, then sailed up Johnstone Strait and past the Broughton Archipelago. Past the Storm Islands and Grief Bay. Then the ship angled right and came out into the open water of Queen Charlotte Sound just beyond Cape Caution. The names of the islands and bays are an indication of what the weather is often like in this region. It's all true. Terrible storms, hurricanes and gales rage around the area for much of the winter and sometimes even suddenly out of the blue on an otherwise lovely fall day. I can attest to it all from the experiences that I gained from my new life of adventure.

We headed into Fitz Hugh Sound as we passed the entrance to Rivers Inlet, and eighteen miles north of it we approached our new home, Addenbroke Island—but kept sailing right past it. My heart sank. Apparently, dropping us off was not the skipper's first priority. Many dark hours later and, no doubt about it, many more tree-covered islands later, we docked at Prince Rupert in the wee hours of the morning and stayed the rest of the night—hallelujah!—in a hotel near the docks.

The next morning the ship was loaded with supplies, and later in the afternoon we finally boarded again and headed back down the coast toward Addenbroke Island. The ship stopped at other lighthouses as we travelled south and delivered freight, groceries and a bag of mail for the eager people living there. This was a time-consuming venture requiring all hands on deck, the ship's crane, straps and nets, and lots of yelling. George and I spent two more nights on the boat in a tiny little cabin with tiny little bunk beds and an even tinier washroom. We ate meals with the crew. The food looked delicious but I was feeling queasy with the constant rolling of the ship and was not able to enjoy any of it. Mealtimes were especially trying when you had to hold on to your plate of food or it slid across the table to the fellow sitting opposite you. Really, I just wanted to shut my eyes and roll up in a ball in my bunk. After the second night and day of travelling south, we were finally getting closer to Addenbroke again but also running out of daylight. By the time we could see the light from the tower, it was too dark to safely get off the boat and onto dry land with all our belongings. Because there was no dock and the little bay was not well protected, the ship anchored in Safety Cove across Fitz Hugh Sound, within sight of the lighthouse, but oh so far away. Safety Cove is perhaps best known as a place where Captain George Vancouver beached his ships for a time when he was exploring the West Coast in the 1790s. We spent another claustrophobic night on the ship.

Early the next morning our ship chugged over to Addenbroke. Once there, we climbed down a precarious ladder on the side of the ship and into a bobbing rowboat and then rowed to the shore right below the wharf. The ship's men used the crane to off-load our furniture and boxes of goods, plus supplies for the senior lightkeepers. They were also delivering the newfangled automation equipment for the light and horn. The Canadian government's plan was to automate all the lighthouses over the next few years. The senior keepers were not pleased to see this equipment arrive because they thought of the island as their home and didn't want to be made redundant once the island was fully automated. (They need not have worried—I am writing this forty years after the fact and the island still has lightkeepers!)

There were two houses on the island, one for the senior keeper Ray Salo; his wife, Ruth; and their preteen daughter, Lorna, and the other for the junior keepers. That would be us! The junior keeper's house had two bedrooms, a very large kitchen and a great living room with a window that covered almost one whole wall facing west toward Fitz Hugh Sound and across to Calvert Island several miles away. We could see snow-capped Mount Buxton perfectly framed by the huge window and a waterfall cascading down into the ocean. People could travel all the way up the wildly beautiful coast in a boat, anchor in the bay, walk up the boardwalk to our house and still, they couldn't help gasping at the spectacular view from our living room.

From the kitchen window we could see south to Egg Island about twenty-five miles away, and on a clear day we could even see the mountains at the north end of Vancouver Island a little over fifty miles away. Beside the big front window was a door that led out to a huge square deck. The deck had been built on the base of the site's original lighthouse, which had been pulled into the sea by ships' winches in 1968 to make room for the new lighthouse and tower on top.

The house was fantastic! We loved it, but there was one little problem. The fridge was missing. We had nowhere to store our fresh produce. Somehow that important detail was not included in the memo from the Coast Guard about the contents of the house. We got to work and made ice in the downstairs freezer and made do with a cold box until a fridge was finally delivered many months later. And, there was more than one problem. There was also no washing machine, just two sinks and no dryer either! Something about the 7.5 kilowatt Lister Petter generator (our only source of power) not being able to handle too many electrical appliances, especially those producing heat. There was a note in the memo that said, "a drying rack of light rope would be very useful indoors." How nice that the previous occupants had left a clothesline outside that we could ... *I* could use. There was also a note for us to apply for and bring with us a CNCP Telecommunications credit card so we would be able to send telegrams. Otherwise we would not be able to send quick messages to family while we were stationed there. We would receive mail about once a month when our groceries were delivered. On top of it all, there were no curtain rods or curtains so we lived without for the next year and a half—but given the wilderness setting, who needed curtains?

In the basement there was an oil furnace, which we would be grateful for when we saw how much work it was to keep the wood-burning furnace going in the senior keeper's house throughout the winter. There was also a workbench attached along one wall, and we immediately started planning which woodworking tools we would buy once we had money. The basement also had plenty of space for storing extra food supplies. We were told to have no less than two months' worth of groceries on hand at all times.

Half of the basement was a water cistern that held fresh rainwater that washed off the roof. There was a pressure pump to push the water upstairs. There was no other water source on the island so we quickly learned to conserve the precious liquid. No leaving taps running while brushing teeth, or washing dishes under running water. Ruth told us the scary story about some lighthouse people who ran out of fresh water many years before and had to have water delivered from a dirty, rusty tank off the Coast Guard tender boat. We were having none of it. To this day I can't leave a tap running for more than a few seconds.

Addenbroke Island is about two miles square, with the houses on a cleared area on the Fitz Hugh Channel side with enough area in front of the houses for two lovely, though time-consuming lawns. Other than the gardens and walkway areas, the rest of the island was covered with a thick forest of huge cedars, yew, a few small shore pines, spruce and alder as well as dense salal undergrowth—but mostly cedar. The bay was only safe to anchor in if there was good weather, which was rare in winter, and there was no safe place to build a dock because of the constant crashing waves. Instead, a wharf was built far above the high-tide line. The wharf was about 150 yards from the houses. There was a small rowboat that belonged to the station and an even smaller skiff, with an ancient motor on it, that belonged to Ray. A hydraulic derrick on the wharf lifted the small boats in and out of the water when they were needed. Halfway between the house and the wharf was a fenced garden on one side of the walkway and a short path that led through the salal bushes to the helicopter pad on the other. When it was convenient for the Coast Guard, they sometimes arrived in a helicopter between the regular monthly boat deliveries and brought our mail. And if we were notified in advance of their delivery, which was seldom, they could bring a little extra fresh produce.

Ray and George split the twenty-four-hour workday between the two of them with Ruth covering a few hours in the morning while I took a turn late in the evening to give George a chance to have a nap. During my late-night shift months later I heard a song dedicated to me on a Seattle radio station, the one channel that our radio could pick up. It made me feel like I was still connected to the outside world. The fact that I was the one who had submitted the song request to the station (by mail) meant little. Even if it was a dedication to myself, I heard my name on the radio!

George worked from midnight until 4 AM and then 10 AM to 6 PM. Ray and George worked together in the afternoon on a variety of projects to keep the lighthouse looking good and functioning well. They made repairs wherever they were needed; they painted the white buildings and the red trim, cut the grass and maintained the machinery. They worked inside if it was raining and outside if it was dry. During the day I could always hear Ray talking while they worked. Ray had a wealth

Me with the Addenbroke Island light tower in the background. Having moved from the flat, open spaces of Saskatchewan and Manitoba to the rugged wilderness of the West Coast, I was ready for adventure. I think I got more than I bargained for.

of knowledge about life on the coast. He was patient and helpful and always explained how something worked or how he wanted the job done. George soaked up the information like a sponge. Ray was like a little old elf, small but agile as he moved quickly and clamoured over rocks and up and down ladders with ease.

Part of George's job was to, once a day, radio the weather to the Coast Guard in Prince Rupert, including wind speed and wave and swell height. And at 6 PM he would take the Canadian flag down. The main duty for the middle-of-the-night shift was to keep an eye out for fog because the keepers had to go out to the generator room to manually start the foghorn if visibility went down to about two miles. The horn had a lovely deep-throated bellow that was easy to get used to. I could drift off to sleep feeling safely wrapped in the fog on solid ground while the sound of the horn washed over me.

George and I spent a lot of time talking. There is nothing quite like being stuck on an almost-deserted island on the Pacific for couples to learn how to communicate with each other. Who needs couples therapy when you have endless hours in front of you with no one else to talk to but your partner? We talked about anything and everything. We talked through our arguments, we talked over our finances, we talked about the past and we talked about the future, always with me curled up in the cozy armchair and George sprawled on the couch so we could both watch the changing scenery through our awesome front window. There was nowhere to go, so we learned a lot about each other. I thought of the saying my mom would quote to us kids when we were having a tough time: "What doesn't kill you outright, will only make you stronger." We decided that rather than killing each other outright, we would make the most of our life together on the lighthouse. We only got stronger.

Gardening, Chickens and Can You Really Eat This?

I was bent over weeding when I heard a noise. I turned to see a doe leap straight up and over the seven-foot-high fence and land three feet from my bent back. I leaped out the open gate in startled panic. The high fence all around the planted area was ostensibly there to keep the deer out.

I was learning how to garden. Ray and Ruth had a great vegetable and fruit garden that required constant care. Ruth was a kind and caring matronly woman who was generous with her knowledge. I helped with the work and learned a lot from them both. My only previous experience with gardening was with an oversized bag of English pea seeds that my big brother gave me when I was ten years old by way of an apology for dragging me around the house by my hair. I planted them in the semi-shade at the side of our house and enjoyed raiding my very own garden a few weeks later. I also picked lilacs in the back lane and sold bunches of them to unsuspecting people walking past our house. Though that might be considered more entrepreneurship than gardening.

The underbrush from the surrounding forest on Addenbroke was relentlessly trying to take back the land. I was constantly pulling little salal plants out from where they had popped up after creeping underground five, ten and sometimes fifteen feet into the garden. I felt right at home—weeding, raking in nutrient-rich seaweed and compost or helping to tie up the beans and raspberry bushes. It didn't matter what the job was, I dug in and enjoyed it all. Except for the slugs—great big banana slugs. So disgusting. They stampeded in from the forest. One night I walked out onto the back deck in bare feet and stepped right onto a huge squishy, slimy one. It popped under my foot and oozed between my toes. I let out a blood-curdling scream that brought George running, terrified that I was being electrocuted. He was relieved to see me hopping on one foot very much animated and alive. Ruth and I sharpened the ends of a few sticks and marched up and down the rows of vegetables poking the sticks through the slugs. We had to de-slug the garden every day. Every once in a while Ruth, Lorna and I walked around the extensive front lawns with our sticks. We each called out the number as we poked into them. "125," "126," "127"! When there were six or seven slugs on a stick we would fling the slugs over the cliff at the bottom of the lawn and into the ocean. One morning we poked over four hundred giant slugs onto our sticks.

Ruth gave me broccoli, cabbage, cauliflower and tomato seeds to plant in flats in the basement. There was lots of light downstairs since the generator ran all day 365 days a year and, because it was diesel, we needed to leave all the lights on for a more even load on the engine. (If we weren't using enough electricity, the exhaust pipe would throw out thick black smoke and all the pipes and anything nearby would get gummed up with oily sludge.) The seeds sprouted quickly, and in a few weeks I planted the seedlings outside. My garden would provide an important part of our diet on the island since we couldn't be sure that we would receive fresh produce more than once a month. This was serious business. There was not a little green grocer around the corner. I added peas, carrots, lettuce, spinach, radish and kale seeds to my next grocery order. I also sent for several gardening books from the library in Nanaimo. The long-distance library service was my new best friend. I studied the gardening books and several seed catalogues during my late-night shifts and acquired a lifelong love of working with plants.

We had brought a dear little sheltie dog named Kobe with us. Friends of ours from Vancouver were going to be out of the country for a couple of years, and we said we would look after him. At first he tried to herd the chickens, but they didn't react the way his DNA told him they should. We told him not to chase them. Then he spied the seagulls flying overhead and became obsessed with getting them into an organized flock. He loved to chase after the seagulls right through a bunch of chickens, scattering them in all directions as they squawked and complained. *What? I didn't see them!* There were a few deer that came down to eat the grass but he learned very quickly that he wasn't allowed to chase them either. He often ran right past the deer as he was looking up at the seagulls, and the deer would then chase him for a few steps reaching to hit his back with their deadly front hooves. He did a great job of chasing the seagulls away from pooping on our roof and therefore our freshwater supply, but we had to keep him in the house part of the day because he couldn't stop chasing after them, and they were everywhere and completely impossible to herd. He would crawl exhausted onto the porch, foaming at the mouth, but if a seagull flew overhead he would take off at full speed and once again try to take control.

We built a makeshift chicken coop after Ray and Ruth gave us a dozen bantam chickens. They had been running free but they settled down quickly and were producing eggs within days of their move into a huge unfenced area behind the house that we covered with fishnet. The net draped over salal bushes and around cedar trees and over stumps and fallen logs. The chickens were comfortable and I'm sure they soon learned that they were much safer under the net. There were eagles and hawks in the area that often helped themselves to the chickens that were loose. Also, the free-range chickens tended to hide their eggs, and when you found them you had to put them in a bowl of water to see if they sank or not to check if they were fresh. You don't eat the ones that float. But sometimes they kind of stood on end and I am here to tell you not to try opening an iffy egg.

We composted everything until we got the chickens. Then we fed everything to the chickens and used their manure in the garden. Straight chicken manure is too strong to use right away. I had a lesson in manure-tea brewing from Ray and could safely use the brew to water and fertilize the plants, skimming the "tea" off the top and leaving the manure on the bottom of the five-gallon bucket.

We took turns picking raspberries. Ray and Ruth let us pick the berries from their well-established and amazingly prolific bushes every second day. They were like manna from heaven. I made raspberry jam for the first time ever and can wax poetic about how wonderful it was with butter on fresh bread right out of the oven. More about the bread later.

During the summer, two of the young chickens turned out to be roosters and started fighting. They were vicious when they fought and gouged great tears into each other before one would back down. Ray said the only way to stop the fighting would be to chop their heads off. Ray was not a romantic. He and George went out one day with an axe and caught both roosters. They walked with them over to a stump by the garden. I didn't watch but was there when George came back to the house looking rather pale, with two dead roosters in his hands. Ray had instructed George on what to do with them. We couldn't waste them. He set up a plank outside between two chairs to use as our worktable, and I boiled a big pot of water in the kitchen. We dipped each headless body in the hot water then ran outside, laid the birds on the planks then began plucking out the feathers. This was not something I had ever pictured myself doing but it was easier than I thought it would be. Then we had to clean the guts out. George made a cut into the first rooster and tentatively put his hand into the cavity. His face quickly turned the colour of the bright green grass we were standing on. When he started to gag I told him to go away, and I finished the job. It was gooey, it was smelly and it was disgusting but I figured that somebody had to do it!

I put the roosters in plastic and then into the freezer. I wanted to distance myself from them, and from the smell of innards that I couldn't get out of my nose, before I would be able to think about eating them. It was months before I had the nerve to cook one. I made the mistake of baking it in a pan in the oven. The poor thing was so tough that we couldn't get the meat off the bones or even the skin away from the meat. It was like trying to eat an India rubber ball. Another few weeks had to go by before I cooked the other bird in a pressure cooker and we had a wonderful chicken dinner that was tender and oh so delicious.

One morning there were suddenly thousands and thousands of herring in the bay where the wharf was. Ray showed us how to use a small net to scoop quickly through them and drop our catch into a bucket. We stood in knee-deep water with the herring swirling all around us and scooped up several buckets full. I cooked a pan of them for dinner but we decided that we didn't like eating fried herring—way too many bones. Ray suggested that we could turn them into chicken food by boiling a bunch with oatmeal. I made a huge batch of herring porridge and after it cooled threw glops of it to the chickens. They loved it, and over the next few days they ate every bony lump. But after the second day, we noticed that the eggs were taking on a distinctly fishy taste. Who knew this could happen? It's one thing to eat fish and eggs, but quite another to eat fishy eggs. The mind boggles at the possibilities here ... oatmeal and bacon porridge for bacony eggs, or oatmeal and mushroom porridge for

Coast Guard ships and helicopters delivered our supplies at Addenbroke Island. Shown here is the buoy and lighthouse tender *Alexander Mackenzie*. Freight day at the lighthouse was always exciting. We received mail orders and letters, care packages from our families and groceries that had been ordered a week before, including frozen meat and fresh produce.

an instant mushroom omelette? I was more careful about what I fed the chickens after that.

The herring had come to lay their eggs on the kelp in the bay. A few days later Ray took us down to the wharf, waded into the water and reached for a strand of kelp that was covered with eggs. He put the kelp in his mouth and pulled the strand out between his teeth, snagging the eggs as it went. Such a funny texture. Like fresh, salty, fishy Rice Krispies. The eggs popped in your mouth in a not unpleasant way. Not my favourite seafood experience, but there would be others that would be worse.

George and I went back down to the bay the next day to try the herring eggs again. I brought a washtub along in case there was something interesting to put in it. Suddenly George shouted, grabbed the gaff and leaned out over the water. I could see an octopus gliding around in the shallows, probably after the same thing we were there for. George snagged one tentacle and started pulling the rest of it toward him. It was looking at us with one huge unblinking eye. He had it almost within reach but the beast wrapped several tentacles around a rock. I was jumping up and down with excitement banging the washtub on the rocks because it just happened to be in my hands. Every time the octopus seemed to be coming closer, it would reach out another tentacle and suction-cup itself onto the rock. George had a good hold of one tentacle but more and more of its appendages wrapped around the rock. George put up a good fight, but the octopus was in its element. Eventually the gaff slipped through the octopus's flesh and it swooshed off into a cloud of deep inky black water. We were not going to have fried octopus for dinner that night. I can't say that I was disappointed.

Clams, Tools and Protecting the West Coast's Inside Passage

Very early one misty morning we went with Ray to a little beach made of broken clamshell. We brought buckets and pitchforks and a shovel. The tide was very low so there was a good mound of beach showing where we could dig. Most of this shore would usually be underwater for at least half of the day. We dug close to the waterline and pulled out big fat butter clams about four inches wide and dropped them in a bucket with salt water. We filled several buckets with clams and sloshed more water on them to wash off any loose shell or sand. When we got back to the bay by the wharf, we poured more salt water on them and put the buckets in the shade. We left them there for a few hours so the clams could clean the sand out of their systems.

In the meantime, we helped Ruth wash and sterilize cans that they bought by the case for canning clams and salmon. After the clams had soaked for the rest of the morning, we hauled them up to the house so George and I could shuck them one by one in our kitchen sink. George split the shell open and I cut the meat out and dropped it into a big bowl. Then we took the bowl of meat over to Ruth's kitchen and filled the waiting cans, which we then fed to a machine that crimped lids onto the cans. We borrowed a very large enamel pot and carried it and our share of the cans back to our house and started the long process of boiling-water bath canning.

My cookbook said that you were *never* to can meat or fish in a boiling-water bath. The canning authorities felt that there was a very real danger of the bacteria that cause botulism contaminating the cans. But Ruth told us that she and everyone she knew over the years who lived on the coast had always used this method. You were just supposed to do it longer than if you were using a pressure canner. So instead of ninety minutes in a pressure canner, something none of the old-timers owned, the cans had to be covered with rapidly boiling water for four hours. I topped the pot up with more hot water every once in a while as it boiled away. Then at the end of four hours, I carefully lifted the cans one at a time out of the hot water onto a towel on the counter. After a few minutes the cans started to *ping,* a sound that indicated that the lid was being sucked down as a vacuum was being formed. When the cans had cooled for a few hours, it was easy to see if one hadn't sealed properly because the lid would not be concave. Also, when you tapped on them, you were supposed to hear a high *ping* and not a *klonk* sound.

One of George's favourite meals was clam chowder, but after handling the slimy things all day, the last thing I wanted to eat for supper was a clam. We piled the tins in the pantry and after a few weeks I was quite happy to make a big pot of chowder with them. I seem to have a short memory.

When we weren't out clamming or catching herring, we liked to get cozy on the couch and read aloud to each other. During our stay at the lighthouse we read through my *Complete Sherlock Holmes* and then the entire *Lord of the Rings* series, including *The Hobbit*. It was a favourite part of the day, to sit down with a nice cup of coffee and read a chapter or two, or if it was raining, three or four. Ray and Ruth's daughter, Lorna, who was a dark-haired, dark-eyed bundle of mischief, would come over and listen whenever she could get away from school work. Of course we had no telephone, TV or VCR or PVR or satellite or cable or computer, and the internet would have been the stuff of science fiction.

By this time both George and I had paid off our credit card bills from before coming to the lighthouse, so George, the only one with a paycheque coming in, was finally able to buy his first tool. We looked at the tools and machinery sections of Ray's catalogues first and finally settled on a hammer from the Sears catalogue. George wrote a cheque and put it with the order form into a stamped envelope. The supply ship wasn't going to be arriving with, or picking up mail for three weeks, so we watched and waited for a boat to be passing by on the way south.

A few days later George could see a commercial fishboat a couple miles up the channel. They don't travel very fast so he had time to run past Ruth's house to collect any outgoing mail that she had and then down to the wharf where he lowered the skiff into the water. He hurried down the steps and pulled the boat in closer so he could jump into it. Then he started the engine and headed out into Fitz Hugh Sound. By this time the fishboat was almost in line with the island but was quite a ways offshore. George headed out of the bay going full speed and happily bounced and bumped over the waves until he caught the skippers' attention. (When George was young, one of his favourite things to do was to use up the tank of gas his dad gave him on a Saturday morning, going around in big circles on their boat in calm Cowichan Lake, making waves to bounce over! When his tank of gas ran out, he would row his boat back to the dock.) The fellow on the fishboat slowed his boat down and George pulled alongside, and with his engine still running, George reached up and handed the little packet of letters over to him with a friendly request that he mail them for us. The fellow shouted out to him that he would drop the letters in the first mailbox he passed but it may not be for a day or two. George thanked him and, slowing his engine, let the fishboat pull away and continue on its way. George then turned his boat around and headed back to shore.

Three weeks later when the supply ship dropped off our mail, there was a parcel from Sears. George's hammer had arrived. We did a little happy dance and would remember this for a long time as the start of a very extensive tool collection. Behind the shed on the wharf, there was a pile of two-by-fours that had been left behind from previous government projects. The government wouldn't bother retrieving surplus building supplies because of the cost of transporting them back to town. George made two coffee tables and a few indoor planters using the old wood. His first big project was to make a bed for us. Until this point, we just had a mattress on the floor. He borrowed some of Ray's tools and, using more of the leftover wood, he made a four-poster bed with a carved headboard and footboard. He spent hours and hours carving the top of each four-by-four post into a round ball.

Our lighthouse living room with George's handiwork with two-by-fours. There were amazing views from the front window. We spent many hours lounging here with one of us reading aloud through *The Complete Sherlock Holmes* and *The Lord of the Rings* trilogy.

During my late-night shift one night when I was the only one in charge of the safety of boats and ships travelling in front of our lighthouse along BC's Inside Passage, I heard a thump on the side of our house. Then another, and another. At first, I thought it might be Ray and Ruth's son, John, who lived in Rivers Inlet and worked as a logger and log salvager and sometimes came to visit his parents. John had a bushy beard and wild hair, and his everyday uniform consisted of heavy wool pants, a grey Stanfield's shirt and suspenders—and he seemed to be joined at the hip to his tugboat. He was often visiting his family here, and now I thought he might be playing another trick on me. Something he and Lorna loved to do. The thumps continued while I crept from room to room trying to see out the windows. It got spookier and more disturbing as I went. Were there a whole bunch of people attacking our house from all sides? But why? I knew I would already have been seen by what sounded like a huge mob because anyone could easily see in the windows at night since the rooms of our house were always lit up like a used-car lot. I couldn't see out, but while standing at the kitchen window, there was another *thwack!* right into the window, inches from my face. It looked like a bird. It *was* a bird—and *birds*! Hundreds! *Thousands!* I was in the middle of an Alfred Hitchcock movie. The thudding on the walls woke George and, curious to find out what was going on, he joined me at the kitchen window.

He was intrigued and wanted to get a closer look. I put on a big sou'wester and, holding my hands in front of my face, followed very closely behind George out the door onto the deck where we could see swarms of birds kamikaze-flying into the house and lighthouse tower. Short of turning off the navigation light, there was nothing we could do to stop the deadly deluge.

In the morning, Ray told us that they were rhinoceros auklets. They nest in burrows along the coast and often feed at night to stay safe from predators. They were being blinded by the lights, especially the huge spotlight that could be seen for miles. Ray said that this strange behaviour happened every few years. Such a sad waste. Some managed to escape with only a bump, but we collected hundreds of little bird bodies in the morning and gave them a burial at sea.

One day, the helicopter arrived with our mail a week before the supply ship was scheduled to be there, which was such a nice surprise. But then when the supply ship did arrive, it was so anticlimactic, since it brought no mail. So disappointing—we lived for the mail service. I began to think that maybe I wasn't cut out for this kind of wilderness of the spirit. Then John arrived with a load of mail for us that had been sitting for two weeks in the post office at Dawsons Landing, our alternate mailing address. The general store at Dawsons Landing has the closest post office and is about six miles south of Addenbroke and eight miles up a side channel of Rivers Inlet called Darby Channel. We didn't realize that it would be so hard for us to get to the store, quite impossible really, since we didn't own a boat. We would have to see if we could borrow Ray's boat once we knew the area a little better.

There were cards and letters and a parcel from George's sister Gery. She had mailed us a bottle of wine! Unfortunately, she didn't want to get into trouble with the feds at the post office if the bottle gurgled en route, giving away its true identity, so she opened the bottle, topped it up with water and re-corked it, then covered the top with wax to seal it! It was not the best glass of wine, but even watered down it was better than no wine, which is the usual sad state of affairs when one is so far from civilization!

We had been there for almost three months and, in spite of the warm weather, we had yet to receive a fridge.

Exploring the Wilderness

George liked to get away from "it all." One day we headed out hiking and I found that it was more like slogging once you were about six feet into the bush. There was a lot of heavy coastal underbrush, mostly salal, amongst the towering spruce and cedar trees. Huge trees had fallen over the years and were hard to climb over or under. Occasionally we had to scramble straight down ravines and then straight up on the other side, clutching at little clumps of roots, young bushes or sometimes prickly young spruce trees to steady ourselves. We then came to an area that was impassable. We couldn't go up or down or over or under and had to turn and claw our way back to the water. We were sort of swimming across the top of the thick salal, our bodies far above the actual ground. I had been so hoping for an easier route back to our house and its lovely expanse of wide-open green front lawn. We finally "swam" our way out toward the edge of the island, which at this point was a rock face, straight down to the water with a thin ledge about sixteen feet above the rocky beach. Waves were crashing and swirling on the rocks far below.

George could see how nervous I was, and said, "Trust your boots. They have a good solid sole and will keep you safe."

I stared down at the thin strip of rock cliff that was little more than half an inch in width. I was supposed to walk back, along this? I would have preferred a skyhook to lift me out of there. I put my foot on the ledge and without letting go of the branch in my hand, I tested my boot by bouncing slightly and could feel that it wouldn't slip off the narrow ledge. I reached over and found another handhold and brought my other foot onto the ledge. This was going to take a while. I carefully reached again and pulled myself over, one boot and one hand at a time. After I had taken six steps across the sheer face, I came to a vertical crack, a fissure in the rock. It was about three feet deep and narrowed as it went in. Peering into the darkness, I could see a little brown bottle stuck near the back of the opening.

I called George to come back and see what I had found. He worked his way back along the ledge to where he could peer in and see the little bottle. It was in as far as he could reach and he tried to pull it out but it was stuck fast. He carefully inched his fingers into his pocket and slowly pulled out a small knife, then he chipped away at the rock around the bottle. After a few minutes he was able to free the bottle from the crack and gently slid it into his jacket. My mind jumped to the stormy wave that must have carried the little bottle and inserted it into the gap without shattering it on the rocks. *Ooops!* I had forgotten for a moment that I was still perched sixteen feet above the waves crashing over the rocks below.

Just past the ledge we came to a wider shelf where we stopped and lit a fire with our usual allotment of one match. George had a competitive streak—that I had witnessed before on the badminton court, baseball field and at the bridge table—which meant we always had to light the fire with only one match. We each wore a small backpack on our treks, with a small jar to keep matches dry, water bottles and a snack. On this trip, George carried the hot dogs and I carried a small pouch of flour. George cut branches to spear the hot dogs on and I mixed flour and water to make bannock wrapped around a fat stick. After cooking the bannock, you pulled it off and stuffed the cooked hot dog in. I crushed a few thimbleberries that I picked from the bushes surrounding our ledge and spread the delicious jam on the extra bannock.

I would have loved a refreshing nap but we persevered, tramping through the woods for another two hours before we eventually saw the red roof of one of the houses. Strangely we had gotten lost on this little island. My sense of direction was born of the Prairies, where, in the wide-open spaces, I always knew which direction I was headed because I could always see, or at least feel, where the sun was. Down in the darkness of the forest surrounded by two-hundred-foot cedar trees, I barely had a feeling of where the sun was supposed to be. And George hadn't brought his trusty compass with him. I was worn to a frazzle. I felt like the cat on the Pepé Le Pew cartoons to George's Pepé Le Pew.

Ray let us use his speedboat to explore around the island. Addenbroke Island is at the entrance to Fish Egg Inlet. This inlet had not yet been surveyed so it was exciting to poke into all the little bays and channels, feeling like we were the first ones there since Captain Vancouver's crew. We weren't though. There were ruins of two First Nations' villages near a great clam beach. Both villages had been burned to the ground in the early 1930s. There was also a small safe anchorage on the north side of Fish Egg with a little wooden sign that read "Joes Bay" tacked on a tree that leaned out over the water.

At low tide in the back of the bay, there is a waterfall more than three feet high coming from a tidal stretch of water called Elizabeth Lagoon. At some points the lagoon is over four hundred feet deep and about a mile wide so, as the tide falls, there is a huge volume of water that comes crashing and tumbling out through a very narrow gap in the rocks. It's very impressive to see but you really don't want to get caught in the lagoon when the tide starts to fall or you will be stranded for many hours. At least until the water calms down around a high slack tide, which is when the high tide changes direction, stops going in or coming out and momentarily stands still so you have a chance to escape the lagoon at last. We almost got caught. But usually George knew enough to read the day's tide table before we headed out in the boat. Usually, but not always! Huge drifts of thick white bubbly foam pile up along the shore just outside the waterfall from the force of the water churning out. I have always fancied that the bubbles are from the grizzly bears having a bath just out of sight. There is a large grizzly bear population in this vast mountainous wilderness area.

We headed back to the wharf at Addenbroke when it was close to low tide. George stopped the boat near the edge of a patch of bull kelp, where you could see the top six feet of the stem ending in a baseball-sized bulb with its long flat leaves ebbing and flowing with the surging of the swell like streams of mermaid hair caught in the current. I leaned over the side and cut several two-foot-long hollow pieces, including the large bulb. I had read that you can pickle bull kelp, so I was going to give it a try. The most applicable recipe that I could find for the kind of texture I was dealing with was one for watermelon rind pickles in an old pickling book my mom sent to me. I spent days boiling, draining, chopping, brining, boiling again, draining, spicing and boiling again before I was finally able to pack the "pickles" into the sterilized jars. In the end, they were actually quite tasty, and I would eventually add them to my Christmas parcel for my mom and dad, which also included salmonberry tea leaves in hand-stitched muslin bags, our canned clams, my fabulous jelly that I would make and canned salmon from the lovely coho that we were soon to catch.

George's sister could order a side of beef from a local butcher in Vancouver that she would share with us. The butcher would freeze our nicely wrapped portion and box it up for Marilyn to deliver to the Coast Guard in Vancouver. Our district manager in Prince Rupert told us that we would have to get the captain's permission to allow this box to be carried on their ship. George checked who the skipper would be for the upcoming trip and learned that it would be the crabby-pants fellow, so it was unlikely that he would grant permission. Also, the boat might have taken two weeks to get from Vancouver to Prince Rupert and might not have stopped here on its way by. In which case the meat would have sat in Rupert for a month before being sent down here. Marilyn's plan just wasn't going to work, so we were back to ordering super-expensive meat from Prince Rupert.

We used Ray's little boat to cross Fitz Hugh Sound and drive up Kwakshua Channel almost to the other side of Calvert Island. There is a narrow slip of land at the end of the channel where Ray said we could safely anchor the boat and walk across to a nice beach. We anchored the boat with an ingenious method using two ropes. George coiled the anchor and one rope over the prow of the boat, then he attached a second rope to the first one and took it to shore when we climbed out onto the beach. George pushed the boat off the beach and when he was satisfied that it had floated to a safe spot, he jerked on the rope in his hand and the anchor dropped overboard securing the boat nicely in deep water. Then he tied his end of the line to a huge cedar tree.

A note about the terminology: Growing up on the Prairies, when I heard someone talking about going to "the beach," I always thought of pretty, blue, calm, fresh lake water and long stretches of white sand with people lying about on towels and lounge chairs, radios playing the latest rock music and five popsicles for a quarter. People in this wild coastal country call anything between the ocean and the lowest branches hanging over the water "the beach." It can be made up of mucky mud, broken clamshell, heavy gravel or jagged, barnacle-covered rocks and still be called "the beach." It was hard to wrap my head around this.

On this beach, there was an old cabin just past the high-tide mark built by people from Ocean Falls about twenty miles away. Anyone was welcome to use it. We followed a trail that led out behind the cabin and crossed the island to the west and the open ocean. The forest here was quite different from the rest of the island, with less underbrush and very large trees but farther apart. It was quite easy to follow the trail between the trees, huckleberry bushes, and barberry and Oregon grape shrubs. We passed a giant cedar tree that had a huge scary mask carved into it that was painted deep red and blue and had a huge pointed nose sticking out. Then a little farther along the trail was a tree that had been bent down and then around so that it grew straight back up. It created an almost two-foot round frame for people to peek through to have their picture taken. There must be thousands of photos of happy faces in that frame. We later learned that a certain Dr. George Darby had slowly and patiently shaped the tree over all the years that he lived in the area. He had been working as a medical missionary based in nearby Bella Bella throughout the year and in the Rivers Inlet area during the sockeye-fishing seasons for over forty years, from his first season shortly after graduating from medical school in 1914 to his last in 1959 when he retired. Many years later the tree was knocked down by an overzealous logger trying to make his fortune with the surrounding trees.

We followed the trail for a few more minutes picking huckleberries as we went, then once again came to a very different type of forest. The trees were smaller and mostly coniferous with old man's beard moss gracefully trailing from the branches in great long tendrils. The forest floor was covered in thick soft moss with low trillium flowers and tiny lady's slipper orchids peeking out. The light filtered down through the trees and gave the area an otherworldly feeling. It was enchanting and I half expected to see fairies dancing about. We could hear the waves rolling and crashing onto the beach but couldn't see water yet.

There was a bit of salal to push through, and then we stepped up onto a log with a clear view of the most magical stretch of white-sand beach and bright blue ocean with waves curling up and breaking onto the sand.

Over many years, medical missionary Dr. George Darby bent this tree on Calvert Island. The tree is situated on the route to what we called West Beach. Everyone who crossed the island to West Beach had to stop and have their photo taken through the frame.

It completely took my breath away. The beach was at least a mile long with logs all akimbo at the high points where they had been pushed up by the tide and winter storms. It curved around slightly with rock cliffs at either end. There were several tiny islands with short deformed and gnarly trees a hundred yards offshore. We leaped off the log and ran and ran and ran. I hadn't realized how much I missed stretching my legs. I felt free and laughed and cried as I ran, the clean white sand squeaking with every flying step.

We then slowed to a stop, turned and stared at the beauty of this incredible place. How could we be so lucky? We hadn't been told how special this beach was. Just past the winter high-tide mark the beach was lined with low bushes and in a few places there were steep, sculpted rock walls. Along the walls there were narrow ledges with wild strawberries growing as if someone had planted them there. The bushes were all slanted away from the water, and the trees beyond them were beaten, twisted, gnarled and pushed in that direction by savage winter winds. Tall grasses were growing high up on the beach with purple beach peas and bright red fireweed safely tucked in amongst them. Lanky columbines, yarrow plants and huge cow parsnips grew above the tide line. About halfway down the beach there were sand dunes that gradually rose fifty feet high that we climbed and then threw ourselves down, stumbling and leaping, shrieking and rolling to the bottom. Then we picked ourselves up and walked along the waterline where the sand was wet, and seaweed and shells were washing up on the waves. The water was icy cold but it felt wonderful when I stood still and it eddied around my bare feet as the sand slipped away from under them.

We walked back to where we came out of the woods and built a fire to cook our go-to hiking lunch of hot dogs. Even looking for bits of firewood felt special as we poked around under logs and cut hot-dog sticks from the shrubbery. We sat quietly on a log and stared out to sea while we ate. We were full of the wonder of this place. It was here on this beach that we first talked about getting married.

Visitors and Visiting

We had the luxury of a few visitors at Addenbroke. Every few months, and if weather permitted, the *Thomas Crosby V*, an eighty-foot ship owned and run by the United Church, anchored in the bay, and the minister would row to shore and climb up to the wharf.

Sometimes his wife and a few of the crew came with him. They had a small library on board, and it was a treat to be able to pick up a few extra books and trade ones I had already read. We didn't discuss religion, but we did enjoy having someone new to talk to. George and I both felt a spiritual connection to the beauty and grandeur of the wilderness setting of the island, and the minister appreciated and understood our feelings. They were often keen to have a bit of a party, and it seemed to us they were just happy sharing their joy with the often forgotten remote communities along the coast.

In the middle of August, George's mom and dad came for a visit. They drove to Port Hardy on the north end of Vancouver Island and then flew in a Gulf Air float plane right to our island. The pilot circled a couple of times before landing on the water and taxiing into the bay. This gave us time to run to the wharf, lower the speedboat and then motor out to meet them. George's dad, Ernie, climbed eagerly down the airplane steps and into the boat, then George and the pilot had a heck of a time manoeuvring George's mom, Irene, out of the plane, down the three steps onto the pontoon and into the little bobbing boat. It was like trying to stuff a cat into a tub of water. I was anxiously waiting on the beach and willing her not to tip out the other side. I couldn't tell for sure, but Irene had the look about her like she might have had a wee dram before climbing into the plane.

Irene and Ernie were great houseguests. They were interested in everything we did, and we were happy to tell them all about our secluded life here and how amazing it was that we were still enjoying spending all our time together. That afternoon, George took Ernie fishing and they caught a beautiful coho. We planned to celebrate with a wonderful dinner of fresh salmon and lots of fresh produce that Irene and Ernie brought with them. We invited Ray, Ruth and Lorna to join us. I had never cooked for so many people before so by the time we were finally sitting down to eat, it was quite late. No one was in a hurry though, since there was no place else to go.

We were having a lovely time when suddenly there was a knock on the door. We all looked around the table to see if anyone was missing. Our glances nervously returned to the door. It was unheard of for anyone to turn up unexpectedly, especially after darkness had fallen. George finally stood up and went to open the door. An axe murderer was wielding his weapon—no, actually it was only John, Ray and Ruth's son. He had arrived from the north side of the island so he hadn't driven past in front of the houses. One of us would have surely seen or heard him go by if he had. Then he had anchored his tugboat in the bay, used his own skiff to get to shore and knowing that we didn't know he was there, he thought it would be fun to knock and give us all a fright! Well, he had succeeded! We all laughed nervously and pretended not to be surprised or scared. I wasn't the only one thinking about the lighthouse keeper who had been murdered behind the wharf shed at Addenbroke in late 1929—a murder that is still unsolved.

George took his dad fishing early each morning and they always came back with huge grins and bright silver coho. They didn't have to go far; just below the lighthouse was the perfect spot. The tide, the lack of early morning wind, the way the feed follows the shoreline—all provided the best fishing conditions. Ernie liked to be the one to clean the fish when they got back, which worked for me, and still works to this day! From then on, I said, "If I cook them, I don't clean them!" One day we canned the fresh-caught salmon the same way that we did the clams, except this time we put the meat into canning jars, not cans, then into a boiling water bath. I'm still here, so I think I have proved that it works!

Ernie never liked to sit still anywhere for long and was perfectly happy to have work to do with George and Ray every afternoon. Irene and I spent hours sitting on the deck crocheting in the sunshine while listening to Ray and Ernie talking about how life was when they were young. Ernie grew up in the Courtenay area on Vancouver Island, while Ray grew up in Sointula on Malcolm Island near Port Hardy and had spent many years on the West Coast of BC. The two men were about the same age and both had an easy storytelling way of keeping us all entertained. Ray and Ernie did most of the talking while George listened and learned.

George and his dad built two watertight wooden boxes with Plexiglas bottoms and handles on two sides. We went out in the skiff and motored slowly along the shore while hanging overboard looking into the boxes. The see-through bottom didn't need to be very far into the water, just far enough to break the surface to make the fascinating sea life so much more visible. We drifted along the shores watching eel grass and bull kelp sway in the current. Dungeness crabs skittered sideways, starfish seemed to glide along the bottom. There were sea cucumbers, little pike fish and eels, limpets and hermit crabs. So many coloured sea anemones that opened like giant flowers then disappeared into their long tube if we got too close. Long siphons stuck out of clamshells, and feathery fingers reached out of mussel shells combing the water for nutrients. We spotted bottom fish almost hidden in the sand and starfish sometimes sucking out the contents of a clamshell. There was always something new to look at.

Irene didn't like to stay too long with family because she didn't want to impose. We were waiting for the float plane to return to pick them up when the *Thomas Crosby V* arrived and anchored in the bay. Irene had already fortified her nerve with a couple of stiff drinks, bracing herself for the flight to come, when the minister came to our door. We invited him in and chatted for a few minutes while Irene tried to pretend that she was drinking plain soda water—on ice with a twist of lemon. The float plane was soon circling in front of our house and we had to hurry down to the wharf. George ran ahead so he could get the boat organized, and I was last out the door as I made a quick check in case they forgot something. I jogged down the walkway and up behind the minister and Irene walking quickly down to the wharf. The minister was kindly carrying Irene's "drink" for her and they were passing it back and forth so she could sip a little more courage. In the end, all went well, and Ernie and Irene were safely tucked into the plane for their return home.

The day after Ernie and Irene left we borrowed the boat again. Ray had told George about the people who were living at the Egg Island Lighthouse. Egg Island was the next beacon marking the Inside Passage for ships travelling south and we could see their light on a clear night. I had no idea at the time how far the island was. We headed out in the little tin boat early in the morning because the trip would take a couple of hours. I felt very small by the time we passed the entrance to Rivers Inlet. At that point you start to get out into the open water and the swells of Queen Charlotte Sound, and the safety of land looks very far away. The swells here are different from waves, they are more like the ocean heaving up in huge round-topped speed bumps. You can have a six-foot swell and ride up and over it just fine, but when you add the chop on top, well, things can get ugly. This morning though, as luck would have it, the sound was flat calm as far as you could see in all directions. I don't think I have ever seen it that calm since. Our little boat was a tiny pinprick on the vast reflective surface that merged with the sky. I didn't know how scared I should have been, and would be, on future boat rides.

We zipped along past the Dugout Rocks and Cranstown Point then past False Egg Island and Table Island. Finally, we approached the west side of Egg Island where the houses were. We could see the lighthouse keepers waving to us and knew that we had to drive around the island to the back, more sheltered side where they had their wharf and crane. When Ray radioed the 6 AM weather report he had sent a message through the Prince Rupert Coast Guard that we would be visiting Egg Island that day. The Coast Guard then contacted the Egg Island light-keepers, Ed and Carlene Carson, and passed on the message. They were expecting us, and they were very excited.

Egg Island is even more remote than Addenbroke, and almost no one ever visits. There is no safe harbour or anchorage so everyone generally just passes by. It's a very small island in the middle of Queen Charlotte Sound and because of exposure to winter winds there is not a lot of greenery or trees growing on it. The first lighthouse there had been built in 1898 but was very badly damaged by a huge wave in 1912. They built a new foundation farther away from the water, but still not far enough! On a cold November night in 1948 the lighthouse was destroyed again by a huge rogue wave during a tremendous storm. That night the house trembled each time another wave hit. At 2 AM the lightkeeper, his wife and young son just barely managed to get out of the house and up to higher ground before a wave hit and carried off their home. They endured piercing rain, frigid temperatures and intense hunger for five days.

Shortly after the storm abated, the father attempted to row for help but he had fallen and damaged both of his elbows so he was not able to get very far. Then they saw a fishboat circling the island and the three of them climbed into the rowboat and rowed themselves to the *Sunny Boy* and safety at last. The crew on the *Sunny Boy* fed them and gave them clothes because they were still in their pyjamas. They then took the family to the hospital in Bella Bella where they were treated for various injuries and exposure. The federal government had assumed that the family of three had been washed away and did not send help to check on them! The family who had helped keep boaters safe for many years was never properly compensated for their ordeal or the loss of everything they owned. They did not continue to work as lightkeepers.

George's dad and a friend with a nice catch of salmon caught off of Addenbroke Island. Our guests would still be fishing this area for the next thirty-eight years from the sport-fishing resort that we would build called Rivers Lodge.

Ed and Carlene helped us lift the skiff out of the water with their crane and swung it over to rest safely on the wharf and ushered us across the island to their home. It was a quick few minutes' walk to cross the entire island. They showed us the foundation of the original lighthouse and told us why it had been destroyed so easily. Apparently when the new foundation was built in 1912, the old lighthouse was moved up onto the foundation but was never actually attached to it. Just simply plunked down on top and that was that.

We sat at the kitchen table while Carlene made lunch and we all chatted at the same time. Everyone wanted to talk, but there was so much energy in the room that it was okay and no one felt left out or shy. It wasn't long before Ed brought out his homemade salal-berry wine. We sipped politely for a little while before he plunked a bottle down beside each person and that was the end of polite. The salal berry doesn't taste very good just picked off the bush, but it can be turned into a great wine. Or so we thought at the time. Why, that wine was some of the best that I have ever had the pleasure of drinking! George managed to keep his wits about him just enough, and asked Ed to call the Coast Guard to pass along a message to Ray at Addenbroke that we wouldn't be returning that day but would come back in the morning. Ed convinced George that he shouldn't worry, that Ray or Ruth could cover his middle-of-the-night watch. I convinced George that we sure as hell couldn't drive back to Addenbroke after we had been drinking all afternoon. It was all Ed's fault!

We did manage to get out of bed in the morning and made our way back to the wharf. Ed lowered our boat into the water and we sadly hugged our new best friends goodbye then scrambled down the rocks to climb into the boat. The trip back to Addenbroke was much longer and more uncomfortable than the day before because there was a bit of a chop on the water that slowed us down, and our heads were still feeling the effects of all that wine.

As we got closer to Addenbroke we were suddenly travelling with a pod of huge orcas. There must have been twenty of them and I think they just happened to be going in the same direction as we were. I was startled at first then scared half to death. We all seemed to be travelling at the same speed. They kept surfacing and blowing great puffs of smelly, fishy mist and because we couldn't speed up in our tiny boat, we couldn't get away from them. I kept watching off the front of the boat in case one came up and we ran into it. I had no plan—I just wanted to be the first one to know if I was going to die.

The whales travelled with us for several miles and then they just seemed to melt into the ocean and disappear. When they didn't reappear anywhere that I could see, I started to breathe a little easier and unglued my eyes from the front of the boat. I turned to George, and he called out over the engine, "Wasn't that amazing, wasn't that fantastic?!"

Oh yes, it was amazing to me, but deep in my heart I am a Prairie girl. About this time I was thinking a farm in Saskatchewan might be a nice place to be.

We had been back on the island for a few days when I decided to use some of the salal berries that were ripening everywhere and turn them into jelly. They taste awful and they had a funny texture but when you added a whole lot of sugar, and strained the lumps out, the flavour was like an intensely delicious blackberry sauce. Unfortunately, I was a little late picking the fruit and little white worms had gotten into the berries. As I boiled the berry and sugar mixture, a worm-filled foam formed on the top as worms floated up to the surface. I stood bent over the pot for what felt like hours, skimming the top and picking out worms. I had to stop occasionally when the salal fumes steamed up into my face and I started gagging with the memory of drinking too much salal-berry wine. Maybe the worms added to the flavour, because the salal-berry jelly that I made at Addenbroke was so good it could have won awards.

We were due to have six weeks' holiday after being at the lighthouse almost nine months. It worked out that we would be in Vancouver through the Christmas season. I had missed being with my family the previous Christmas and couldn't possibly miss another one. We flew off the island on the Coast Guard helicopter. What a thrill as it lifted straight up off the helicopter pad. I was surprised to see from the air that the island was completely green. Other than the few buildings on the west side, the island was lush forest. No clearings, no streams, no meadows, no wide-open valleys. No wonder we got lost! We went to Vancouver and visited our friends before I flew to Winnipeg and George went to Lake Cowichan to spend the rest of the Christmas holidays with our respective families. One afternoon in Winnipeg before New Year's, there was a knock on my sister Marcia's door. There was George with a big grin on his face!

We had a great big reunion hug. We missed each other so much after living together where we were practically joined at the hip, day after day, morning, noon and night for nine whole months. I made a pot of coffee and we sat in the living room telling each other everything that had happened in the last week and a half. I couldn't believe how much I had missed him. I had trouble taking my eyes off him when he tried to show me something. I finally saw that he was holding a ring in his hand and was trying to give it to me. He asked me to marry him, and I said, "Yes! Yes! Yes!"

Lighthouse Keepers Sometimes Save Lives

We headed back to the lighthouse at the end of our holiday. George liked to say, "We had six weeks of holiday after nine months of holiday." We got right back into the daily routine of more holiday. Since it was now mid-winter, there was no garden work for me so I spent a lot of time reading about gardening, and knitting and cooking. I looked after the chickens and wrote a lot of letters documenting our life. I didn't get bored with the routine, there always seemed to be something interesting to read, learn about or do. I became fascinated with food and studied all the cookbooks that I could get my hands on. George was my very willing guinea pig and was happy to try anything that I put in front of him. There were a few hits: roast beef with Yorkshire pudding, carrot cake, Manhattan clam chowder. There were also a few misses, like canned-salmon soufflé. "I feel like all I'm eating is air," George said, which of course was the whole point! I've already mentioned the awful fried herring, and I won't go into what he said about the stuffed and baked green peppers, but he would hold on to a long-lingering hatred of green peppers after that.

Another miss, for some reason, was that my bread would not rise. For the most part, I did what the books said. I mixed the ingredients well, I kneaded the dough for as long as they told me to, I left it for ages hoping it might rise more on the counter before putting it in the oven. I even thought, *maybe it will rise after I put it in the oven.* Once I put the loaves into the oven, though, what few bubbles there were would flatten and not rise again. George started calling them "bricks of bread" instead of loaves. Many years hence, after having made thousands of beautiful high loaves with perfectly proportioned air pockets, I now know part of the problem was that I was trying to make super-healthy bread and it was simply too heavy. All those great ingredients like whole-wheat flour, oatmeal, bran and wheat germ cut through the air pockets made by the rising yeast and elastic gluten. You really can't substitute all of those ingredients instead of white flour and expect to produce a nice high fluffy loaf. And I no doubt heated the liquid too hot and mostly killed the yeast. I might as well have been making porridge. But hard and flat or not, it was healthy. And with butter slathered on and homemade jam heaped all over it, my bricks of bread were a real pleasure.

While we had been off the island for our holidays, mechanics came to the lighthouse and hooked up the new foghorn. They didn't hook up the automation equipment that would turn the foghorn on, but it was now set up for us to push just one button to manually turn the fog siren on. They had pointlessly replaced the lovely low rumble of the old horn with a new high-pitched, screechy, dentist-drill-shrill siren that would jangle my nerves every time it was foggy. Every twenty-five seconds for a full five-second blast. Making it almost impossible to fall asleep. On a foggy night I would find myself levitating off the bed for five seconds every twenty-five seconds, until it was either not foggy anymore or until morning had arrived to drag me out of bed.

One chilly evening we looked out our big front window onto the most beautiful, sparkly, snowy night that had come to envelop our island. When it snowed, visibility for ships in the channel was almost non-existent, so the loveliness of the evening was shattered by the shriek of the new foghorn. For five seconds … every twenty-five seconds. Great huge flakes were drifting down and glittering each time the light from the tower swept past. We watched as the snow built up and covered the walkway and how it left a huge white square on the helicopter pad. We showed Lorna how to make snow angels and covered the front lawns with them. Enough for an entire angelic choir!

In the morning, Ray found their old-fashioned sled and we all piled on and went flying down the winding walkway to the wharf, doing about fifty miles an hour. Only on the last hairpin turn did we lose the top two people, who went skittering off in a hysterical pile of loose hats and mittens. After a childhood of sledding on the gentle Prairie landscape, this was the best sledding ride ever! Our shrieks of laughter were muted by the low-slung clouds and the thick covering of snow. After the snow stopped falling we could see the mountainsides on Calvert Island well defined by the blanket of snow, and the world seemed to be only soft shades of grey and white. Even the calm ocean was monochromatic grey as the dense snow mixed with the frigid water on the surface.

John stopped by, towing a firewood log for his parents' furnace. He tied it onto the beach under the wharf. He salvaged logs for a living, but this one had some rot in the end and he thought it would be rotten all the way through, therefore not good for a building or a float. John left, and the fellows started cutting the log into rounds. As they went, the wood became stronger and better. There was not one knot or bit of rot in the rest of the log! It was forty feet long and a good three feet thick at the butt end. Ray and George used the crane to lift the heavy blocks onto the wharf. Once they started chopping into the log there was no stopping them. Lorna and I stacked load after load of wood into the tractor wagon and drove it up to the house, then stacked the wood again in their basement. George liked to say, "Our firewood warms us twice. This time when we chop and stack it and again when the Salo family heats their house with it." Over the next week we chopped and stacked our way through the entire log. John felt sick when he heard that the whole log was not rotten and they had cut it up for firewood anyway. Apparently it could have been worth a lot of money. It was a great fir log though, and fir makes some of the best and hottest fires. Ray's family was warm the rest of that winter and most of the next, while our house stayed cozy all winter with the oil furnace in the basement.

One nasty dark and windy night I caught a glimpse of a twenty-foot sailboat as the beam of light swooped past. It was bouncing and dipping in the waves in front of our house and then rearing up on the next swell. I put a jacket on and went out to the edge of our deck. The wind was howling so I couldn't hear what the people on the boat were yelling. One of them grabbed a jacket and started waving it in the air. In a pinch, this is an international distress signal. I ran and woke George to come and signal that we would help. George yelled for me to grab his rain gear and ran out the door. I grabbed his jacket and boots and raced behind him. He was already lowering the skiff with the winch when I got to the wharf. It was bitter cold, and I was frozen with the fear of him going out into the storm in that ridiculously inadequate tin boat. He grabbed life jackets and climbed down the steps then pulled the boat onto the beach, stepped into it and pushed away from shore.

I was afraid to watch and afraid not to. I ran back to our house and stood on the deck so I could warily follow the rescue. After many minutes of slowly pounding through the waves, with water sloshing over the sides, and wind tearing at his clothes, George pulled up close to the sailboat and threw a rope to the fellow who was on his knees in the back of the boat. It took a few tries but the guy finally snatched the rope with a long gaff and secured it to the back of the sailboat. Once the two boats were tied together, the fellow hauled in more line and was awkwardly able to tie the rope to the front of the sailboat to make it safer for towing. Meanwhile, George had made sure that the rope was secured to the stern of the skiff, and he let out a lot more rope before he cautiously turned back toward the bay and very slowly towed the sailboat through the storm to safety.

The couple on board were so thankful. They thought they were going to end up washing out to sea but then they realized that their boat was being pushed closer and closer to the lighthouse. Their engine had stopped working and they couldn't put sails up in the stormy wind and high seas. That's the funny thing about sailboats: they almost always passed us using an engine and rarely did we see one go by with the sails up. We found out that they had no flares, or charts, or life jackets, or life rings, or extra rope or radiophone—and apparently no sense whatsoever to head out onto the ocean so ill-prepared. They stayed with us that night, and in the morning Ray and George and the fellow tinkered with their engine and got it working again. We gave them flares, some rope and life jackets and showed them how to get to Dawsons Landing where they could pick up more necessary supplies. They were so lucky that I just happened to look out the window when I did. Just a few minutes later and they would have been around the point and out of sight and no doubt crashing onto the rocks.

After the storm passed and the swell settled down, we used Ray's boat to visit a couple that were caretaking the BC Tel relay station on Calvert Island, Andy and Nell Olsen. I was always perched at the very front of the boat, so when we travelled through rough water I took a terrible pounding up my spine from the hard wooden bench. For weeks after each trip across to Calvert my back felt like someone had strapped hot coals under my shirt. But I had no knowledge of how to run a boat through waves and swells, so my spot was always up at the front, taking ten times the pounding of the happy driver who sat at the back holding onto the motor's tiller arm. It was the price I paid for our excellent adventures.

There was a huge tidal flat in front of the Olsens' house so we tied the boat to the dock on the other side of the peninsula and walked about a mile and a half to their place on a little-used but very rutted road. All along the road there were signs of wolf—tracks and poop. As we approached the Olsens' house, we could see a young wolf sitting about twenty feet from their kitchen window. Andy had intended to shoot any wolves he saw come around because they kill all the deer, but when this one showed up on his lawn, exhausted and starving, he didn't have the heart to. So he fed it that day, and the day after, and it stuck around ever since. As we got closer, the wolf loped off to the edge of the lawn with its tail streaming out behind it, then turned and stared at us with huge yellow eyes.

I had seen more wildlife in the year since I arrived at Addenbroke than I had seen in the rest of my life. Every day was an opportunity for new and often unexpected encounters with forest animals, whales and dolphins, as well as the tiny sea creatures that I was finding as I scrabbled along the rocky shores. The love that George and I felt for each other grew along with our sense of adventure and our growing sense that we really belonged in this wild country.

In the middle of March of 1974 we wanted to get some mail out, but the supply ship would not be in for another two weeks. Ray told us we could take his boat to Dawsons Landing. The day looked clear and the weather forecast was good, but I bundled up in my warmest Prairie winter clothes and we headed off early in the day to make the trip to the store. Dawsons Landing consists of an assortment of buildings tied to shore in a sheltered bay just off the main channel of Rivers Inlet. The general store is built on a huge log raft locally called a float, and the building sits about three feet above the water. On another float is a gas station with the fuel tanks secured on the hillside behind it and great long hoses draped down the hill and across the water to the dock. There were other floats for the storekeeper's house, generators and storage sheds. The whole place was floating.

We handed in our mail to Lucky, the storekeeper, and turned to see all the wonderful goods for sale. The store carried everything that would be needed in town: clothes, shoes, rain gear, tinned food, books, housewares, tools, boat parts, plumbing parts and fishing gear. And if you timed it right and arrived just after the freight boat had been, there would also be some "almost fresh" produce. They also had the only post office for over fifty miles in any direction. The only thing missing was that in those days, there was no liquor for sale anywhere in the Rivers Inlet area or, as with the post office, for over fifty miles in any direction! The store was a little quiet in March but extremely busy in the summer fishing months with the hundreds of commercial fishermen living for weeks at a time on their fishboats. In the middle of the sockeye season, there could be a thousand commercial boats in the area.

A fishboat drifted in to the dock then a couple climbed off, tied up and came into the store. I could hear them talking with familiarity to Lucky and I heard an English accent. A happy, rosy-cheeked face was smiling and stepping quickly toward me. Right behind her ambled a jovial-looking fellow with a blond curly mop holding fast to a pair of reading glasses. We walked to the front of the store and introduced ourselves and said that we had just come down from Addenbroke Lighthouse. They introduced themselves as Sheila and Richard Cooper, then Sheila turned to me and blurted out, "Are you the kelp-pickle lady?" I had to laugh. I was known for making kelp pickles? How would people have heard about them? Sheila turned red with embarrassment, but I insisted it hadn't been an insult. We were all having a good chuckle when a couple of fellows came in to the store.

We were introduced to Ken Moore, a commercial fisherman who lived full-time in Finn Bay near the mouth of Darby Channel, and the other fellow, John Buck, the owner of a fishing resort who wintered in Finn Bay after the sport-fishing season was over. Everyone finished their shopping and we were all leaving about the same time. While we had been standing around talking, the sky had darkened and by the time we walked out the door, snowflakes had begun to fall. Ken asked if we would like a tow as far as Finn Bay and we gladly accepted. They were in a thirty-foot cruiser with a nice warm wheelhouse and cabin. George sat up front talking to the resort owner, and I sat below at the table having tea with Ken—the first of many cups of tea shared with him over the years. When we were almost at Finn Bay, George leaned through the small door and yelled to me over the engine noise, "Do you want to cook for eighteen people at John's fishing resort this summer while I manage it?" I shrugged and shouted back up to him, "Sure!"

PART TWO

Rivers Lodge

Working at a Fishing Resort

Two months later we left the lighthouse. We had been there for almost a year and a half. We had been perfectly happy there, but when a chance encounter with the resort owner turned into a job offer, we both were excited to try something new.

It was 1974 and we listened to ABBA and the Beach Boys as we packed our few belongings into boxes and loaded them into the tractor wagon for the ride down to the wharf. John Salo and his tugboat, the *Robert G II*, were anchored in the bay, and George and Ray used the hoist and a net to lower our things down to him. The most important piece of furniture that we had to take was our bed that George had so patiently and lovingly carved. There were also the two very heavy coffee tables, wooden planters and various jars of jellies, jams, pickles and canned clams and salmon. Also important was our record player, with quite a few records, that had been a godsend for me on crushingly quiet winter evenings.

We pulled the netting off our makeshift chicken coop and let the banty chickens run free. They were very adaptable and would be hiding their eggs in the woods again shortly. We left the chicken house for future junior keepers. I had scrubbed our temporary home from top to bottom and now walked through the rooms feeling just a little sad to be leaving. We had had such a wonderful time here and I didn't quite know what we were heading into. But I was sure it would be more exciting exploits. I stood looking out the big picture window in the living room and memorized the vista: the always interesting and changing ocean as it rolled and roiled up the channel. The mountains rising three thousand feet on Calvert Island to the highest point on Mount Buxton, the lush shades of green of its tree-covered flanks and the contrasting starkness of the treeless craggy rocks at the very top. I had no premonition that one very sad day I would land in a helicopter on the very peak of that mountain to fulfill an important wish for George.

I finally turned to go, and bumped into Lorna, who was also unhappy to see us leave. She loved to have someone to play tricks on and would miss listening in on our story time. We walked over to the senior keeper's house to say goodbye to Ruth, who was just sending the 11 AM weather report. She came into the kitchen and wrapped a bundle of cake for us to enjoy on the trip to Finn Bay. In the *Robert G II*, the trip would be a little over an hour. We had hugs all around on the porch and headed down to the wharf. John was waiting on his boat, which was gently swaying on the swell. They had everything already tucked safely on the boat, so we headed down to the shore where John could pick us up in his skiff. We climbed aboard the tugboat and with a forlorn wave headed out of the bay and on to our next excellent adventure.

The resort in Finn Bay was called North West Safaris and was built on log floats like the Dawsons Landing store, only on a much smaller scale, and was safely tied to shore in a corner of the bay just off Darby Channel in Rivers Inlet. The entrance to Finn Bay was about 150 feet wide, and the bay itself was a half-mile long by about five hundred feet wide in places and was surrounded by low tree-covered hills. The resort was there for the winter because the spot they tie to in the summer was too rough on the floats in the winter winds. John dropped us and our belongings off on the floats and headed out of the bay, leaving us in the stillness of the beautiful late-spring day. The lodge owner had a little cabin that we would stay in for the summer, so we carried our things in and piled them in the corner. The cabin was one room with a clothes rod along one wall, and a saltwater marine toilet and sink in a cubby hole in the corner. You pumped sea water in to flush the toilet but the sink wasn't hooked up to fresh water yet. Very simple accommodations compared to our comfortable house back at Addenbroke—and it definitely didn't have anything comparable to that incredible picture window. But I was excited and anxious to get started.

We had arranged to leave for a holiday in Vancouver before the fishing season started, and our flight was arriving shortly to pick us up. All commercial flights into the inlet landed on the water, so they either had long metal floats underneath the body like on a Cessna or Beaver, or they landed on their belly like the Goose. Also, most of the float planes had wheels underneath so they could land on the tarmac at the Port Hardy Airport. These are called amphibious planes. If they didn't have wheels, they had to land on the water in the harbour, which was ten miles from the main airport and made it nearly impossible to make your connecting flight! We had very little time to look around the camp and get our bearings before we hopped on the Alert Bay Air Services Goose and flew to Port Hardy and then on to Vancouver.

We arrived back in the middle of June from a lovely month-long vacation and jumped right into getting the fishing resort ready for the summer season. The lodge had already been towed to its summer location in Kilbella Bay at the head of the inlet. The floats were tied to shore with stiff legs, which were usually at least sixty feet long and straight and attached to a series of logs that held everything away from the rocks like the Dawsons Landing store floats, almost but not quite out of the afternoon westerly. There was a mountain rising up right behind our cabin, and our view out the front was of the Kilbella/Chuckwalla River delta with the snow-capped Coast Mountains all around. In the distance we could see the Monarch Icefield and Silverthrone Mountain. We were the only crew hired. George was hired to be the manager/handyman. I would be the cook and housekeeper, and John and Norma Buck served as the hosts. There was a lot to do to clean up after the long months in storage and to sort out all the boats and fishing equipment. The boats were all piled on a float and each one had to be pulled into the water and then have the small motor attached. After each boat and motor was assembled, George took it for a test run, bouncing across the waves and sometimes zipping up the river, hair flying and grinning from ear to ear when he returned to the dock! Meanwhile, I spent a lot of time on my knees scrubbing the kitchen and its equipment and then making beds and cleaning bathrooms. *Hmm!* I thought and squinted out at him through narrow slits.

Every sunny day there was an afternoon westerly wind that brought waves crashing into the floats. Our little cabin heaved and bobbed and banged, first into the float that it was tied to, and then into the logs that were holding us in place. There was just enough time for the floats to all drift back out toward the churning sea, before the next wave crashed them backwards again. The worst of it was that all this bumping always made the needle skip across my much-loved Jim Croce and Carly Simon records if I tried to listen to music. If there was a stormy night, sleeping was not an option and there were quite a few stormy days and nights throughout the summer.

One lovely and, thankfully, calm night I got up to use the washroom. When I flushed the toilet, the water flashed bright enough for me to "read my lover's letters." I flushed again and again and finally woke George with the noise. He told me that it was phosphorescence—a natural light emitted by micro-organisms in the ocean water. He said that you can sometimes see from far above that there is a trail of phosphorescence for twenty miles behind a large ship travelling at night. So now every time I flush the toilet I'm bringing light-emitting organisms into my bedroom? I felt like I had entered the Twilight Zone.

I was cooking and cleaning for eighteen guests plus George, myself and the owners, John and Norma. It was an endless job from 6 AM until 10 PM. Cutting, chopping, baking, roasting, washing dishes, serving, making beds, cleaning bathrooms, laundry, more cutting, chopping, serving, washing dishes, day after day after day after day. There was about an hour in the middle of each afternoon that I had to myself when I could catch my breath and, most of the time, as long as there wasn't a westerly blowing, I would just drop on my bed and sleep. I felt like a zombie when I first headed into the kitchen in the morning. I never got enough sleep and relied heavily on the first pot of coffee to get me going and I still felt like a half-dead carcass when I finally left the kitchen late at night.

One morning before the guests had started to come in off the water for breakfast, I was standing in the quiet kitchen washing a bowl in the sink. There was a door behind me and a counter with a coffee thermos where people would come to fill their coffee cups. I had a sudden feeling of warmth slide along my leg and had a moment of panic thinking someone had come up behind me and put his hand up my pant leg! I looked behind me and no one was there. Then I felt my leg and there was a bump in my jeans. The bump turned out to be a pair of my underwear that I had missed when I dressed in a stupor in the dark before coming in to make breakfast. They had been stuck up my pant leg and had finally made their way, warmly down the inside of my jeans. I looked around to make sure that no one was watching as I snatched them up and stuffed them into my pocket.

Later that day I sat on the steps of our cabin sewing a button back onto my shirt. The afternoon was full of sunshine and light and as I reached for the spool of thread my hand knocked it off the edge of the step. No problem, right?! I watched as it rolled across the plank. I watched as it kept rolling and suddenly dropped overboard off the side of the float. I leaped up to rescue it as it floated off and was about to disappear under the next float. This was going to take some getting used to!

Before working at this lodge, the only cooking I had ever done was for George and myself at the lighthouse and fluffy egg and tomato sandwiches as a kid before that. I was stretched beyond my comfort zone, but being the only one available I just had to keep going. Whether or not I had any skill, I had acquired the necessary confidence from watching my mom. Everything she made was delicious and she never seemed bothered by the mechanics of cooking—except on goldeye night. With five kids in the family and half the neighbourhood kids wanting to eat at our house, Mom was a wreck by the time we all had "boneless" portions of iconic smoked Winnipeg goldeye. Getting the bones out of those fish in order to safely feed half the neighbourhood children was a loathsome job.

One lovely cloudless afternoon near the end of the summer, when there was a bit of a lull and not very many guests, I put on a life jacket and took a little skiff for a ride. George had shown me how to run a boat and this was the first time that I was trying it on my own. The floats were tied up only a few hundred yards from the mouth of the Chuckwalla River, so I headed across the tidal flats dodging half-sunken logs and continued a couple miles up the river. The river valley was about one mile wide and surrounded by mountains, which by September no longer had snow on them. There were soft sandy beaches in many places and lots of logs jammed into the sand. The water was very clear and I could see the clean sandy bottom and lots of salmon as they darted away from my boat. I couldn't get very far up the river because it suddenly became very shallow and I didn't want to hit the bottom with the leg of the motor and get stuck so far away from everyone. I put the engine in neutral and drifted back down the river, listening to the birdies chirping and lots of rustlings in the bushes that I couldn't identify. I felt brave and refreshed by the time I headed back to the lodge. All of a sudden I understood why George loved being out in a boat so much.

In the meantime, George had been working longer days. I was only half joking when I said that he would have to show his identification before I let him into our cabin at night. He spent a lot of time cleaning boats and fish, but he spent even more time out in the boat guiding guests into catching fish. A part of his job was to take guests on sightseeing trips. He would run three or four people up the inlet pointing out interesting local sights, like where there used to be canneries or where there was once a hospital years ago when the inlet had thousands of summer residents, all working in the commercial fishing industry either catching or canning salmon. There was even an old jail site to point out. The metal bars were still clearly visible where they had sunk when the float the jail was on broke apart in a storm. Sometimes he would take the guests up the river in a flat-bottomed, jet-powered riverboat to see the beautiful valley. He spent a lot of time with guests out on the water and the country just grew into his soul. My soul was still deeply seated in the Prairies, but I loved our experiences, the incredible wild country and the man. Before the summer was over, he was talking about staying in the inlet for the winter on our own.

Late in September when the last of the fishing guests were long gone, the floats were tied together and towed back to Finn Bay. George and John Buck had been fishing first thing in the morning before John Salo and his tugboat arrived, so I spent a lot of time cleaning the beautiful bright coho while the floats were being towed. Of course the fellows needed a nap after their early morning fishing! It was silly of me to expect help. The discordance of living in this man's country where the men, George, had so much fun, and the women, me, had the cleaning and cooking to do, was really getting to me now. It was perhaps the last time I cleaned a salmon. The tow was long and slow, taking about seven hours to finally arrive in Finn Bay. We stayed in the little cabin while the owners went to town and we were able to catch our breath and visit some of the people who were living at the mouth of the inlet. One day while we were picking up mail at Dawsons Landing we met Jack Rendle, a friendly, toothless old commercial fisherman who had a small house on a float that he wasn't using. He agreed to let us rent it for the winter. At that time, it was tied up in Sunshine Bay, on the west side of Ripon Island, about four miles from Finn Bay and about one hundred feet from John's own collection of floats. We would move our belongings again sometime in the next couple of months, after we were finished working for the lodge.

Wilderness Wedding

In the month before I left Winnipeg for the West Coast in 1972, I had been looking for a particular piece of music that I heard on a TV show. The music spoke to me, and I wanted it at my fingertips. In the credits of the show, the piece was called the same as the title of the program, *Narcissus are Forever*. I can't recall details about the show other than that I loved the music and that Canadian actress Margot Kidder starred in it. I had asked for the song in many record stores since then but received many blank looks and no luck. I was surprised one night at a dance at the Winnipeg Cabaret, when the piano player of a local band started noodling on the piano during their break and he played my piece! I worked my way over to him on the stage and asked what he was playing. "Étude in E, Opus 10 No. 3 by Chopin," he said.

Now that I knew the true title, I looked in music stores in Winnipeg expecting to have no trouble finding it on an 8-track tape. But no luck. Shortly after, I crammed my meagre belongings into my car and drove west. On the way, I picked up a friend in Regina who also wanted to escape to Vancouver. I had an 8-track player in my car and we sang along at the top of our lungs to my tapes on repeat all the way across the Prairies. We decided to pick up another Cat Stevens tape to fill out our repertoire. We checked a few stores in Saskatoon, then Edmonton, Kamloops and anywhere else we stopped and picked up more music to sing along with, but I couldn't find my favourite Chopin. We listened to Cat Stevens all the way to the coast. Once we left the flat Prairies and the gentle rolling foothills of the Rockies behind, my friend and I chain smoked as a way to cope with the fear of driving off a cliff, and she covered her eyes through some of the most beautiful scenery on earth.

And now, two years later, I flew with George sixty miles north of Rivers Inlet to Ocean Falls where we could pick up a marriage licence. The little town was virtually closed. The mill that created the once-thriving community had shut down and the co-op store was barely surviving with a bit of tourist boating traffic in the summer and a few local people in the winter. I flipped through a cardboard box of records in the store, though I didn't expect much but I always checked anyway, just in case. And there it was! Chopin's Étude in E, one of the most romantic pieces of music I have ever heard. We picked up our marriage certificate and the music we would play at our wedding, in the almost deserted town of Ocean Falls.

We were near the end of September, the fishing season was over and we were looking after the lodge until it was time to head to Vancouver with the lodge owner and a couple of boats. We were organizing a party to celebrate our wedding. There was a bit of a problem with the logistics though because we didn't have a firm date for when the *Thomas Crosby V* would be in Rivers Inlet with the minister on board who would marry us. Like most traffic on the coast, they had an unpredictable ETA. Our guests would be coming from miles around and sometimes it was difficult to get a message to people that lived far away. There was no reliable phone service in the inlet and we were trying to contact people who lived outside of local VHF radiophone range. We finally decided on a date that was around a time we figured the *Thomas Crosby V* should be in the general area and that's what we told people. "Come for a party to celebrate our marriage, and we may be married or not, depending on whether the minister can get here before the party." We were going to be the first non–First Nations couple in twenty-six years to be married in Rivers Inlet.

We planned the party for Friday, October 11, 1974, and let everyone know to be at our place on that date, minister or not. People started arriving in the afternoon in skiffs, speedboats, fishboats, tugboats and private planes. Everyone was bringing food and drinks and plenty of good cheer. About 6 PM, we had a call from friends at Dawsons Landing who said, "The *Thomas Crosby V* just pulled into the dock and the minister wants to know, should he come down now and marry you?"

Wedding day, 1974, with the *Thomas Crosby V* in the background. Humpback whales, orcas and chum salmon joined us for the ceremony.

Well, there was so much bustle and banter and people were already drinking and eating and the music was blaring. We didn't want to ruin a good party so we told them to tell the minister to come on down tomorrow. The party was grand, and there were so many people dancing and bouncing on the float that we actually made waves that rippled and flowed out across the bay.

We were still at the fishing resort so there was room for people to stay the night. Some people who lived close by left in the wee hours of the morning, some stayed on their boats and quite a few slept in the extra bedrooms. The next morning I made a big pancake breakfast for the fourteen people who had stayed overnight, and then everyone started heading home. Just in time, I suddenly realized that we needed witnesses for the ceremony, so we asked the last of our guests, the Broom family, to stay and be the wedding party.

The church boat finally arrived, and the minister, Bob Ferris, and his wife, Celia, joined us for tea and we went over the plans. Darcy Broom would be in charge of the music, Étude in E of course; Jack Broom would film the ceremony to show our families; and their daughter, Shannon, would be our flower girl with a bouquet of wildflowers picked from between the logs and around the floats.

Darcy started the music, and she and I walked outside to where the minister was standing with George. George was dressed in his jeans and brown corduroy sport jacket and looking a little nervous. I was wearing the full-length colourfully embroidered white cotton dress that I had bought on a very quick trip to Gastown in Vancouver. I was carrying a little white Bible and the pretty wildflower bouquet. Two humpback whales had just passed the floats in search of a good rocky shore to rub against and the bay was full of chum salmon. While the minister was conducting the ceremony, the background music changed to the constant plopping and splashing of fish leaping out of the water and belly-flopping back in.

The sun was shining and an hour later there was a rainbow over the *Thomas Crosby V* as it chugged out of the bay surrounded by orcas that were on their way into the bay for a feast of salmon. I had married my sweetheart. The honest, charming, principled, funny, hardworking love of my life. A lot of water would flow under our house before we were parted.

Our First Crossing

The front of the boat plowed into the huge swell of water, and the wave crashed over the bow, washed up and over the windshield and along the top. I was cringing in my seat, holding on for dear life. We rose up on the next swell and the water moved on, leaving our boat suspended in air. We crashed down into the hollow between swells and the entire thirty-foot length shuddered as it seemed to haul itself back up for breath. I kept wondering how long this boat could take such pounding.

The waves were relentless. How long can *I* take this pounding? *I'm sorry, Mom*, kept going around and around in my head.

We were running the boat from Finn Bay to Port Hardy for John Buck. He had headed out in his smaller and faster speedboat and was possibly already in town. There had been a terrible storm over the last few days and the fifteen-foot swell was what was left of it as we headed out early in the morning. Because of the poor water condition, we had to go very slow, with the speed barely registering, and we had about fifty miles to travel across Queen Charlotte Sound, which was open water all the way to Japan. By the time we were almost halfway across, the wind started to strengthen and there was a large chop on top of the swells. I wanted to go back. George couldn't turn the boat around or we would have been swamped between the swells. We were already going as slow as he dared to go but we had to keep some forward speed to control the direction of the boat and keep it from wallowing and possibly sinking. At this point I was thinking, *If I die out here, Dad's going to kill me!* Wave after wave crashed over us, and the boat shuddered and shook, squealed and groaned. Or was that last part just me? I couldn't tell anymore.

While I can't say that George was exactly happy that we were in this predicament, he was very confident in his ability, and he viewed the waves and swell as a challenge. He has a profound sense that boats are made to float while I had simply acquired a pathological fear of boats and water and drowning. I could taste it. Salty and desperate and *I'm sorry Mom, if I'd known this could happen I would never have agreed to be here!* The water was a dark, angry grey, and now large whitecaps were forming on top of the waves on top of the swells.

When the waves washed over the top there was a feeling that the boat was going down. Tons of water held the boat like a huge hand pushing down on us. We didn't talk, we couldn't talk. The noise of the wind and waves was thunderous. The wind shrieked in the crack in the window that I kept trying to push closed but most of the time couldn't coordinate with all the jerking and crashing. I kept trying because salt water was forcing its way in with each wave and I was getting soaked with freezing cold water. We pounded with every wave and now the tops were being blown off the whitecaps. Tops are blown off when the wind is over thirty-five miles per hour. "Please make this stop!" was now my mantra. I said it over and over, mixed with "Please send me a skyhook that can pluck me out of this boat and put me on dry land!"

There were no other boats out here. Everyone else must have listened to the weather report. No one crosses the sound when a storm is forecast, which is something I know now, but especially not in a slow boat. The weather can change a lot in the six hours that a normal trip would take. And it did. When we rose to the top of a swell I could just make out the lighthouse on Pine Island through the mist. I knew that just ahead of Pine Island was a stretch called the Storm Islands and then the relative safety of Goletas Channel. I had to hold on for a while yet. I dug down deep inside me and brought out more reserves of strength and determination and started deep-breathing to maintain control of myself so I didn't end up a pool of jellyfish sloshing around on the floor of the boat. Then I started singing in my head. I was too worn out and still being slammed around to be able to sing out loud. I sang every word to every Christmas song and every folk song and every pop tune that I could remember, and then I sang them again. This deep-breathing and singing is what I now call my "safe place," which I have gone to many times over the years to get through some pretty harrowing situations.

We were passing Pine Island very slowly, and we were making very little headway. But wave by wave we plowed our way forward and headed into what I hoped would be the relief of Goletas Channel. There is a lighthouse at Scarlett Point, right at the corner of Christie Pass, which leads into Goletas Channel, and as we passed it I could see several people waving encouragement to us from the deck of the tower. The water was different here, with very little swell, but the waves were higher and coming faster. I had hoped for a feeling of safety when we turned into the channel but we were still in danger. We were no longer dropping heavily between swells, but now we were crashing and crashing through the waves. The sky started darkening, and I felt my heart plunge again. *How can we do this in the dark?*

The last hour of the trip from the channel into Hardy Bay and finally to the dock was agonizingly slow. Every bone in my body was aching, I could hardly hold my head up and I was numb and chilled to the bone.

I had not even been able to reach for anything to put over my shoulders to fight the frigid onslaught of spray. It was pitch dark until we turned the corner into the bay and could see the lights of Port Hardy, nestled safely onshore. George's eyes were fried from focusing so hard on the water and his arms were ready to fall off. Later we discovered a blister that covered his whole hand from working the throttle for twelve gruelling hours. We finally tied up at the government wharf in Port Hardy and stumbled up the dock.

What kind of life had I gotten myself into?

First Days in Sunshine Bay

I survived the epic boat trip to Port Hardy, and we went on to Vancouver, where we could have some fun and buy supplies for our new life spending the winter on our own in Rivers Inlet. And here we were, three months later, waking up for the first time in the cabin we rented from the elderly fisherman, Jack Rendle. George and Jack had agreed on the rent for the winter. George would build a counter with a sink and taps and shelves underneath. That was our rent. At that time, there was no kitchen sink, but we had very limited groceries so having no kitchen sink didn't bother me. This was our journey! We were on our own! And whatever didn't kill us outright, would only make us stronger. Right?

There was frost on our sleeping bag that first morning. My clothes were warm from being tucked under my pillow the night before, but it still hurt to climb out of our warm nest so I dressed quickly in the stinging air. The sun was shining and the outside air was brittle and clear. January in Rivers Inlet with no central heating and no electricity was going to be a challenge.

The day before, we had flown into Dawsons Landing just hours after the freight boat had dropped our belongings off there. Everything we bought while we were in town was tied into a ten-foot skiff that was left sitting on the store's dock. Lucky, the storeowner, was not pleased with us because amongst our supplies we had boxes of groceries in the boat. His actual words to us were, "Either shit or get off the pot." Which I assumed meant that if we wanted freight dropped at his dock, we should have bought our groceries from him. We paid a freight charge to him and hoped we could continue to do business. We unloaded all of the cartons and bags and a twenty-five-horsepower Johnson outboard engine. George put the plug in the bottom and then pushed the empty boat into the water. He learned at Addenbroke to always check for the plug in the bottom because three men, probably talking too much, once lowered the skiff into the water far below the wharf and quickly scrambled to lift it again as it started to sink. He hooked the motor up and we loaded some of the goods back in and headed to the cabin that was tied to a standing boom in Sunshine Bay. A standing boom is a series of logs tied together and to another set of perpendicular logs called "stiff legs" that act like a hinge to keep the floats away from the shore as the tide goes up and down. We unloaded the freight at the cabin and headed back to Dawsons to collect the rest of our gear.

There was a two-inch black plastic water line coiled up behind the cabin and George wrangled it to shore while walking along the stiff leg behind the house and up the hill about thirty feet to a natural little pond. After covering the end of the pipe with a chunk of one of my nylon stockings, he weighted the end of the pipe down low in the water with rope and a rock and scrambled back down and across the log to the float. Then he sucked on the end of the pipe to kick-start gravity to carry the water down to the cabin. After he was finished spitting out a few squirmy, buggy-type pests, the water finally arrived. He jammed the pipe onto the hose that was sticking out of the back of the house and water spluttered out of the tap into the bathroom sink. Even with the tap turned off, water still dripped into the sink. This was lucky because it kept the water moving overnight, which was just enough to keep it from freezing in the line. We weren't so lucky with the toilet though: overnight the water froze solid in the bowl.

George got the oil stove working while I cleaned the tiny one-and-a-half-room cabin that had a bathroom behind a curtain, which was actually a step up from the door-less toilet cubby we had recently been using at the resort. I made the bed by zipping together the two sub-zero sleeping bags that we had traded for George's design and drawing skills when he designed an office extension for an outdoor-equipment shop in

Vancouver. We had two Aladdin lamps that were our only light in the late afternoon and evening. We had water and a little heat plus our love to keep us warm. We were happy.

That first night, the oil stove had quietly slowed and finally stopped during the pitch-black evening and we decided to climb into our warm and cozy sleeping bags and deal with it in daylight. In the morning, George took the carburetor apart and cleaned the firebox and got rid of quite a bit of dirty grease and managed to get the oil flowing again. He turned the oil stove up and put the kettle on for coffee. Then he went in and chipped through the ice in the toilet. Once I started moving around, I could feel the heat coming from the stove and was warmed in my soul again when I heard the water start to boil.

We didn't have a fridge, but we didn't have trouble keeping things cold. We just stored them at the far end of the cabin, away from the stove. There wasn't a lot of fresh produce to keep cool anyway. The freight boat *Tyee Princess* delivered groceries to Dawsons Landing every two weeks and there was never much produce to choose from. We had root vegetables, cabbage, apples and oranges. The rest of the vegetables and fruit were from cans. We also ate a lot of brown rice, which was easy to ship, store and cook and was full of nutrients. I could make a fresh healthy loaf of bread though. George still called it a brick of bread. It didn't make a very good sandwich. Well, maybe an open-faced sandwich.

Shortly after we settled into Jack's cabin, a friend of ours came for a visit. Chas Bowman was an architect in Vancouver and an adventurer always looking for new, wild and wonderful things to do. We did a little fishing while he was with us and had fabulous fresh cod and chips for dinner. George took Chas beachcombing and the two of them came back beaming and full of the beauty of the inlet on a sunny winter's day. The air was crisp and clear and the snow on top of the Coast Mountains created a stunning contrast between the blue sky and the evergreen slopes.

I was quite content for the two of them to go on their adventures without me since it was only a ten-foot boat and having an extra person on board made it go too slow. And it was a boat. In the morning, we were taking our time at the breakfast table and just lounging with a second pot of coffee. I happened to look out the window and saw the *Thomas Crosby*

V coming into the bay. Not a chance was I going to let them catch me in my pyjamas at 10:30 AM! With a squawk, I grabbed the milk jug off the table and scooped the corners of the tablecloth up with the rest of the dishes and breakfast things and ran clattering into the backroom. I raced back past George and Chas, who were still sitting at the table watching me with their mouths hanging open. Had I suddenly gone crazy? Apparently they hadn't looked out the window. I ran to get dressed, and all was well and presentable by the time the minister and his wife were tied to the dock.

The *OM*

George just had to have the boat with the FOR SALE sign on it. It was a twenty-four-foot very, very old wooden double-ended boat that looked to me like it leaked. Double-ended meant that the boat was pointed on both ends. George saw it as a great opportunity. I saw it as a disaster waiting to happen. The boat belonged to a young fellow named Ken Hall, who lived with his mother on floats tied to shore across the bay from Dawsons Landing. Ken called the boat the *OM*.

Ken was interested in selling and moving to town, so one afternoon we bought the boat and towed it home. George didn't understand why I couldn't muster any enthusiasm for working on it. He started to think that I was just being lazy. I couldn't stand the thought of going anywhere in what I considered to be a hazard to navigation. The whole thing needed to have work done on it. The engine wouldn't start, and it needed to be pumped out constantly to keep it from sinking. George built an A-frame at the stern and started the long, slow process of raising the engine so he could move it off the boat and put it undercover somewhere where he could work on it.

After hours of struggling with the engine, daylight was fading and he left his work to get ready to go out for dinner. We took our skiff to our log-salvaging friend John Salo's cabin, which was about thirty yards away and tied to the same boom of logs that we were tied to. In actual fact, we were tied to John's standing boom. We had an enjoyable dinner with John, then, at about 9 PM, headed back to our place. There was a very light, soft snow drifting down that seemed to mute even the sound of the skiff engine. I had a strange feeling as we came toward our float. I shone the flashlight onto the cabin and could see the whole end of it. The *OM* wasn't there! As we neared the float George didn't even stop to tie up the skiff; he leaped onto the float and ran to where the *OM* had been sunk. It was still tied at both ends but it was covered almost completely with water. After tying up the skiff, I joined him where he stood ringing his hands while I was wishing that I had an axe to help it sink the rest of the way. There were a few things floating up to the windshield, and in the flashlight beam I could all too clearly envision myself floating up to that window with a silent scream on my face. There was nothing we could do in the dark so we went to bed.

The next morning, George found a spot in the bay where the tide went out and left a natural beach that would support the *OM*. At low tide, he built a crib that would hold the boat upright as the tide went out around it. Then he cut down two alders hoping to use them to help keep the boat floating, but they barely floated themselves. He then borrowed two buoyant cedar logs from John and strapped them to the sides of the boat so he could tow it to the crib on the beach. He had to wait until the next high tide to move the boat. Finally, about an hour before high tide, he cut through the ropes that were holding the *OM* to the side of our float. It didn't sink any further. *That's too bad*, I thought.

Then he towed it over to the spot he had prepared and tied it to the trees that were hanging off the shore. As the tide went out, water poured from hundreds of different places on the sides of the boat. We had borrowed a pump to drain the water out as the tide went down, but we didn't have to use it. This was not a good sign, confirming my opinion that this boat was definitely not seaworthy.

We borrowed a small empty float that belonged to another fishing resort. It was in Sunshine Bay for the winter for safekeeping. George worked day after day, building a proper cradle to hold the *OM* upright after it was pulled onto the float. He used his brand-new chainsaw and cut down several small trees and also used the first two alders that he cut down. When the boat was empty of water, and before the tide came back in, John helped pull the boat up onto the float with his tugboat. He used lots of ropes tied carefully into a harness and around the *OM* to protect the boat so it wouldn't fall apart as he pulled it out of the water. I was somewhat dismayed by the care he took, as I was hoping that it would crumble with the force of the pull. George then built a frame around it, which he covered with plastic so the whole boat could dry out.

Once in a while I made dinner for John and another friend Warren Nygaard, who also lived in Sunshine Bay. The two fellows would come over for supper, and then through the evening we would play hearts, which I usually won. The three guys were all very competitive and watched the cards being played while I was up and down getting tea or treats and chatting while I had a captive audience. I never paid much attention to the cards, and this kept the fellows constantly guessing about my strategy and me constantly winning. Sometimes I won just because I ended up with 101 points, which is an automatic win! One afternoon I made a Chinese food dinner for the four of us. I spent three hours chopping, slicing, stirring, mixing and sautéing. We sat down to dinner and the food was gone in less than three minutes. What on earth had I just spent three hours on?! I don't know if anyone even tasted it. But it was worth the work to be entertained by Warren's stories of

The ill-fated *OM* hauled out on a borrowed float. George thought I should help work on it but I never had the confidence that this boat would ever safely carry us without sinking.

growing up in the wilderness of Rivers Inlet and the long Robert Service poems that John memorized while he was towing a boom of logs for thirty hours at a time.

Other than winning at hearts and cooking or serving tea, it was hard to get noticed when I was always surrounded by men who were logging or fishing or hunting, or doing any number of real "men's pursuits." I spent a lot of time alone in the cabin, and when someone arrived I would be so excited and anxious for some real conversation that I would become tongue-tied. I usually sat quietly listening to all the guy talk, and when I did speak up, the fellows would turn to look at me and then get right back into their own stories. Every so often I would start talking and then they would all turn and stare. Then I would lose my train of thought and stop mid-sentence. I needed to do something or I would go crazy. I observed the men in conversation over time and learned a few tricks. When I felt I really had something to say, I would step one foot into the group, lean forward and speak in a loud voice about the "lube job that I was doing on my sewing machine." This would be enough to catch their attention, and then I could launch into what I really wanted to say. Once I had them, I had to talk quickly or I would lose their attention.

We had met an older couple, Ed and Dottie Searer, when we were working for the resort the previous summer. One day we saw them again at the store and they invited us to visit them and stay overnight. We drove our skiff up to their cabin at the head of the inlet on the side of the Wannock River. Ed had been a TV announcer in the States and they had retired to the inlet for a change of pace. They introduced us to the most amazing breakfast: fried bacon, scrapple fried in the bacon fat, fried eggs, biscuits and gravy—made from the bacon drippings and a can of condensed milk—and toast. Dottie's scrapple was made from cornmeal mush and the meat and gel from pork hocks boiled for hours. These ingredients were ground all together with spices. We poured syrup on the scrapple after it was fried, just for good measure. It was an authentic Deep South breakfast and absolutely delicious, but you really needed a four-hour nap after eating it.

Ed was an amazing fisherman. In the summer, they catered to paying guests who came from the States to have Ed guide them to the huge chinook waiting to spawn in the Wannock River. He always seemed to have the best luck. Possibly luck *and* skill—with a little deviousness thrown in. He had a boat that was painted green on one side and yellow on the other. One of his best tricks was to motor slowly away from the rest of the fishing boats as soon as he had a fish on the line. He would hold his fishing pole underwater so that no one could tell that he had hooked a fish. Once he was away from the tourists, he would turn his boat so the other colour was showing. People would usually only be fishing at the head for a couple of days so were never able to figure out exactly where he hooked into the big ones.

There was another couple who also lived in Sunshine Bay that winter. Bob and Joan Ryder lived on their own classic wood cruiser and were the caretakers for the American-owned Rivers Inlet Resort. Bob told us that he had helped train commandos who were involved in the Bay of Pigs invasion in 1961. He liked to throw cans and bottles out into the water, and after they had drifted for a few minutes he would blast away at them with an automatic rifle. Warren and I traded notes about how we would dive into our cast iron bathtubs when we heard him start shooting. Bob also said that he was suspicious of anyone entering our bay. He said, "I watch the boat approaching through the scope on my rifle, ready to shoot if I don't trust the look of it."

Small Boat, Deep Water

I decided that I needed to overcome my fear of being in boats on the ocean. I wouldn't last very long in Rivers Inlet if I couldn't comfortably travel around in them. We were surrounded by islands, and if you did go to shore, you didn't exactly walk around as much as slog, slip and scrabble through the underbrush, and over or under fallen logs and up and down ravines. There are no roads in Rivers Inlet. If you want to get from one place to another, you have to go there by boat. Most people lived miles apart and on separate islands. I use the term "most people" loosely since there were fewer than fifteen people living at the mouth of the inlet at that time.

Growing up on the Prairies I loved nothing more than to walk for hours out of town into the dry, dusty, flat fields. You could see all around you and miles away to where the horizon is swallowed up into the sky. I felt that I could see forever when I stared out the window of my elementary school class. From my desk, I could see one little copse of trees on the otherwise bald prairie and once watched a deer dive into the bush to hide in the only cover for miles in any direction.

I have a long stride. George always hurried to keep up when we walked together on a city street because his stride was short and uneven from his years of scrabbling through the coastal bush, and I had trouble keeping up with him when we headed onto shore and up into the woods.

I'm a Pisces, but having the sign of the fish doesn't help me here. I learned from my first big boat trip that the ocean is something to be feared and now I had to try to unlearn this. I wanted to be able to help George rebuild and refinish the *OM*, but unless I could get a better feeling about being in boats, I would not be able to bring myself to work on it.

One afternoon while George was working under the frame covering the *OM*, I took our small skiff out for a ride. I slowly motored out of Sunshine Bay and picked up speed as I entered the large protected area called Klaquaek Channel. Klaquaek is surrounded by many low, tree-covered islands, and some people say it reminds them of the Lake of the Woods in Ontario. It was a beautiful sunny day with no wind to create even the slightest ripple on the water. When I was in the middle of the channel, I stopped the boat and drifted for a while. Then I shut the engine off and drifted along in the sudden peace. This would prove to be a big mistake!

There was absolute silence as the boat gently floated along with the tidal current. I sat up straight on the seat in front of the motor with my hand on the tiller bar. I knew the water was very deep here—between 450 and 550 feet at its deepest. And the water was very dark and I was all alone and far from shore. My heart was pounding and I started gasping for breath. I grabbed at the pull cord to start the engine. I had to stand up to get enough momentum to pull hard enough and yanked the cord three times, four times, five times and it still wouldn't start. The darkness seemed to envelop the boat and I could feel it rising up to surround me. I braced my foot against the wooden seat and pulled with all my might. The engine kicked in and I dropped quickly onto the seat, threw the gearshift into forward, thankful that I hadn't left the engine in gear or I would have been catapulted overboard while the boat took off on its own. I zoomed back into Sunshine Bay as fast as the boat would go, and not wanting to slow down I almost ran the boat up onto the float. I hadn't even slowed down to let Bob, our neighbour with the automatic rifle, see who I was. I staggered into the house and threw myself onto the bed. I hadn't quite cured my fear of water and possibly I had added fuel to the fire.

After that, every once in a while, I would have another panic attack, which is what I decided I had that day out in the boat. It's funny how your mind can play tricks on you. They would come out of nowhere, sometimes in the middle of the night, or sometimes just before we were supposed to go out in the boat. George took his boating comfort for granted and thought that I was just being irrational. He had spent so much time in boats that he thought everyone should love them. "What could possibly be so scary about being in a boat?" he asked. Maybe nothing, but at times I thought my heart was going to jump right out

The beginnings of our lodge, 1976. The building with floor to ceiling corner windows is on a float that was built in 1938. This building became our house/lodge. The building/float to the right of centre originally had one room, a breezeway and a workshop full of fishing and logging gear. The *Om* is on a float to the right of the guesthouse.

of my skin. I wrote a letter to my doctor in Vancouver describing what was happening to me. He prescribed pills that would settle me down. I thought there must be a better way.

I read about "behaviour modification" techniques. It was not unlike meditating your way through your greatest fears. I started practising the technique—deep-breathing while focusing on something completely outside of what is happening—and was able to rein in some of the worst attacks that I had that didn't even seem to have anything to do with water. It was a good place to start.

Fishing for Rockfish

Contrary to popular belief, it isn't cheap to live in the wilderness. We needed money. That winter we asked everyone in the inlet if they needed any help or had any jobs that we could do for them. Ray Reese was a commercial fisherman who lived in Finn Bay, right across from neighbours Ken Moore and Gus Erickson. He came over to Sunshine Bay one day to discuss getting our help to commercially fish for rockfish. It was January though and not the best time to be going out on the high seas in his pint-sized green wooden boat but George thought it was a good idea, mainly because we could really use any money that we could make. I figured that Ray, at fifty-eight years of age, knew quite a lot about the weather and waves and what his boat, the *Janet*, was capable of handling, or he wouldn't still be around. We decided to become temporary commercial fishermen.

We started working with Ray at his place in Finn Bay the afternoon before we would go out on the fishboat. There were a lot of details that needed to be organized ahead of a fishing trip. We had to get all the hooks and lines out and coil them carefully into buckets, then prepare small chunks of frozen squid and herring by the bucketful, ready to be hooked onto the lines as bait. We made sure our rain gear was all there and ready to be jumped into. Rain jacket, bib rain pants, knee-high gumboots and a big black sou'wester. We fuelled the *Janet* with diesel and put a jug of drinking water on board, made sure all knives were sharp and the gaff was hanging within reach. These preparations took several hours and we headed home by 3 PM so we wouldn't have to travel back to Sunshine Bay in the dark.

When we got back to our house, I raced in to get the stove heated so I could make supper. I contemplated making out my will. It wouldn't take long. I started cooking brown rice by Braille while George worked on lighting the lamps as the darkness filled the cabin. I was not feeling confident with the fishing plan. Ray wanted to have a large tank on board that he would fill with salt water as we travelled. He wanted to keep the rockfish alive because they would be worth more. His plan was to travel to Port Hardy as soon as the tank was full of fish. We were really relying on his expertise here and thought he knew what he was doing. We ate our dinner of rice and canned fish and went to bed early. We would have to travel in the dark to Ray's place so we could leave there by 5 AM for the fishing grounds.

There are two things that I dislike more than travelling in a small boat and that is travelling in a small boat in:

1. freezing weather
2. the dark

Ray's float was tied up in Finn Bay about four miles from ours, a long cold trip in the dark. George was driving our small skiff very slowly in case there were any logs or rocks in our way. Even when it is pitch dark, you can still make out the shape of the shoreline and we followed the shore as much as possible, but at times that was even scarier because we knew there were reefs of rocks in several places between our house and Ray's. I actually felt a little relief when we finally stepped onto the larger *Janet* and chugged out of Finn Bay toward Fitz Hugh Sound.

The *Janet* was a very slow, roly-poly boat and with the swell that was working its way into Fitz Hugh Sound from the open water, we were dipping and rolling and dipping and rolling all the way out. The cabin of the *Janet* was designed for one person, with a small bunk in an area that was ahead of the steering wheel and down a couple of steps. Tools, batteries and emergency cans of food were stored under and above the bunk. Ray had his little oil stove going, and with the heat and the rolling and the horizon disappearing I didn't last very long inside the warm cabin. Holding on to anything I could grab, I made my way up the back steps and out onto the deck. This wasn't much better because diesel fumes would envelop me and make me gag. Occasionally, a gust of fresh air would swirl around me and I would gulp it down as fast as I could.

Diesel fumes remind me of all the times that I took the bus in Winnipeg after we moved there when I had just turned thirteen and had to lunge at the back door to get off before I threw up. I would walk a mile, breathing the fresh air and then catch the next bus that came along. Sometimes it took three buses to get home. Sadly, there was no getting off this bus—we just kept chugging along toward Calvert Island. I don't think I need to remind you about how cold it was sitting on the back deck. It was January and the salty spray that blew up from the boat's wash froze onto the windshield, the fishing gear and me.

Ray finally slowed the boat down and came out on deck to get the gear going. No one had come out to make sure I was still there. I'm sure they knew that I would be holding on for dear life. Or they were very deep into a good story. Ray was full of them. At one time Ray was a heavy drinker. He was one of the old-timers who helped his neighbour and friend Gus Erickson (more about him later) drink large crocks of homemade beer. He didn't have far to go at the end of the night so he had always made it home safely. One night, Ray was very drunk and very annoyed with his other neighbour, Ken Moore, who was running his generator for lights. The rumble of the engine was loud and clear, coming across the bay. Ray finally ran out of patience and shot out Ken's living room light bulbs from his own float, one hundred yards away. Ray had been a sniper in World War II. He had wanted to be a paratrooper, but he had a bit of a heart murmur so they made him stay on the ground. It wasn't long after shooting out Ken's light bulbs that Ray decided he should quit drinking. Thankfully he wasn't drinking when we were fishing with him.

George was steering and Ray started hooking small bits of bait onto the longline before he dropped the line overboard. I pulled big rubber gloves on and sat hooking up the bait as fast as I could to keep ahead of him. There was a Scotchman, or big bright coloured buoy, that went over with the end of the longline and floated on the surface so we could find the line later. We kept loading hooks and dropping them for several hours, and then Ray told George to switch with me so I could steer. Sitting in the captain's seat and watching the horizon kept me from feeling ill, and I was able to steer for the rest of the short afternoon while George and Ray hauled in the lines using the net drum on the back of the boat.

We didn't catch very many fish that whole day. Most of the fish that they brought in were dead. Rockfish do not do very well when they are brought up quickly from deep water. Their air bladder expands, sometimes right out of their mouth, and it doesn't deflate. This did not bode well for Ray's live tank. We headed back to Finn Bay and decided we might as well eat some of the fish since it had just been caught. Together we cooked up a delicious feast of deep-fried rockfish and chips that could not have tasted better or been fresher. Unfortunately, we ate most of what we caught, so we didn't even cover the cost of fuel for the trip.

I was just about falling down I was so tired, but Ray wanted to show us how he was training his Brittany spaniel hunting dog to not be afraid of his gun. He sat at one end of his cabin and held the dog between his legs. Then he blasted away at the far wall while he held the dog down and we held our ears. He figured he had to do it until the dog didn't flinch any more. The only way that was going to happen was when the poor dog went deaf from the noise or dropped dead from the fear.

Ray went on to become the oldest person at the time to become a helicopter pilot in Canada. He had always wanted to fly a helicopter and after a gold rush–type fishing season, in which he made boatloads of money, he bought one and enrolled in flight school. Living along the coast all his life and travelling exclusively by boat, he had never even had a driver's licence. He had to have someone drive him to his classes. He passed all his tests and, after years of practice, was able to fly on his own. He built a new float that stuck out from his house float so that he could land his helicopter right in front of his home, which was still tied up in Finn Bay. At this time, commercial fishermen had a guaranteed income from what was then called unemployment insurance, so after fishing ten two-day openings throughout the summer they would be eligible for government cheques. He may have been the only person who regularly flew a helicopter to the post office to pick up his unemployment cheque. A few years later, Ray crashed the helicopter beside a mountain lake and was rescued a day later by John Buck, who flew his own float plane and landed on the lake. That was the end of Ray's helicopter adventures.

As for us, it was the end of our fishing adventures. We went fishing for two more days and finally gave in to the sorry fact that we were not going to make any money at it. We helped Ray clean his gear and put it all away on the third afternoon and said goodbye to our Commercial Rockfish Caper. George and I could go out into sheltered water in our skiff and in an hour we could catch more fish than we caught in our three days of commercial fishing. We didn't have refrigeration so we didn't keep too many fish, just enough for a couple of meals plus a few pounds to salt for later use. We ate a lot of fish that we easily caught, and with the dry goods and tinned foods that we brought in on the freight boat, we never went hungry. We had enough money saved to buy oil for the stove and gas for the skiff, but we were looking forward to making money again when the steelhead season started and we would work for the fishing resort again.

Steelhead and Grizzlies

We worked at North West Safari's camp (later Buck's Camp) again the following spring. This time it was steelhead season in April and May. The lodge floats were again towed to the head of the inlet to be closer to the Chuckwalla River where the steelhead would be spawning then heading back out to the ocean. Unlike salmon, which die after they spawn, not all steelhead die, and they can head back out to sea and sometimes make it back to spawn another year. Once again we were working our asses off with so much to do and long, long hours. It was harder to work for someone else like this after we had spent the winter in the wilderness, relying on ourselves to get through the days safely, as well as working to keep ourselves warm and fed. George and I felt that we were such a strong unit after surviving the cold, the dark, the loneliness and each other. But we had told John that we would help with the steelhead season and here we were.

Once again, I was cooking and cleaning and George was spending the days outside, running guests up the river and dropping them off to fish at different spots along the banks. At times, it was very cold outside with sleet flying horizontally into his face as he stood at the wheel of the open riverboat. April at the head of the inlet was still affected by the snow-pack and quite a bit cooler here than where our rented cottage was at the other end of the inlet. I packed thermoses of hot soup and hot coffee in an attempt to keep George and the guests warm. There were days when everyone returned to the lodge soaking wet and completely frozen. I had to question the sanity of the guests paying a lot of money for this abuse. Some days I was happy that I was inside cooking and cleaning.

One night at the end of steelhead season, George and I went with John Buck in his flat-bottomed riverboat, across the bay to the logging camp to visit some of the staff that we had met during the summer. It was a warm evening in May, and the weather looked like it would stay calm for the next few hours at least. We had a fun evening with our new friends, but I noticed as the evening went along that I could hear wind rattling their windows. By the time we were leaving, there was a gale blowing and I was already feeling sick at the thought of getting into that low-floating, flat-bottomed boat. Both George and John cajoled me into getting into the boat and, in the pitch dark and the blowing gale, we headed away from the dock. It was only several hundred yards across the bay but we were not making any headway against the wind and waves. The tops of the waves were flying off and drenching us with freezing cold water, and the front of the boat was lifting way too high with each gust. We were only about thirty feet from shore when I had had enough and begged the men to take me back to the dock. I knew the boat would flip in that wind and I would die out there in the wild, dark water. They finally relented and, after angrily mocking my foolishness (though I think they realized that I was right), carefully turned the boat between gusts and headed back to the dock. We spent an uncomfortable night on couches and the floor, but I felt like I was cradled in the lap of luxury and happy to still be alive to see another day.

A few days later, George and I took a skiff up the Chuckwalla River. He knew a good spot to pull the boat up onto a sandy riffle where we could get out and walk a little and explore the shore. On the beach, I bent over and watched a giant footprint in the sand fill with water. A grizzly had just left the beach. The bushes were twenty feet away and our little boat was pulled up on the shore twenty feet away in the other direction. As I straightened, I could feel the hairs on the back of my neck standing up, a good indication that I should get the heck out of there.

We were two miles up the Chuckwalla River and, at this point, the river is about eighty feet wide and lined with salal, huckleberry and salmonberry bushes with lots of alder trees in behind. There were worn-out carcasses of fish washed up on the beach and tired steelhead half swimming and half drifting in the gentle clear pools at the side of the river. I looked up and stared hard into the bushes. Nothing was moving except George, who was backing up to where I stood frozen to the spot. Even the birds seemed to have stopped their chittering as if holding their breath with us. George moved his head slightly, and I followed his gaze to a spot just under an alder log that had one end in the water and the other stretched across the beach with its branches mingling with the bushes. I stared harder and finally saw the two yellow eyes looking in my direction. It was a cougar, and it must have been waiting for the grizzly to leave before coming out to feed on the fish carcasses.

I could only imagine that it was not very happy when we showed up. George reached for my hand and we slowly backed down to where the boat was beached. My mind was racing trying to think of what we could use to protect ourselves if the cougar decided to attack. We both still had our life jackets on which might provide a bit of extra protection, and if we could reach the boat we could grab the paddles. We were almost there when the cougar burst out of the bushes and dove down toward us. We leaped at the boat, pushing it back into the water as we jumped aboard. With my back to the cougar I felt my heart pounding in my chest. As soon as the boat was free of the sand, it started drifting away and down the river. We both seized paddles and paddled as fast as we could away from the beach. When I looked back, the cougar was turning away toward the bushes with a great chunk of fish in its mouth. There is a tiny possibility that the cougar hadn't even noticed us on the beach—it was so set on steelhead for dinner!

We finished the end-of-season cleanup at the lodge and let John now that we would be working elsewhere for the summer season. We had both applied for and gotten jobs looking after the sport-fish float for the federal Department of Fisheries for the summer. We would both be issuing permits in an area at the head of Rivers Inlet called the "permit area." The permit area had a boundary line that kept fishermen from fishing too close to the mouth of the Wannock River, where the trophy chinook were heading to spawn. Fishermen were required to bring their chinook catch back to the float, where we would weigh the fish, take scale samples and record the information under each permit. We made a quick trip to Vancouver to pick up food and supplies since we would be on our own but living in the Fisheries cabin at the head of the inlet from early July until September.

We stayed with George's mom and dad at Lake Cowichan and while we were there, I happened to pass the animal shelter. There was a sweet little dog that seemed to be a cross between a border collie and an Australian shepherd. After much wheedling and cajoling, I was finally able to convince George that it would be a good thing for me to have company during the endless hours that I was alone. We brought little Tuki, named after my Icelandic mom's term of endearment, home to Sunshine Bay with us in our next boat, which George found through the Vancouver Island *Buy and Sell* newspaper.

The boat was old, eighteen feet long and had a hardtop over the front seats, a 110-horsepower engine on the back and a flat bottom. It moved over calm water very fast but, because of the flat bottom and George's propensity for speed, it was the most uncomfortable boat I had ever been in when travelling over choppy water. I felt every wave jangle up my spine and crack and crunch the vertebrae in my neck. Where, oh where was that skyhook when I needed it? We drove the boat up the coast from Nanaimo to Port Hardy, tied up to the government dock and stayed overnight at the Seagate Hotel. We planned to get a super-early start the next morning. I was dreading crossing Queen Charlotte Sound again, but since we had spent just about every dime we had on the boat, if I was going back to the inlet, I was going in a boat.

We headed out at first light with the boat loaded with supplies, the dog and me. George wanted to get away before the afternoon westerly started to blow. It was now the middle of June and the weather was clear and sunny. I jacked up my deep-breathing, sang songs in my head and held onto Tuki. There was not much swell as we turned out of Goletas Channel and onto the open water, and there was almost no wind. The crossing was quick because George didn't have to slow down very often, and we were safely back in our cabin in Sunshine Bay in time for a late breakfast. I had survived another crossing of Queen Charlotte Sound.

We visited Ed and Dottie Searer at the head of the inlet again. Most of the fishing guests that they had with them in the summer were from the Deep South and loved the way Dottie cooked. She fried everything in hot fat and served just about everything with delicious baked beans. Everything she made was delicious. She told us that she packed a lunch for her fishing guests with the leftovers from the previous night's dinner. If there were baked beans left over … they got baked-bean sandwiches. One guest was moved to tears to be given a wrapped baked-bean sandwich just like his grandmother gave him when he was young.

The Searers' cat had several wild kittens, and we were hoping to catch one. Dottie went out behind their cabin and threw a box over the head of a tiny grey one. Then she quickly taped the top of the box closed with air holes in the side so the cat could breathe on the way back to our place. When we got home, I opened the box inside the cabin. The kitten was wild all right. It ran along the perimeter of the wall looking like a rat, ran out the door and hid under the cabin for the next two days. I knelt down near the steps with a dish of milk and called, "Here Kitty, Kitty, Kitty." The name stuck. I don't think Tuki liked having a kitten around. I happened to look out the window and saw her walking gingerly across the stiff leg to shore, carrying the kitten in her mouth. I think she wanted to get rid of it. We had to go to shore and poke around under logs and roots to find the kitten before the mink, marten, otters, eagles, cougars or grizzlies found her. Kitty was staying very quiet just like her new mom would want her to, but we finally found her stashed in a little hole in the moss at the bottom of a huge cedar.

I was looking forward to starting work for Fisheries in a few weeks. The sport-fish floats would be tied up at the head of the inlet in the permit area. I knew that I would have more time to explore the area with George since the permit office had hours posted and we would work in shifts. We loved living in the inlet and so in the meantime, we made plans to earn enough money to pay our expenses so we could continue to live in the wilderness.

There were not many jobs available in the area. George had done his share of logging during his university days and was not about to go back to it, and I would never make a good commercial fisherman given my fear of the open sea. That left the sport-fishing industry, which we had experience with—and working for ourselves made sense to us. Why work sixteen-hour days for someone else when we could work eighteen-hour days for ourselves? We would start our own fishing resort.

Lady Pamela

The first thing I heard was "Lady Pamela!" in a loud, anxious British accent. It yanked me out of a deep sleep, and then I heard it again, more strident this time. I had to find out what was going on. It was my turn to sleep in but this could be fun. I leaned over and pulled the curtain back just enough to be able to see to the front of the float where the permit office was. There were several people milling about, including our friend Warren Nygaard, who worked as a fishing guide for the Good Hope Cannery Lodge.

The fellow calling for Lady Pamela was dressed in a very spiffy sporting outfit—with a vest full of pockets with spots for hooking fishing gear to—as well as an ascot and lovely shiny shoes. Very dashing sort, but possibly a little too dramatic. We were on a floating raft about forty by one hundred feet with two small buildings on it. Lady Pamela could not be too far away, and was even less likely to be lost. Indeed, Lady Pamela had walked to one side of the float and was mesmerized by the towering cedar trees that were draped in Spanish moss. She didn't answer because she didn't feel like answering. She didn't feel like answering because she was *Lady* Pamela.

As I headed out the door of the cabin, I could hear the British fellow sweetly asking Her Ladyship if she would please sign the permit. Warren started to explain that she required the permit in order to fish in the area. Lady Pamela turned away from him mid-sentence as if he wasn't speaking. Apparently she didn't think she required a special permit. I thought, now I understand the British class system. When one is part of the upper class, one would no more talk to a working-class person than talk to a cow. This was a new concept to me in reality—it was funny in movies, but not so funny in person. George was quite delighted though, and was able to explain with quite sincere remorse that unfortunately, Lady Pamela would not be able to fish for our monster chinook salmon without signing for a permit.

One of the lodges nearby often sent out several boats carrying guests to fish at the mouth of the inlet. Each boat also had a "guide." One day, one of the guests hooked into a huge halibut. There is no easy way to pull such a big fish into the boat, and it's not a good idea to do so anyway. The fish is one huge muscle and can break the seats out of the boat—and possibly fishermen's legs—if it starts flopping around. We had learned to use a long-handled harpoon to kill the fish, then disconnect the wooden handle from the harpoon head, which is attached to a long rope attached to the boat. This rig works well and you don't have to try to lift the big fish into the boat; you can tow it home. The commercial fishermen usually shoot the larger fish as it is pulled close to the side of the fishboat. On this day, the guide in the guests' boat hauled the huge halibut into the little metal skiff, and while the guests were leaping out of the way of the thrashing, the guide shot the halibut as it lay—in the bottom of the boat! Yes, we have had fun telling that story over the years.

Another day, right at dinnertime, a Fisheries officer pulled into the dock and yelled at George to "get in the boat!" George hopped aboard, and they took off at full speed. I got the story later. They pulled up to the dock at the lodge on the other side of the inlet, barely took any time to tie up and raced together up to the kitchen. There, all over the griddle in all their fresh, net-caught glory, were dozens and dozens of pieces of sockeye salmon. The lodge had bought "Indian food fish" to feed their guests. Very much against the rules. The salmon caught by First Nations people on fishboats could not legally be sold to non–First Nations people. The officer wrote the owner a "notice to appear" and had the staff scoop all of the salmon into buckets and carry them to his boat. I still wonder what they fed their guests and crew instead that night?

One afternoon, George watched as a Seabee float plane broke loose from its mooring and started floating toward the shore. Earlier in the day, the fellow who owned it had landed in the bay and quickly dropped his anchor just fifty feet from the shore, unstrapped a little boat from the side of the plane, climbed in with an armload of gear and headed out fishing. There was quite a chop on the water because of the afternoon westerly, and later in the afternoon the airplane dragged its anchor and was quickly heading into the rocks. George grabbed a rope and jumped into our skiff. He carefully pulled up beside the plane and threw the line around a spot that wouldn't get damaged when he towed it away from imminent disaster. He slowly pulled the plane over toward our floats, and I helped get it to a place along the front of the dock where the wings wouldn't bang into either of the buildings. A Seabee plane's propeller is situated behind the aircraft's cabin so we didn't have to worry about the propeller getting damaged. George secured the plane to the float, and we waited with anticipation for the owner to return. "What would the reward be?" we wondered. Many hours later the fellow finally returned and climbed onto our dock to retrieve his airplane and to thank George. He said, "I want to give you a little something for rescuing my airplane." He pulled his wallet out and thumbed past hundred-dollar bills, then past fifty-dollar bills, past the twenties and the tens. Then he picked out a five-dollar bill and two one-dollar bills. Seven dollars for saving his airplane that was worth well over $100,000. He really did mean "a little something." George almost handed the money back.

One of the perks of working on the permit float was getting to eat fresh salmon without even putting a line in the water. And I don't mean like the two women who ran their boat all night through the fishing fleet and made more money than the fishermen without ever getting their net wet. Since all chinook that were caught in the area had to be brought in for us to weigh and take scale samples, there was a good opportunity for us to eat as much salmon as we wanted. Many private boaters arrived to weigh their fish and then used our cleaning table to either fillet their fish or even just cut the head and tail off so the fish would fit in their cooler. We often asked if we could have the parts that they cut off for bait for our crab trap. Sometimes there would be several pounds of beautiful fresh salmon on these pieces. We didn't actually have a crab trap, but we sure enjoyed eating for supper the salmon that they would have thrown overboard!

Late one day I took over operating the weigh scale while George worked on our new/old flat-bottomed and hardtop speedboat. The boat pounded so hard in any waves because of the flat bottom that George wanted to strengthen its floor beams and floorboards. We called our new boat *The Page*, after the boat that George painted on a batik picture when we were at the lighthouse. He liked the idea that this new life of ours was a new page in our lives. Someone later said, "Oh, it's the first two letters of your names!" We stored *The Page* in the Fisheries boathouse where George could work even if it was raining. He dismantled the seats and then cut the floorboards out. He didn't have the wood for the beams or floorboards yet, so we used the Fisheries boat until the end of the season and we would finish the job the following spring. He did continue to

Me on our first speedboat, *The Page*, in front of the cabin we rented in 1974. George loved to drive fast, so my spine took some brutal jarring as we pounded through the waves in the afternoon westerlies and bad winter weather. He wasn't called Hurricane Ardley for nothing!

prepare the inside while he had the cover, so he used a power sander and sanded the fibreglass all around where he had removed the framework. This created terrible drifts of very fine dust that worked its way into George's beard, his shirt and up his pant legs. Fibreglass dust makes you very itchy, and it was a nasty, messy job. After a couple of hours, George came out to get me and asked for my help. I was glad that he had asked me and excited for a job. When we walked into the boathouse, George handed me a broom and pointing at the piles of dust inside the boat, said, "Would you please sweep that out?"

I won't say that he was acting like the nobility, but I had the distinct feeling that I was being treated like a lower-class person. We were in the middle of the wilderness, we had to rely on each other, we were both doing the same job working for Fisheries, and the only time that he wanted my help was to sweep? I don't think so! This was where I drew the line. *Okay, you want to live in the wilderness. Okay, you want to start a fishing resort. It's not okay to think of me as your underling.* If I was going to make it in this man's country, I was not going to do it as a servant. As I handed the broom back I told him, "Call me when you have a real job for me," and I marched out of the boathouse.

Fisheries, Old-Timers and Floats

On our days off from the Fisheries job, we took the Fisheries fourteen-foot Hurston speedboat and followed the shoreline, poking into every little bay and channel toward the mouth of Rivers Inlet. We were searching for our own space to start a fishing resort. We had decided this would be our next adventure, and it would finance our love of living in the wilderness. We needed a safe, calm bay that would have plenty of fresh water even after several weeks of dry summer weather.

Following close to the shore you could sometimes surprise animals if you zipped around a corner quickly. We saw mink, otters, occasionally wolves, black bears and grizzlies. Several times over the summer, we watched pods of fifteen or more orcas working like a coordinated wolf pack as they gobbled every salmon that was unlucky enough to be in the area.

On the Darby Channel side of Rivers Inlet, there are many small, low islands and several larger islands with tree-covered hills reaching up to about six hundred feet high. There are many safe little channels and bays tucked into the lower islands, but they didn't all have a freshwater supply, which would be necessary for a resort. A safe place to tie up floats in winter and a good freshwater supply that was still flowing at the end of summer were our two main criteria for continuing to live on our own in Rivers Inlet.

One day, we motored into the back of a little bay known locally as Sleepy Bay. It was on Walbran Island, just across Darby Channel from Stevens Rocks, just south of where the channel narrows, about halfway between Fitz Hugh Sound and Dawsons Landing. The bay was about 150 yards wide and about the same in length. On the east side of the bay, there was a narrow channel that went past a tiny island, and we could see a small bay on the other side of it. The small bay was shown completely blue on our chart, which means the depth of the water is shallow at low tide. Over the summer, we went back to that bay every chance we had. The water supply was low by the end of summer, but there was still water coming down from the surrounding hills.

During the summer of 1975, we heard about two old fishermen, long-time residents of Rivers Inlet, who were anxious to sell their floats and move to the city. We visited both men and bought their buildings and floats as well as the contents of each. Our plan was to continue to work for Fisheries till the end of the fishing season and then start working on the buildings and floats and turn them into a first-class fishing resort. Our intent was to open our resort the following summer.

First we bought the floats—which included a house float, a wash-house float, a tool shed and boathouse with a small skiff—from Axel Johnson, an old-timer who had been mauled by a grizzly bear a few years earlier. He had been on his way home one day after felling trees when he was attacked. He pretended to be dead as the bear flipped him over and chewed on the calves of both of his legs. He remained motionless and finally the bear covered him with leaves and moss and wandered away. Axel dragged himself down the hill to his rowboat and rowed three miles back to his cabin. He managed to make it to his bed where he immediately passed out.

Unfortunately, his three floats were tied up in Draney Inlet. There is a ferocious riptide in and out of Draney, so few people actually enter the inlet. Fortunately, it was only a few days before someone pulled up to his dock to bring him groceries and mail. The fellow bundled Axel up in his blood-soaked blankets and took him to the "one-doctor hospital" at the Wadhams Cannery fish camp, about eight miles away. Axel survived but had a pronounced limp for the rest of his life. He had trouble getting around after that and was ready to sell his buildings and floats to us. He left everything except what he could fit into a small suitcase. Of the items he left behind, my favourite was a zither in good working order in a purple velvet–lined case with music books and instructions on how to play it.

We also bought the buildings and their contents and floats from Gus Erickson. We had met Gus a few times over the previous winter and he was happy to sell everything he owned to us. He didn't trust banks and cheques so we paid for everything in cash. We didn't think to get a receipt. Lucky for us, he had no intention of tricking us out of the sale.

For many years previously, Gus had lived in the Yukon, had a trapline scattered over many snowy miles of the country and seldom made trips into town. One fateful night he was in a bar fight and broke a bottle over the other guy's head. The RCMP threw him in jail and waited to see how the injured fellow was after he was taken to the hospital. Sadly, for both men, the fellow died from his head wound. Gus spent a few more days in jail before he escaped and fled the Yukon, leaving everything he owned behind, which included his secret caches of food, furs and money.

He had now lived in Rivers Inlet for twenty-five years, fishing and handlogging and making beer for his friends. He had a thirty-gallon ceramic container that he brewed beer in, and all his friends would come over to help him drink it. They drank until they couldn't hold any more and most passed out somewhere in his cabin or out on the float. Some crawled to their boats and headed home, often not making it there. One of these friends had been living on his boat tied to a float in the back of the bay that we had picked out for our resort, just two miles from Gus's place. He headed home one night but didn't answer radio calls the next day. When someone checked on him, he was "drownded." He had stepped off his boat, missed the dock, landed in the water and was so drunk, he didn't even kick off his slippers. Gus told us, "I used to make beer for my friends but they all drownded so I stopped making beer."

The not-so-sentimental Gus was waiting for "an old man to die" so there would be a bed available for him in the Finnish Manor old folks' home in Burnaby. We would have to wait until he left the inlet to collect his floats. We were happy with the arrangement since we were working at the other end of the inlet and hadn't yet secured a place to put the floats.

We didn't have to wait long because the turnover in the Manor was pretty quick. At the end of the summer and fishing season, John Salo used his tugboat and towed Axel's floats then Gus's into Sunshine Bay near the cabin we had rented the previous winter, where we were able to tie everything to John's standing boom. Now in addition to the skiff and *The Page*, the yellow flat-bottomed speedboat, we had a couple of buildings on floats,

We acquired this twelve-foot speedboat that George dubbed *Patty's Page* in a futile attempt to entice me into the thrill of being in a boat. I did use it for a number of years for bottom fishing near the entrance of our bay and for picking up the mail from the Dawsons Landing post office.

as well as an old boathouse, an old very heavy-duty sixteen-foot-long work-boat with a forty-horsepower Johnson motor and the ten-foot skiff with a twenty-five-horsepower Johnson outboard engine we'd had shipped up to Dawsons Landing when we first arrived. I am not counting the *OM*, which I didn't believe would ever be a viable boat for us to use.

We also acquired a twelve-foot red speedboat from Axel, with a windshield, a steering wheel and a twenty-horsepower Mercury engine on the back. George dubbed the vessel *Patty's Page* in a futile attempt to entice me into the thrill of being in a boat.

Each of the old-timers that we had bought from had left a well-stocked workshop with electrical parts, boat and motor parts, some very old carpentry tools, logging tools including ropes, blocks and tackle, hooks, dogs, six-inch heavy metal staples, Gilchrist jacks, and winches, fishing equipment, trapping gear, buckets of plumbing parts, and in one shop there was a forge and a stretcher. It was time to start our own business. Now all we needed was money.

Bankers Wear Such Nice Shoes

Regular bankers laughed at us. The thought of a couple of kids in their early twenties using their money to start a fishing resort in the middle of nowhere was endlessly funny to each banker, who would inevitably usher us to the door.

"Where is it?" they would ask. "Floating?" They would chuckle. Then we got in touch with the Federal Business Development Bank, known as the "lender of the last resort"—in this case, literally. They reviewed our business plan and must have decided they would at least look at what we had. What we had was several rundown floating log rafts with poorly built cabins that we had already started to strip the insides from. That and a couple of old fibreglass boats with old motors, a couple of sheds full of tools and a lot of confidence in our abilities.

With no way to contact us other than by regular mail, someone at the bank went ahead and booked a flight into Sunshine Bay for one of their loan advisors. We were still in Sunshine Bay waiting for John and his tugboat to tow our floats into Sleepy Bay. One bright crisp day in the late fall, an Alert Bay Air Services float plane landed and taxied into Sunshine Bay. There was no clear place for the pilot to dock the Beaver so he drifted around in circles waiting for someone to bring a boat out to him. Anxious to know who was on the plane, we jumped into our skiff and went out to meet it in the middle of the bay. The bottom of the boat was awash with several inches of water with a thick slick of oil floating on top. I bailed as fast as I could, trying to make the boat a little more presentable for whomever was arriving on the plane.

The pilot threw the door open for the passenger to climb out, and I was shocked to see beautiful, highly polished soft leather shoes reaching tentatively out for the top step of the ladder. I was usually in gumboots in the boat because there always seemed to be greasy water sloshing around in the bottom. The poor fellow climbed down and I helped him step gingerly from the plane's pontoon onto the wooden seat of our boat, and I suggested that he sort of hunker down so he didn't tip overboard and ruin his lovely shoes and banker's suit.

We helped him out of the boat and took him on a grand tour of our holdings. We painted expansive pictures for him of what we planned to do to improve the cabins, how we would do it and when we hoped to be finished. We would definitely be ready in time for next season's fishing. We showed him the work we had already done, which was mostly demolition, George's drawings of the improvements still to come and a list of equipment that we still needed.

Our proposal for the bank read like this, "World famous Rivers Inlet! Home of the legendary giant chinook salmon and the spirited coho, chum salmon and the feisty pink salmon, which also spawn in the many streams and side channels of Rivers Inlet. The nutrient-rich waters washing out from the icefields turn the ocean a milky green and feed the young salmon well before they head out into open waters. There are three fishing resorts in the Rivers Inlet area and ours will be the fourth. Now with more flights into the inlet, ease of access is a huge bonus for our new venture." We went on to show that we had a good grasp of income and expenses over the short term and the long term.

I nervously poured Earl Grey tea as we discussed the logistics of putting our plan into action. We also chatted about how surviving a long cold winter in the wilderness had toughened our resolve to succeed. The man was interested in our background of working at a resort and also the experience we gained from working for the Fisheries Department. He was also impressed by my grade-twelve accounting skills. The pilot circled around over the house to signal that he was back, landed and taxied into the bay to pick up our guest. I slipped out of the cabin ahead of George and our guest to bail the boat more completely so I could show our dapper banker our great customer service.

As the plane taxied out of the bay, George and I both let out heavy, disappointed sighs. We felt that it was not terribly likely that they would lend us money either. Well, we had that wrong. There must have been something that tipped the banker in our favour—maybe the enthusiasm, or the confidence or maybe he thought it was a great idea too. Maybe he was even a fisherman. We received a letter telling us that we were eligible for a loan for twelve thousand dollars—the full amount that we were asking for.

First Days in Sleepy Bay

George spent the next couple of months beachcombing for logs to make a standing boom for us to tie our floats to in Sleepy Bay—our very our own bay. (Within a few years of arriving in Sleepy Bay, George started the paperwork necessary for a foreshore lease. He patiently filled in the paperwork. Letters went back and forth between the Lands Branch and us for well over a decade in order to finally be given the foreshore lease in our bay. The name, Sleepy Bay, would finally be marked on charts of the entrance to Rivers Inlet.) George collected enough logs to string together for a standing boom that we could tie our floats to. There would be a long line of logs that the floats would be attached to, and attached to this long line would be logs that pointed toward the shore at right angles, that were tied with cables, boom chains and heavy rope at both ends. These were called stiff legs and they would be tied to huge cedar trees and act like hinges to keep our floats from getting too close to shore as the tide went down. One afternoon, he and John towed the logs into Sleepy Bay then worked together and tied the logs securely into the most sheltered corner of the bay. The new standing boom (named perhaps because it was like a boom of logs that would stand in the same place forever) would go from east to west so we would see the sun as much as possible as it moved across the treetops on the other side of the bay about sixty feet away. The bay was ringed with low hills covered with two-hundred-foot cedar trees, but straight across from our house was a handlogged area, so the new-growth trees were only about thirty feet tall.

The next morning, all the floats that we owned were disconnected from John's standing boom and then strung together. John towed them from Sunshine Bay to Sleepy Bay. He and George scrambled around tying all the floats together and to our standing boom, while I danced around shouting encouragement and hauling ropes, huge logging staples and sledgehammers to the next place they would tie to. This was so exciting! Our own buildings in our own bay. Now the adventures would really begin!

Later that afternoon, after John had left, I watched as a ripple flowed across the flat water making the reflection of trees and shoreline wobble and waver. A small, round, shiny black head poked out of the water, creating a new set of ripples. The seal had a curious look around then sank straight back down and, moments later, popped up again ten feet away. The reflection of trees shimmered some more. All of a sudden, a little open skiff zoomed around the corner with the Dawsons Landing storekeeper's son Rob holding up a shotgun, ready to shoot. After lowering the rifle, he headed over to where I was standing. "I always shoot ducks in this bay!" he complained when he got over the shock of a bunch of buildings occupying his usual hunting ground. He used the birds as bait in his traplines.

The water in the bay was actually about thirty feet deep at the front of the floats and shallower at the back, closer to shore. Driving toward the back of the main bay you'd pass a small island, which we quickly named Pat's Garden Island. This little island with three low hills of varying heights on it protected us from any ocean swells, large waves and most winds, and many years later from several tsunamis. This much protection and a freshwater supply—which miraculously came down the hill behind where we tied our floats to—was a very rare find in Rivers Inlet.

I worked on Axel's old cabin every day, tearing out the wainscoting, layers of wallpaper and then the walls and some studs, leaving only what was needed to support the roof. I scraped and dug at the layers of linoleum. The top layer of flooring was so rippled and lumpy that I marvelled at how Axel, with his bear-chewed legs, could have shuffled his way around on it.

This cabin was originally used as a logging camp building, and for us it would become the main house and lodge. It was built like a train, where you walked straight through the middle of one room to get to the next. I was taking down the extra walls to open up a larger living area, a good-sized kitchen and a small room at the back for laundry and food storage. We acquired a kerosene fridge along with Axel's cabin (hooray, we finally had our own fridge!), which worked quite well but the top freezer compartment didn't freeze things well at all. One day I tried to freeze some extra bread dough and when I came back after a couple of hours, the dough was squeezing out around the freezer door and dropping into the fridge. I called to George, "Come and look at the bread dough that ate Chicago!"

That was one of the best things about our life in the middle of nowhere. Either George or I could come across something really interesting and call the other to see. Then we would be able to sit and have a cup of coffee to discuss our find, or our hopes and dreams, as well as our plans for the next twenty-four hours or six weeks.

We had an oil stove in the kitchen that we only used for a little while. Axel must have felt that it was an improvement over the wood stove that was stored in the shed. It was no doubt easier for him not to have to carry firewood, but I thought it was a dirty beast, so—after scrubbing the oily mess off the walls and ceiling several times because of a backdraft that caused the stove to poof out dirty, oily smoke into the kitchen—we changed back to the wood stove. A backdraft from a wood stove is much easier to clean. It's not greasy like the oil soot. The old wood stove had a container close to the firebox that heated several gallons of water while the fire was burning and two propane burners attached to the other side that were very handy when I wanted instant heat.

Axel had a cabin on a separate float that he called his wash house since he had a bathtub, a gas wringer washing machine and a sauna in it. The gas engine of the washing machine had a flexible pipe that you hung out the door when you ran it. We wanted to pull the cabin off the wash-house float and onto the main house float and join the two together to create an attached bedroom for ourselves. There was lots of space at the side of the main house toward the back of the float. This was a huge undertaking because we only had hand tools, but we did have a come-along, which was a hand-operated winch, and several sets of heavy blocks and tackle. The block-and-tackle system helps lift or pull heavy loads. Each block that is added helps pull more weight. There were lots of other tools and heavy handlogging equipment in the workshop, things like metal dogs that you pounded into a log, attached a rope through the open end and could then tie it up or tow it home. There were also wedges, blocks and peaveys—equipment still in use forty years later.

George tied the wash-house float in front of the main float and rigged the come-along to pull the building, which was on one-foot-thick log runners the full length of the cabin. The only rope we had was too stretchy. George would heave and crank on the come-along until he couldn't get another inch of stretch, and finally, but suddenly, the building would hop three inches. We were moving the building sixty-five feet, from the back of the float it was on, to the back of the main house float. It was mind-numbing, back-breaking work. Now only 777 inches to go!

People who lived in the inlet would drop by just to watch. They would have popped in every day if they hadn't needed to get some work of their own done. How were we going to move that? When would the supplies arrive? What could we do without electricity? We continued to work and build no matter what problems came up. Some we could antic-ipate, others—like when the fellow who later swallowed the needle valve of our five-kilowatt generator—we could not. At one point, there were five people watching us work the come-along. Thanks, people. George had put a pipe over the winch handle so we could both haul on it and the longer handle also gave us more leverage. One afternoon George was cranking by himself when the pipe jumped off and the handle slammed into his leg just below his knee. He dropped like a rock. "Damn!" he gasped, "I lost all the stretch in the rope," as he lay writhing in pain. We found out that if something is too heavy to move, you just need to add more blocks and tackle. You can use seven blocks before you start to lose efficiency on the line. We had so many blocks set up there was little room left for rope.

We found crab traps amongst other gear in Axel's shop. I imagined how great it would be to have crab for dinner, but we didn't have any bait for the traps. I was washing our lunch dishes in the sink when I looked out and saw a few ducks swimming behind the house. I tiptoed into the next room and picked up the .22, then crept into the bathroom. The window was open a few inches so, without making a sound, I propped the rifle on the windowsill, aimed and fired! Even a .22 is quite loud when fired in a small bathroom, but I got the duck, and we would eat crab tonight! I dragged a small wooden rowboat across the float to the back and skulled my way over to retrieve the dead bird. All the guys were interested to hear that I had shot a duck. When asked where I got it, I said, "Well, I was aiming for the left eye, but I shot it in the heart." I could feel my worthiness go up a notch. This is man's country after all! I would forever be judged on how I could handle an engine, chainsaw or rifle.

Pat's Garden Island

As soon as we settled into our new location, I started to clear a patch for a garden on one of the low hills on my island. I would step out of the workboat onto the rocky shore at whatever tide it was and climb up to the clearing carrying the heavy weight at the end of the rope that was tied to the front of the skiff. One turn around a bush with the rope and the weight was enough to keep the boat near the shore, but if it was going to be a super-low tide, I would have to keep an eye on the boat or it might get hung up on the rocks as the tide went out. I worked a path through the salal bushes up the side of the medium-sized hill to the largest flat area at the top.

I didn't trust planting on the lower flat, grassy area just in case the salt water of a winter high tide reached that point. I hoped the garden would supply lots of fresh vegetables, but I didn't realize how much work it would be for years to come as I slaved over taming that patch of cedar peat, roots, salal and moss. Over the years, there were times during a super-high winter tide with a low pressure that brought the water level two feet over the lower grass area, splitting the island into three, with only the hills showing above the water. During the highest tide, the water was so high George ran our work skiff right across the island through the middle of the hills. It's always good to trust your instinct.

There were a couple of huge cedar trees, a lovely yew tree, several smaller hemlock, lots and lots of salal, a few wild crabapple, salmonberry, huckleberry and thimbleberry. Also a twinberry bush that produced terrible-tasting berries that George liked to trick kids into tasting. There was a thick, deep, soft moss that would later be dotted with trillium, yarrow, fritillaria and pretty little daisy-like chamomile plants.

I also found saskatoon berry bushes and wild roses after I cleared away some of the salal. Under the moss, the salal roots created a layer that was as solid as concrete and almost two feet deep. I slaved over those roots for months with a mattock, hacking and chopping and tossing the pieces over the side of the hill. A mattock is sharp like an axe but the heavy head is turned sideways so it worked better for heaving up over my head and crashing down through the roots. Bit by bit I opened up the ground and made a garden space about fifteen feet by thirty feet. It was good, healthy outside work instead of just demolishing and deconstructing inside the dusty, old buildings. It also made me feel good to be on solid ground again.

One side of the island sloped gently down toward the water, and there was a very thick covering of rock cress that I was sure would be a good fertilizer. I raked this into piles at low tide, filled five-gallon buckets full, then hurried the buckets across the shore, over boulders and rocks, then up to the garden and back again before the tide came back in. This made the start of an amazing compost heap. There were also plenty of starfish and huge twenty-six-legged sunstars in the bay that I collected and added. I found a small shell beach at low tide where the sunstars were piled on top of each other, and there were so many that I went into a frenzy lifting them on my rake and dropping them onto the bottom of the workboat. Later I lifted the slippery mess into buckets to carry up the hill.

I wrote to the Agriculture Department at the University of British Columbia and asked about the combination of seaweed and starfish. They wrote back and said it would make very healthy compost. The only problem would be the bad smell for a few months. My compost was far enough away from our house that we were not affected by it. The Ocean Falls fire chief and his wife visited us one day, and he loved my compost idea. Back at home he made his own pile of seaweed and starfish, but all of his neighbours grew mad at him because their dogs would roll in the stink and then come home reeking of the dead sea.

After many months of hard labour, I had the medium hill a little under control and I started working on the big hill. It was too early to plant and we didn't have our building supplies yet, so I had plenty of time to work in the garden. The top of this hill was much farther to climb with buckets of seaweed and soil. There was no real soil up that high, just deep cedar peat moss. I broke the moss up, chopped the roots apart and went in search of a patch of soil I could bring over in buckets to add to the mix.

There was an area we called "the slough" at the very back of the bay. I hiked about fifty yards into the woods and up a tiny creek where I came to a pond. There was nothing that I could dig up, but I did find the most interesting flower of all, way back in the marshy woods: a sundew, or *Drosera rotundifolia*, which is an insect-eating plant with the most amazing shape. It looks like an alien with lots of red-tipped antennae.

Thankfully I had passed a large cedar tree right at the edge of the shore with the dirt falling away from it and into the water. At high tide, I could grab shovels full of black soil and, beneath that, real sand, and I could load the workboat with buckets of the heavy mixture. I struggled up the hill with bucket after bucket, and the only thing that I ever grew up there, and not very well, were potatoes. The medium hill was much more productive.

Ken Moore, a gentle old-timer friend who lived in Finn Bay, often came in for tea, or we went and visited him. One day Ken told me about the diet he was on. A doctor had informed him he needed to lose weight, so he cut back on his candy habit and treated himself to only one

There was something about the soil in my garden that produced wonderful turnips that were sweet and crisp like apples. I brought bags and bags of goat poop from a trip back to Addenbroke, where the new lightkeepers kept three goats. The broccoli and cauliflower were also amazing.

chocolate a day. And that was enough for him to lose twelve pounds. It was years later that I found out that his one chocolate a day was a Rogers' chocolate, which are two inches across, at least an inch deep, are loaded with delectable fillings and are easily equivalent to four or five ordinary chocolates.

Ken wasn't only interested in cutting back on his own sugar intake. He tried to stop the juncos from eating his delectable cherries one year. He sat at his open kitchen window and shot at them, killing one after another. He would hit one and the rest would fly out of the tree for a few seconds and then land again to continue eating. He shot every last one in this way. He wasn't a mean man. He was actually quite kind and had a soft spot for birds and animals and had two pretty budgies in a birdcage on his kitchen table. He just didn't want those juncos eating his entire crop of luscious cherries.

One day I looked out and Ken was on the sloping shore of my island with a rake and was stuffing my seaweed into sacks. I did what I had to do. I picked up a rifle, walked out to the corner of the float and pointed it at him. This is the only language that these old-timers understand, especially from a twenty-two-year-old girl. I called out to him, "Ken, put the seaweed back or I will have to shoot!" In a split second, Ken made the right decision and dumped out the burlap sacks and climbed back into his boat. Then he came in and we had tea.

First Renovations

There was a public timber-cutting area set aside a few miles from our bay where George was allowed to mark quite a few big cedars for our own use. That was something that Rivers Inlet had lots of: timber. There were lots and lots of cedar trees covering every slope of every hill and mountain right up to the head of the inlet, where there are also huge fir trees mixed in with the cedars. People from the Ministry of Forests would check the trees out and charge us a stumpage fee based on the estimated board feet in each tree. This would be a nominal amount that we were happy to pay, and we could then legally cut down trees. We needed big logs for building floats and smaller logs for cutting into lumber. We could burn the scraps in the kitchen wood stove and the soon-to-be-ordered fireplace for the living room.

Rivers Inlet had been handlogged for years. If you scramble a hundred feet up and into the forest behind our floats you can still see stumps of gigantic cedars with notches cut in the sides for the fallers' springboards. The springboard was a diving board–like platform and would be pushed into the notch sometimes ten or twelve feet up from the base of the tree. Risking life and limb, the faller would then climb up, stand on the board to put an undercut in the side facing downhill, then move the springboard around to a notch near the uphill side and, from there, cut the tree down.

The senior lightkeeper's family from Addenbroke Island had handlogged around Sleepy Bay twenty years before we arrived. Years later when George was diving in the back corner of the bay, he came up to the surface with a potty-training seat—covered with barnacles. We gave it back to John with a chuckle and said, "No wonder you're so tough!"

While George was in the short-lived business of falling trees for our new endeavour, limbing them, then getting them into position with the use of peaveys and jacks and finally sliding them into the water with the work skiff, I was tearing apart the inside of Axel's wash house. Right in the middle of the main room was a gas-powered wringer washing machine and a big claw-foot cast iron bathtub. Behind the main room was a smaller room that was completely lined with cedar boards with a very dodgy old barrel used as a wood stove that turned the room into a sauna. A wall-mounted bench had to go, and so did the barrel stove. The chimney pipe was falling to pieces as I moved it out, no doubt from using salty beachcombed wood for so many years. I stripped the back-room bare and painted the floor, then we moved the tub back there and hooked up a little oil-fired Dickinson boat stove with a coil in it to heat water. George ran an extra water line to the back of the building but hadn't hooked up the line yet.

The front room of the wash house would be our bedroom and the backroom would have our bathtub and a space for storing dry goods. It just needed cleaning and painting but not yet. We had to build a connecting hallway between the main part of the house and the wash house now that it was moved into position. This was complicated by the fact that the main building's top plate above the wall studs was only about five feet eight inches from the floor, so George couldn't make the door any taller than that. It worked for us because we were both short enough to walk through the opening, but we would have to make a taller door for the main guest entrance. Over the years, many a taller friend bumped his head at the family entrance. The main building that we were working on had been built almost forty years ago with no insulation other than tinfoil-backed paper and it had small windows. The very low top plate also meant that the small windows could only be opened about four inches before they bumped into the plate. This would make for a stifling kitchen in the hot summer months.

More complications were time consuming because the floors of the two cabins were not even, and the roof on each building had to be cut open to create a proper covering for the hallway and small washroom that would be built off the hallway. To put in a proper main door, George had to cut into the existing roof and build a new section that extended out and across the new porch. The porch was made of beautiful nine-foot two-by-twelve-inch planks that George had cut on my island.

Once the roof over the porch was built, I attached the shingles around the opening. The wall studs were about twenty inches apart and nailing the shingles was tough because the wall bounced under my onslaught. When I was at the top of the ladder and reaching as far out as I could, I hauled off and slammed the hammer into my left hand completely flattening the end of my index finger. I looked at it thinking, "This should really hurt." I carefully climbed down and walked around the building to call George back from the island. As I walked, I pushed and pressed the wound around and reshaped the skin and nail so it once again looked like a proper finger.

George rushed back, knowing I wouldn't call for his help unless I really needed it. He walked me over to the tap and started to run cold water over my hand and then *Whomp! Whomp! Whomp!* It started to hurt. We didn't have time to stop for injuries. George just bandaged my finger and gave me a couple of aspirin, and we both went back to work. I didn't climb back up the ladder that afternoon though, since

I was feeling rather light-headed. Instead, I sorted the nails that I had pulled from the walls into a good pile and a those-too-bent-or-rusty-to-be-reuseable pile.

Christmas was just around the corner and George's mom and dad and sister Gery were coming to stay with us. We were still living in the cabin we rented from Jack Rendle, which had been towed along with the other building from Sunshine Bay, but we could squeeze a few more people into it and sleep in our new not-quite-finished bedroom in the wash house. Before our company arrived, we cut down a seven-foot pine tree and decorated it with keyhole limpet shells that naturally have a perfect hole in them for a ribbon to slip through. The keyhole in a live limpet helps move sea water out of the shell. Jack came over for tea and noticed our rather bare tree, so the next time he came by he brought two strings of very old lights and a box of pretty baubles. We had a 2.5-kilowatt generator that we could turn on in the evenings, and the decorated tree truly sparkled in the corner of the main room.

As soon as our family arrived we had a party. We also hosted the Coopers, friends from Sunshine Bay, and Andy and Nell from the Calvert Island telephone station. At one point, Nell wanted to get another bottle of rum from their boat. I asked one of John's crew to go with her since we had all been drinking, and there was only a narrow plank walkway over to where their boat was tied. A few minutes later they walked into the cabin with silly grins on their faces and presented a dripping-wet and shivering Nell. She had stepped off the walkway and into the water. She went down right over her head, but on the way she managed to place the rum bottle onto the walk. They were both so proud of themselves that they had saved the rum! And there was a round of applause because we were all so glad that she did!

We had very little money to spend on Christmas gifts, but I did have a spinning wheel that I had built from a kit ordered from the Mother Earth catalogue while we were at the lighthouse. I also bought two carding paddles—that looked like wide flat hairbrushes—that were used to prepare raw wool or in my case, my hair, for spinning into a long fibre. I had been saving hair from my hairbrush for months, and while George was out, I carded my stash of hair then spun it on my spinning wheel into a nice thin thread. There wasn't very much but I added a bit of wool and managed to crochet a little folding key-chain holder to give to George as a present. In the meantime, George had found an almost perfect heart-shaped rock and glued a small ring onto the back of it, then spliced a leather thong onto the ring to make a beautiful necklace. Who needed money?

Shaking All Over

I once woke up in the middle of the night in our new bedroom in Axel's former wash house and couldn't feel my hands. I rubbed the back of them together for several minutes to get the blood circulating again. Both of them were seized in the shape of claws. Actually, my right hand looked like it was still holding a hammer and my left hand looked like I was still holding a bunch of shingle nails.

George had cut down a nice straight cedar tree and after limbing it and removing the bark, he cut it into fifteen-inch-long blocks and then squared each piece ready for me to make shakes. The chunks of wood were too heavy for me to move so I cut the shakes right there in the woods where the tree had fallen. I used a froe, which has a fifteen-inch sharp cutting edge fastened at right angles to a wooden handle. It was part of the equipment that Gus had left behind. I would line it up with the straight edge of the cedar block and smash down on it with a rubber mallet. The grain of the cedar was very straight and the froe would only need a few more hits to make it slide right through to break off a nice straight shake.

My left hand and wrist shuddered from each froe-slam and my right hand up to my shoulder vibrated with each bash of the mallet. I was cutting shakes in the winter months, with freezing-cold rain falling on me most of the time. I had a bright yellow rain jacket on, rain pants and a big black sou'wester, but nothing could keep the rain off my wrists and hands. I would work until I could hardly lift the mallet again and then would spend some time piling the shakes into tidy piles. I wrapped the piles with wire and carried the heavy bundles down through the brush and fallen trees and scrambled down the rocks hauling the bundles to the water's edge, one bundle at a time. I tried to time my shake-cutting so that I was finished for the day at high tide so there would be less rocky shore to clamber down. I hoisted the bundles over the side of an old wooden, flat-bottomed boat that we used as a barge and then paddled the boat back to the lodge. I had to unload the old barge when I got back or it would definitely sink overnight. Sometimes George was there to help unload but he was most often busy with his own projects.

After unloading the barge I quickly headed into the half-finished kitchen to get the wood-stove fire stoked and ready to cook supper. Once the fire was roaring, our kitchen would finally be a welcome place to warm up in. The copper coil at the side of the firebox heated water while the fire was burning but while I was out all day, the fire would slowly die down. There was never enough hot water to enjoy a hot bath, unless I went to another huge amount of effort to boil great big canning pots full of water to help fill the bath. We had moved the cast iron bathtub into the backroom and would soon have a hot-water tank hooked up. So getting warm after a long day out in the freezing rain was a slow and arduous task.

George's dad had stayed with us for an extra week. He couldn't bear to just leave when he could see how much work we had ahead of us. He was such a jolly presence and tackled any job that George handed him with wonderful good humour. I was sad to see him go. Sadder still that he took my dog, Tuki, with him. George didn't like the dog and deemed it untrainable. Ernie agreed, so off Tuki went.

We next renovated the cabin that we bought from Gus Erickson, and that involved changing the outside of the building and filling in a breezeway to be part of the new guesthouse. We made the original room that Gus had lived in into guestroom number one and the area that we closed in became guestroom number two. Each guestroom had lots of space for three beds and would have its own washroom with a toilet, sink and shower. The area between the rooms would make a good-sized entrance with an oil heater to dry guests' rain gear. This room was forever called the drying room, not the usual mud room, since there was no mud—just lots of rain. There was another long narrow room at the other end of the cabin into which George put a door from the outside, and that room became the tackle shop.

Renovating Gus's cabin had been a challenge for George because it was originally built by someone who apparently didn't understand proper building practices. They must have built the walls flat on the float and then lifted them. This is how the cabin was originally built:

Approximately every twenty-four inches they laid an alder pole to be used as a wall stud. Then they nailed poles perpendicular to the uprights about six inches up from the bottom and several inches down from the top. These top and bottom poles were used to tie the uprights together but should have been attached across the very top and bottom of the upright poles as what is called the "plate." They flipped these framed walls over and nailed thin shiplap planks to the outside, trying but not always succeeding to centre the ends on an upright pole. They managed to lift the wall and brace it to others that were built the same way. Then they nailed hand-cut shakes on the outside. There was no finish on the inside walls. The roof joists rested on the top alder pole and the roof was finished with shiplap planks and hand-cut shakes.

As a result of this curious building technique, when there was any amount of snow load on the roof of this cabin, the entire roof and walls sank down under the weight and rested on the walkway on the bottoms of the shakes. This also created a problem for me as I nailed my cedar shakes onto the new outside walls of the building. I had cut close to a thousand shakes to cover the new walls, and I was hammering into something akin to a soft mattress. The studs should have been sixteen inches on centre instead of twenty-four inches apart, so the whole wall would bounce when I hammered making it difficult to hit the nail a second time. George had bought a huge box of really cheap nails used for nailing plywood. They had rings around them so they wouldn't pull out of the wood, but this also made them bend very easily. Using bendy nails on a bouncy wall defied logic.

The first wall that I worked on, I just followed the way that Gus had put his shakes up and found out quickly from George that that was not the right way. Gus had just started with a shake on one side of a wall and overlapped them across, then without measuring, started another row above. I

Heavy snow weighed down the floats. One of the old cabins was built in an unorthodox way. The bottom plate was attached to the side of the wall studs, which were simply alder poles, so we had to remove the snow from the roof before the weight made the building settle onto the bottom of the shakes that covered the walls. We put aluminum roofing on all the buildings so the snow could slide off quickly. We could then shovel it off the floats.

learned to attach a long, one-by-one board or stringer across the bottom of the wall, then a row of shakes beside each other and then covered the gaps between them with another row of shakes across the bottom. Then I used a chalk line to attach a long narrow board that created the straight edge for the next row about eight inches up. All of this was done in the pouring rain and of course there were no gutters to keep the water from continuously inundating me. This is where the hammer-and-nail claw-hands come in. It was like a wartime torture to have to work as the winter cold water cascaded down on my wrists hour after hour.

George had to go to Port Hardy to be a witness for the Fisheries officer's seizure of the illegally purchased Indian food-fish sockeye fillets from the fishing lodge the previous summer. The lodge owner "defendant," Mike, sauntered into court looking very dapper and well tanned from his recent month in Mexico, George told me. George approached Mike to ask if he wanted the float we were borrowing to support the old leaky boat, *OM*, while we repaired it, or if he would sell us the float outright? "Sure," he said, "how much is it worth to you?" George said, "A hundred dollars?" Mike said, "How about two hundred?" George then said that it wasn't worth it, but for the convenience of not having to pull the boat off "and having it sink again," he agreed to pay him two hundred. Shortly after that, Mike pleaded guilty to one charge and the Crown decided to drop the other two charges. His defence was that "people are out to get me because I'm an American—and everybody gets fish from the Indians all the time." The Crown asked that he be severely fined with the maximum, which could be as high as one thousand dollars. The judge announced that his fine would be two hundred dollars! Poor George. He was really choked at having to pay Mike's fine for him by buying that scrap-heap float.

The Page Hits the Water

George had been working harder and longer trying to get the boat repair finished and get *The Page* ready for the water so we could take it outside of our bay into the main channel where we could use our VHF radiophone. Once it was ready we would use *The Page* for long-haul trips, for carrying freight and for carrying guests after we opened the lodge. Since we didn't have a high antenna, we had to get away from the surrounding hills to have better phone reception. The phone on the boat was registered under the name, *The Page,* but when we made a phone call during high-traffic times, we would quickly answer the operator's query with "*Page.*" It was short and sweet and the operator often heard our boat name before picking out a longer name. This would be very important later when there would be hundreds of boats in the inlet, and we might be fiftieth in the lineup to make a call.

We had hauled *The Page* up onto the side of our house float using our handy little come-along. Then George used the hand jacks called Gilchrist jacks, which handloggers had used to move gigantic logs in the woods, to raise the boat, one side at a time, onto blocks so it was two feet above the deck so he could work under it. He built a frame around it that he covered with plastic so he could work on it in any weather. The covered frame also helped to keep heat in when it came time to set the fibreglass layers.

Once the boat was covered, he attached the new and much stronger floor joists that he had cut from a log on my island. He then put a new floor on top and lots of layers of fibreglass to make it really sturdy. He also sanded the outside of the boat and added strips of fibreglass down the prow, along the bottom, on the sides and all around the motor well so the boat was incredibly strong and heavy. He finished the outside with a shiny, smooth gelcoat that made the boat look very professional.

We ran the little generator for long hours so he could use electric lights the last few nights as he finished the final bits of fibreglass work and painting. We were bound and determined to be on the water by 7 PM in case someone phoned us. We had planned to be out in the boat between 7 and 8 PM on Wednesday evenings to receive calls and to phone friends and family. George ran everywhere, ten steps to get a screwdriver, five steps to get the sander, eight steps to get a piece of wire. No time for walking. No time for meals. We had lowered the boat two days ago so it was sitting on metal rollers with a few wooden blocks keeping it balanced and steady. The afternoon was speeding by as I called out the time in half-hour increments. As I pulled a meat pie from the oven and stashed it in a box with salad and wine, George was attaching the last bit of wiring, ready to connect the radiophone.

Everyone who had stopped by to watch us work in the last few weeks had asked how we would get the boat back into the water. They were all doubtful that the rollers would work. "The boat is too heavy ... There will be too much drag ... You'll need more people to push." Needless to say, after removing the blocks, we were holding our breath as we exerted every ounce of our combined energies for the first push. *The Page* started to roll as if we were pushing a little red wagon. It hit the water at exactly 6:35 PM. Just minutes to spare in order to be in position to hear if anyone would call us at 7 PM, the time we had told people we would be available for calls. We suddenly had to scramble since neither one of us had thought to put a rope on it. I jumped into my boat and started the engine, hooked a bowline onto *The Page* then onto my towing harness, and I headed out of the bay pulling the boat behind me. George was already on the floor installing the radiophone.

I laughed all the way out of the bay because *The Page* was sitting so high on the water without an engine to weigh down the stern that it fishtailed and danced around on the surface, but I had to drive far enough out of the bay to be away from the surrounding hills. George must have been getting dizzy but didn't stop working until we were minutes from where we could pick up good reception and I saw him raise the antenna. I tied the two boats together then shut the engine off and scrambled aboard *The Page*. The sun was still quite high above Mount Buxton on Calvert Island, so the evening was lovely and bright with the slightest breeze pushing us along. We drifted on the current with just the sloshing of water as it splashed on the side of the boat, and the tranquil water sparkled all around us. Then we heard the haunting call of a loon as we gently glided out toward Fitz Hugh Sound—the perfect soundtrack as we toasted the almost-finished boat. It still needed the seats, steering wheel and engine installed, but it was now built like a tank, and the little finishing bits wouldn't take too long.

Every Wednesday evening, I boxed up dinner and we headed out and drifted around in Darby Channel hoping that someone would call between 7 and 8 PM. If no one called by 8 PM, we usually called someone just so we could be in contact with the outside world. George's dad had found a travel agent in Duncan on Vancouver Island to whom we would pay a commission for sending fishing guests our way. We hoped that we would hear from her but it was still early, and we hadn't actually advertised yet.

We could now use the phone to call George's mom and dad, who still lived in Lake Cowichan, and who would be doing a lot of grocery shopping for us to make sure that we had fresh produce and dairy delivered on a regular basis. Lucky, the owner of the Dawsons Landing General Store, told me that he would not put in a special order for me on a continuing basis. I wanted to cut down on the fresh produce that we would have to fly into the lodge, and I loved working with the soil on dry land. I had my garden looking really great now. I planted seeds in the house and set out tiny kale, Swiss chard, spinach and lettuce plants on the island. I planted carrots, turnips, beets and Brussels sprouts straight into the ground. I started zucchini seeds and planted them in five-gallon buckets beside the

The view from outside the main bay in front of our lodge where, in the mid-1970s, we drifted around in order to find reception good enough for making phone calls. A few weeks after re-launching *The Page*, we were able to lift an antenna high enough to get reception right in our house, just in time to receive a call from our first guests.

house. I also had tomato plants that I would move out to the front of the house very soon. We carried an old rickety wooden rowboat onto the front corner of our house float and I filled it with soil and seaweed. We enjoyed the sun-warmed lettuce that I pick to thin out the plants growing there. I will have lots of fresh vegetables to serve our guests this summer. Our first guests would arrive on June 25, and we were both looking forward to finally getting our resort started! There was still a lot of work to do though.

Carburetors and Kenny

The look on his face told us what had just happened. Our friend James had swallowed the needle valve from the carburetor of our broken-down generator. He had insisted that, "You have to take the carburetor apart three times ... no less than three times." George had already stripped and cleaned the parts several times and the generator was still not getting enough gas to keep it going. James took it apart again and said, "the needle valve is probably just clogged," and blew into it. Then he sucked on it and the teeny tiny valve disappeared—right down his throat.

We had been rushing to put the finishing touches on our main house/lodge building and our first guesthouse before the new fishing season started and now we had no power to run the table saw, and, well, no power. The saw was set up in the dining room of the lodge so we could cut all the finishing pieces right where we needed them. The generator was a five-kilowatt Busy Bee that we had ordered from the Princess Auto catalogue. Where on earth would we find the part that we needed? James was one of John Salo's deckhands in Sunshine Bay and had come over to catch the flight to Port Hardy from our "Sleepy Bay International Airport Dock." He was leaving and taking that very important piece of equipment in him. I wanted to nail his foot to the floor. George hinted that we would even be happy to receive a parcel from him in the mail.

George headed out of the bay in *The Page* so he could use the radio-phone. He made several calls and tracked down a carburetor in Florida and asked the company to "air-freight" the package to us in Rivers Inlet.

There was so much work to do and very little time, so George started "ripping" one-by-sixes with his chainsaw. We needed one-by-ones and one-by-twos for finishing the walls in the kitchen and around the edges of the floors. This would take ten times as long as cutting with the table saw but we had to keep working. Ripping through a one-by-six lengthwise is a very slow process and is very hard on the chain. The wood heats up, the saw heats up and the language heats up, so I would make sure that I was working on something far, far away. There would be a cloud of blue smoke coming from the overheated saw and a cloud of blue air hovering over George's head. I learned very early to read the warning signs and beat a hasty retreat. As soon as George finished a nasty job though, his usual carefree and happy self would return and I could work beside him again.

Five days later the part still hadn't arrived at Dawsons Landing. George called the company from the boat on his way back from the store. There was an air-traffic controllers' strike, and freight was not being flown anywhere. We had to work with what we had, which was a very small 2.5-kilowatt gas generator that would power the paint sprayer, the hand drill and not much more. I started painting everything in sight, inside and out. It is much easier and faster to paint in an unfinished room with a paint sprayer than with a paintbrush and roller. There is nothing to cover and protect except the windows, which I taped and covered with plastic before I started spraying.

My brother Kenny and his friend Alvin arrived from Winnipeg to stay with us for a couple of weeks. Kenny loved fishing and every time he put a line in the water, he caught something different. We ate well while Kenny was with us. He was in fisherman's heaven but we had to put them both to work. I put a paintbrush in Alvin's hand and pointed him toward the miles and miles of white trim that needed to be painted outside. Kenny and I worked together in the kitchen painting the rough chainsaw-cut trim. Most of the pieces hadn't been attached yet, so to save time I cut them to size with the handsaw and we would paint them, put a couple of finishing nails partway into the wood, and then holding onto that nail, we then nailed them to the wall where it joined the ceiling. Kenny is taller than I am and could reach most of the spots where we were attaching the boards. I had to perch on a paint can so I could pound the nails in.

Kenny could remember every funny line from every funny movie he had ever watched, and he entertained me with humorous skits. We were running out of time so we made up for it by not letting the paint dry before we stuck the boards up, and we were having a hell of a time holding onto the wet wood. I was on my tiptoes on a paint can, reaching way over my head, holding on to one end of a nine-foot board that was still wet with paint and trying to hit a tiny finishing nail with a hammer that was already slick with paint. My hammer would slide off the nail and splat into the paint, spraying white specks all over my face and hair. I started giggling. At the other end of the board, Kenny started snickering. Before long we were doubled over hooting and snorting when George walked into the kitchen. He looked at me, then he looked at Kenny, and in an absolute fury, he stormed out of the kitchen yelling over his shoulder, "It isn't funny!"

The poor mini generator just couldn't work that hard. We burned out the brushes, which conduct the current, and essentially crippled the generator. Now I couldn't even use the paint sprayer, and we still had to paint many rooms on the inside of the lodge and guesthouse as well as the cedar shakes and shingles on the outside of all the buildings. George bought the only available set of the wrong brushes at Dawsons Landing. He carved them to fit using his jackknife, and we had a little power again. Still no needle valve for the bigger generator though.

We were using Aladdin lamps in the evening to conserve the generator for using tools in the daytime. Aladdin lamps are nice and quiet (as opposed to the Coleman lamps that had to be pumped up and hissed from the pressure the whole time they were lit). They were also very bright, but if the mantle was a little crooked the flame would start to make soot on one spot and if you didn't notice right away, the soot patch would get bigger and bigger until it started a flame burning. At this point, the light in the room would grow dim and little specks of black soot would start drifting down onto the page that you were reading as you slowly brought it closer and closer to your face because you could hardly see it. Someone would finally notice and with a shout of "The lamp! The lamp!" would leap up to rescue us from what was now a flame shooting a foot high out of the top of the glass.

While still waiting for the generator parts, George used the chainsaw to cut a hole in the living-room roof to put the metal chimney through for the new fireplace that had just arrived. It was a Franklin fireplace from the Sears catalogue. At this point the only heat in the house was the old wood stove in the kitchen, which wasn't quite enough to heat the whole house on a cold day. The fireplace arrived with a removable screen, a set of fireplace tools and two brass balls that we were supposed to screw into the top of the stove for decoration. I didn't like that idea so I cut a chunk of Styrofoam from the packing box and screwed the brass balls into it and put the sculpture on a shelf in the bedroom. I liked the idea of having brass balls.

We finished the trim in the kitchen and Kenny and I started painting the outside of the main lodge building. We had had several days of good weather and decided the shingles would be dry enough. We both had thick, wide paintbrushes and a bucket of milk-thin red stain. The old shingles were very dry and soaked up the paint like sponges. We painted for about four hours and had only managed to paint one and a half outside walls. I was thinking *Please, oh please be there!* when George left to check if the part had arrived at the store.

Hallelujah! The needle valve had finally arrived. The company had put the part on a bus to Vancouver for furtherance on the freight boat to Dawsons Landing. George quickly put the generator back together and, while we crossed our fingers, tried starting it up. It worked! We could get back to using power tools. In the next four hours, using the paint sprayer with a tube going into a five-gallon bucket of stain, we were able to finish painting the outside of all the buildings. I carried the bucket along while George sprayed the walls. Even with having to move the ladder every few feet, we were still able to finish painting all of the outsides of the buildings in less than four hours. Hooray for electricity!

George cut huge cedar planks to make dining tables, a beautiful bar, the porch steps and beds for the guestrooms. He cut stacks of planks to completely cover the open spaces on the floats and to make a heavy walkway between our lodge float and the guesthouse float as well as a bridge over to the generator shed. Putting the planks down across the logs was a slow job. Each plank had to be levelled just right across the float logs, which were a mishmash of uneven surfaces. He used cedar shingles to shim up the planks on any low points and used the adze to chop down through logs that were too high. Amongst our first guests a few weeks later would be a couple of fellows who were timber buyers in the US. They walked around our floats with awe on their faces. They were almost in tears when they talked about our beautiful walkways. And the cost of those walkways if we had to buy those planks in town—they were a full twelve inches wide by a full two inches thick and eight or ten feet long. They didn't feel that they should walk on this beautiful, straight, clear lumber!

When the walkways were finally done, George made a huge plank box with a heavy lid and lined it with Styrofoam sheets for an icebox to hold the fresh fish for guests while they stayed. George had repaired the Francis Millard fishing company's floats during the winter and they agreed that he could get ice from them during the summer. The Millard's fish camp consisted of several large floats tied together in the back of Finn Bay, where commercial fishermen could safely tie up during bad weather and stretch out their fishnets over racks if they were in need of repair. The company had ice available during the commercial fishing season so it would be a short trip for George to pick up several tubs of ice at a time.

We were finally feeling legit, since the freight boat was stopping at Rivers Lodge in Sleepy Bay now, and we would no longer have to travel to Dawsons Landing to pick up our supplies. The freight boat called *Tyee Princess* arrived with our first two open skiffs with motors as well as our order of fishing rods and tackle for our guests. A washing machine, dryer and a dishwasher also arrived. I insisted on the dishwasher. Most of the money we had spent so far was for tools to make George's life easier. The dishwasher, good knives and a beautiful set of canary yellow (just like my car) Copco pots would make my life easier. I was studying the Escoffier cookbook and learning as much as I could. Did you know that in classic French cooking, they suggest that you should not use the core of a carrot? I was paying one thousand dollars freight on a two-thousand-dollar grocery order delivered to Rivers Lodge from Vancouver. If I had to pay that kind of freight on my carrots, I was darn well going to use the whole thing! One very important lesson that I learned from this world-class cookbook was that for the most part, French cooking is about being good at using leftovers. They prepare most of the meal early in the day and mostly rewarm what has already been precooked! Then they add a sauce. Busted!

Now, with the buildings all a uniform red and the white trim getting done, the lodge was starting to look really good. It was time to celebrate!

There was no liquor store in the inlet. There was no one like old Gus making beer anymore, so the only time there was beer in the inlet was in the summer when the people on the Fisheries patrol boat, the *Falcon Rock*, would pick up orders for us. The rest of the year, if we wanted a bottle of wine or rum, we would take the boat to the general store, buy a money order for the price of the wine plus the return postage, and mail it to the liquor store in Port Hardy. About a week after sending in the money order, we would receive a box in the mail with our bottle or two. It was quite amazing how fast the news travelled that liquor had arrived in the inlet. People suddenly dropped over late in the afternoon. It would have been rude not to offer them a drink.

Some folks arrived with food, and we suddenly found ourselves putting the tools away, pushing the table saw against the wall and pouring drinks at the new kitchen counter. We plugged our 8-track player into the extension cord and immediately everyone was dancing to Bob Seger, the Bee Gees and KC & the Sunshine Band. In the middle of "Get Down Tonight," the chimney pipe crashed down and with a *whoosh*, soot shot across the living room. The dancers moved back in each direction but continued hopping and gyrating while George went for the Shop-Vac, vacuumed up the mess, and the dance floor filled up again with the party-starved dancers. Then the booze was gone and we waved goodbye until the next liquor order arrived in the mail. Until then, it was back to offering company a simple cup of tea.

Rivers Lodge Is Open

We didn't celebrate for long. We still had to finish painting inside and clean away all the building debris. I set up the kitchen with my lovely Copco pots and our Wedgewood dishes—given to us as wedding gifts—that would help me produce and beautifully present fine hotel-style dining. When it came to our food and service, we sought to emulate the Four Seasons Hotel. We wanted to look after our guests and anticipate their needs before they even knew what they wanted.

One of Lucky's sons arrived to see how we were doing as I was pushing, pulling and shoving a huge cabinet into place in the kitchen. He leaped in the door and started pushing the heavy cupboard with me. I was so unaccustomed to having someone help with the heavy lifting that I tried to shoo him away. But I quickly realized that it would be great to have his assistance. I had become too independent over the last many months working my way around manual labour and I didn't know how to let go.

We had changed the configuration of the small backroom behind the kitchen and it now held the washer and dryer, and fridge. The room had originally been closed in with no outside access. Axel had used the room to store cans of paint and other items that he didn't want to freeze. There was a low wooden bench along one wall with a large round hole in it and a note was painted above it reminding himself the last time he painted this rather uncivilized toilet, that it had "Vet Paint" and he shouldn't sit down any time soon. The colloquial name for this type of toilet on the coast was "the aquarium." When you looked through the hole, you could see fish swimming around below the logs under the house, and at a super-low tide, you could watch starfish moving along the bottom. Not your bottom—the bottom of the ocean. This bench was the first thing to go when I was tearing the house apart, but I hated to paint over the "Vet Paint" sign. We added a door to the back wall. Just outside was a small shed that we had pulled onto the back of the float for extra food storage. In the kitchen, the cupboards had to be kept well organized since there wasn't time or wood to make doors for them.

George built the beds for the guesthouse and I set up the rooms. I had splurged on down comforters so the guests would be warm in cool weather and cool in warm weather. I tacked cardboard boxes onto the wall of the backroom of our house to pile the extra linens, sheets and towels. George started the oil heater in the guesthouse entrance to take the chill out of the cabin.

He set up the two twelve-foot open fishing skiffs that were for the guests' use and organized fishing gear in the tackle shop beside the guestrooms. I had made a grocery order for the freight boat and had the menu planned for our first guests, who would arrive in a little over a week. As long as the air-traffic controllers' strike was over. But we kept working, hoping that everything would be settled and planes would be flying again.

George had cleaned up the float from which we had pulled the wash house. He filled in places where there were no planks with his hand-cut ones and towed it out to the main bay. Then he used a massive anchor from Gus's shop to keep our new Sleepy Bay International Airplane Float safely anchored away from shore.

Most airplanes could not manoeuvre into the small bay where the lodge was tied to shore. I say most, because over the years there were a few planes that actually did come in and tie up right in front of our house. One was flown by John Salo, who had an inordinate skill with equipment, including airplanes. The other was flown by a pilot who tied to our house float in the Cessna that we chartered to carry three hundred pounds of halibut we bought from Scarlet Point Seafoods in Port Hardy to feed our guests. And later, a pilot who simply didn't know any better came right in to tie up in front of the lodge float.

A few days before our guests were to arrive, George went out in the boat and called the Duncan travel agent. He came back in looking utterly dejected. The strike was still on so the guests had to cancel. We had no other guests lined up. The travel agent didn't know any fishermen, and fishermen didn't know her. George's and my combined marketing skills were less than zero. We had been on our heads with construction and naïvely hadn't done any advertising.

Old Jack Rendle came in for tea in early July. The first sockeye opening was coming up and there were quite a few commercial fishermen tied to the dock at Duncanby Landing in Goose Bay on the other side of Rivers Inlet. Duncanby Landing had fuel available for the fishboats, as well as a small store and washroom and laundry facilities. Jack was the winter caretaker but was able to stay in his cottage during the summer seasons, when he wasn't out fishing himself. I asked if he would like to bring a few of the fellows over for a nice home-cooked meal in exchange for some sockeye. He thought it was such a great idea that he organized six men to come over a few nights later. They were super happy to be fed because they were away from home for several weeks at a time and cooking for themselves. I was super happy because sockeye is the best salmon to can. The night after the fishing was closed for the week, the men all arrived with three sockeye each and had a delicious four-course dinner. We continued with this exchange for the next ten years until Jack left the inlet.

I canned all the sockeye in half-pint jars with just a pinch of salt on the meat. During World War II, even when food was scarce, people didn't want to eat canned white chinook salmon as they assumed there was something wrong with the fish. It's simply due to the genetics of different salmon runs. One year there was a terrific run of white salmon and one enterprising company wrote on the cans: "Will not turn red in the can." They managed to sell all they had. My salmon, canned in a boiling-water bath, was bright red in the jars! The very best canned salmon ever!

Fog filled the bay with a delicious moist air so thick you could almost cut it with a knife. Only the graceful ghostly tops of the trees could be seen as the mist grew lighter with the heat of the sun that we could feel but not see. Once the fog burned off it was going to be a beautiful day and the water on the sound would be flat, so we planned a trip to explore the beaches around Hakai Passage. I still like the water to be calm when crossing Fitz Hugh Sound because it's a long way over to Calvert Island and I feel so vulnerable and exposed out in the middle. The fog was gone by the time we were passing the BC Tel station.

We went around to one of the outside beaches where we could anchor *The Page* and use the dinghy that we carried in the back to row right onto the beach. The sand here is lovely, fine white shell. It was still very early in the morning with a super-low tide as we walked along the slippery kelp-covered rocks and hunted for abalones on the shore on the other side of the bay. Sometimes you could see one stuck to a rock, and other times you would find one when you pulled the long kelp leaves out of the way. The abalones can't get away, they sort of flutter along by the frilly edges of their thick meaty "foot" so slowly that you can barely see them move.

There were also a few rock scallops here. Rock scallops filter feed in somewhat the same way as abalones so you often find them in the same area. I found two beautiful scallops where they were attached in a crack of a rock shelf very close to the waterline. I chipped at the shell and cut the meat out. Beautiful! The meat was over two inches deep and two inches across. I couldn't wait to cook them lightly in butter for supper. The tide was now quickly covering the kelp, so after finding about a dozen abalones, we climbed into the dinghy and headed over to the sandy beach where we lit a fire and propped a piece of salmon close to it. The salmon was stuck on a cedar board full of nails pounded through from the back. Before we left home I had covered the meat with brown sugar, and it had been marinating in the sun while we foraged. After walking the length of the beach to see what else we could find, we came back to the fire with a handful of gooseneck barnacles. Then I leaned the salmon closer to the fire and balanced a couple of abalones and barnacle skewers over the coals. We had a seafood feast with fresh bread and salad. The perfect meal, on the perfect beach, after a perfect day.

On our way back home in the afternoon, we stopped the boat outside our bay to phone the travel agent. No news, no new bookings. With a little extra time now, George was determined to put up a good high antenna. He cut down a tall thin alder, cleared the limbs, then dragged it through the water to the side of our float. He attached the antenna to the top of it and using a block and tackle and me, he raised the whole contraption beside the house and hammered a brace around it and to the side of the building. We raced into the house to see if it worked. Sure enough, George contacted the operator for our telephone channel. We could now make phone calls from inside our house! We would still be using our VHF radiophone for many years until Telus decided not to service the equipment due to cost.

Not only could we make phone calls, but we could receive them too. As long as someone was beside or near the phone when Coast Cone, the BC Tel VHF channel in our area, called our vessel name. "Coast Cone calling *The Page*, Coast Cone calling *The Page*, Coast Cone calling *The Page*, Coast Cone out …" Sometimes I would hear "*The Page*" and start running toward the phone, and by the time I got there all I would hear would be "Coast Cone out …"—the death knell since we had no way of knowing who had called. The radiophone was in our bedroom which was close to the kitchen, but it was still just chance that I caught the call from our first real guests.

I was in the kitchen getting ready to can the abalones that we brought back from the beach. We didn't have very much freezer space so canning was the best way to keep the meat. I heard "Coast Cone calling *The Page* …" and ran to accept the call. It was from a couple from California who were in Port Hardy and were looking for a place to go fishing. I still don't know who gave them our boat name and told them how to call us. They had to dial "0" to contact the long-distance operator and get put through to the marine operator in Campbell River who then voice-called us on our Coast Cone channel. Now that I think about it all these years later, it's amazing that we had anyone call us that year! I told them that, "Yes, we have room for you and would love to take you fishing." They were going to fly into the inlet and land in our bay the very next day—they were anxious to get fishing and we were ready.

Our First Guests

There was such a flurry of activity as we ran in all directions at once. I had a menu already organized for the first couple who had to cancel, so now I just had to execute the plan. Here is my first lunch menu, from July 15, 1976, for our very first two guests, Barbara and Jim.

Homemade Corn Bubble Bread and White Bread
Meat Loaf with Chili Sauce
Devilled Eggs • Crab Quiche
Sausage Rolls • Kelp Pickles
Walnut Squares and Coffee

George raced off to pick up ice for the fish box. He re-started the heater in the guesthouse to take any chill or dampness out of the air and got the water running and the hot-water tank started. I had to finish canning the abalones, which was an awful lot of work for so few abalones, but it would be worth it in the end because it would probably be a year before we were in abalone country again. I saved two abalones to cook for our guests and put the rest in a bath of warm water. I always told people that I also put on soothing music so the abalones were totally relaxed when I cut them out of their shells, which made for very tender meat. I had tiny little jars and put two abalones in each with a bit of water and salt. Then I covered the jars with boiling water and boiled them for four hours while I started on my lunch menu.

Fifteen minutes before we were expecting the guests to arrive, George made his way over to the old boathouse where we kept the garbage to be burned. He was carrying a couple of big cardboard boxes that partially obscured his view. He took a step off the generator float and missed the boathouse, which had drifted slightly away, and went straight down in between the floats and into the water all the way over his head. After clambering out, he sloshed his way back in the house with seaweed dripping off his head and beard. After that, he made a habit of waiting to dress in his good clothes only once he'd heard the plane fly over the house.

I was feeling very organized and had plenty of confidence from watching my mom cook. I had spent the last year studying cookbooks to learn the art of making sauces and cooking meat and fish. I had fresh vegetables and herbs to use and by now could make beautiful bread of any kind. My first dinner menu was:

Green Salad with Fresh Herb Dressing
Halibut Steak with Béarnaise Sauce on a Bed of Spinach
Sourdough Bread
Glazed Carrots • Château Potatoes
Lemon Meringue Pie

Our guests finally arrived and were delighted with the accommodations. They had their lunch, and then George took them fishing in *The Page* for the afternoon and gave them a tour of the area. When they came back to the lodge, they brought back a couple of silver bright coho that they had caught. They were very excited. They came in for dinner at about 6 PM and then they headed back out very eager for the evening fishing. When they came back at 10 PM, they had three beautiful coho and a good story about the big one that got away. (A story I would hear many more times over many more years.) I helped George clean and ice the fish, and then everyone headed to bed. It was going to be an early morning. I was the first one up to start the fire in the kitchen stove, make breakfast and pack a lunch for the fishermen to be able to head out by 4:30 AM. They were going to travel up to the head of Rivers Inlet where they heard the fish were bigger. Even in 1976 the head of the inlet was crowded with boats. Everyone had heard that the fish were bigger at the head. There were a few guided resort boats plus private boats that had travelled over from Port Hardy, all scrunched into a very small area hugging the boundary line, full of engine exhaust and careless drivers cutting each other's lines.

Occasionally orcas would follow the fish up to the head of the inlet and into the confined space of the bay, the fish could only get away by diving very deep or rushing up the river before they were ready to spawn. Fishing could die off for hours, or even a day or two, after the whales had been through. One day the whales were actually weaving through the sport boats and one of the resort owners pulled out his rifle and started shooting at them. This created pandemonium amongst the boaters and the fellow was shamed into never doing it again. The orcas and fellow boaters never saw justice for his actions. Nothing ever happened to him because this was long before today's world in which every person would be holding up a cell phone filming his careless and unconscionable behaviour.

Our guests did not like the competitive nature of fishing at the head of the inlet so they decided to fish near our lodge, as George had first suggested. That evening, Barbara caught a thirty-pound chinook. It's amazing how much energy is in the air when someone catches a big fish. They came back into the lodge and were toasting their good luck late into the night. The next day, George took them to fish along an area known as The Wall on the other side of the inlet. There were several guided boats already fishing when they arrived. The others tried to run over George's lines and push him away from the best spots. This just made him mad. Only he knew how strong *The Page* was after he rebuilt it. In comparison, everyone else's boats were thin Tupperware. So George did what was best for our guests. He set a course for where he wanted to go, then turned around and put his head down to fix bait on the guest's hooks. Everyone scuttled out of his way at the last minute as *The Page* plowed toward them, but once again, the atmosphere was too competitive. Our guests loved the peace and tranquility of fishing on our side, where they caught as many fish as anywhere else in the inlet without the hassle of competition. George loved being out in the boat no matter where he was. If he had to add to the conversation once in a while or fix bait on a line, he was okay with that. He just loved to troll along watching the shore and the way the clouds drifted above while feeling the water gently rocking the boat.

In the meantime back at the lodge, I was cleaning toilets, making beds, doing laundry, washing dishes, topping up the wood box, baking cookies and bread and getting lunch ready. There's a pattern here, right? Each day during that first summer when we had guests, and for years to come, the guests headed out between 4:30 AM and 5 AM when it was just starting to get light, and I worked through the rest of the morning to have all the chores done before they came back in for lunch. I made a pot of wonderful clam chowder with bacon and vegetables and fresh clams and had fresh bread just out of the oven to go with it. Our guests never went hungry.

Around the corner from our lodge where we liked to fish, you might see a bald eagle swoop down to pluck a fish out of the water. Or you could watch orcas, grey whales and dolphins passing by. Whale traffic didn't affect salmon fishing at the mouth of the inlet like it did at the head where the fish were collecting in a small area just before heading up the river. There were more directions the fish could go to get away from the whales, so they didn't completely disappear after the whales had gone by.

Our first guests left very happy at the end of their adventure, with lots of fish to put in their freezer and a promise to be back next year. The plane left the airport dock in the main bay and George rushed back into the house. "We've got the undercut in 'er now" he said, and we danced around the kitchen so proud to finally be running our own fishing resort, even though it would be a couple of weeks before our next guests arrived. As it happened, this booking was more by chance than our first. A plane arrived in the inlet and taxied up to the Dawsons Landing store dock, and five men climbed out. They asked Lucky where they could find lodging, and he showed them on a map how to get to our bay. Suddenly there was a plane at our dock and George headed out to the float, and after a quick chat he very slowly tied up the plane. Then I watched as he helped all five men climb into *The Page* and he very unhurriedly drove into the lodge. I realized he was stalling so I had enough time to clear the living room and get the kettle on.

They were a great group of friends from Oregon, who on a whim boarded a plane and flew in to the area and were so happy to have found a place to stay and fish. I made lunch for them while George got them set up with fishing gear and boats, and when they were ready, he led them out to the best place to fish nearby. Some of these men continued to fish with us for over thirty years and became our good friends.

We had one more group of fishermen that first summer. Another plane arrived in the inlet, tied up to another lodge and asked if they could stay and fish. Luckily the resort was full at the time so they had sent them over to us, knowing we might go hungry if they didn't. The resort called us on the boat-to-boat channel so we had about twenty minutes' lead time to get ready. We were used to running in all directions at once so we looked quite casual when the plane arrived. Once again, George took his time tying up their plane and slowly motored into the lodge with his boat full. I was quite ready for them this time.

It was September and the end of our first fishing season. We had to figure out how to make more money. It's surprisingly expensive to live in the middle of nowhere, and we needed money for some advertising. There was no work to be found in the inlet at the time so, very reluctantly, we decided that we would have to go to Vancouver to find work. We found a basement room to rent in an old house near Cambie Street and Vancouver's city hall, with a shared fridge and bathroom. There

The lodge as it looked at the start of our first season. The centre building is the lodge/house. We had one guest cabin with two guestrooms plus the tackle shop. There is a work-shop/generator shed on a float on the left side. We had a small shed behind the lodge for food storage and a paint shed beside the workshop building. At this time we had a little boathouse, big enough for my boat.

was a little hot plate and a sink in our room. I had canned the last few pieces of meat from the freezer and left them for the caretaker, who would live at the lodge while we were in town, and who was a friend of a friend without a job; but for some strange reason, there were quite a few pounds of cheese left, so I dipped one-pound pieces into hot wax and brought them to town. We ate cheese sandwiches for lunch for the next two months.

I answered an ad in the paper and was hired as a cocktail waitress at the Waldorf Hotel lounge, a dressed-up term for the tiki-themed dive bar. There was some very interesting entertainment there, with scantily clad women (they didn't see my wardrobe before they hired me), and the clientele seemed highly questionable with some very scary-looking dudes at the dark tables. It was a crazy, busy, noisy job where tips were everything and the hotel really didn't expect to pay wages. On the third night that I worked there, George came in to see what the place was like and almost punched several patrons before grabbing my arm and hauling me out the door past a very angry bouncer and a lineup of customers.

I found a temporary job at the city hall instead. The manager in the tax department wanted to hire a few extra people because tax time was coming, and he thought his department would be super busy. Really, there wasn't enough work to keep me there but he hired two more people after me. I worked there for three months and never had a very busy day. The best part was that the city hall staff worked four days a week, ten hours a day. Meanwhile, George found work building sets for the CBC TV variety program *The Wolfman Jack Show*. It was interesting and challenging work and he often saw superstars like Dionne Warwick, Tom Jones and Lou Rawls as they wandered around in the studio. We managed to save a good chunk of our wages and were able to head back to the inlet at the end of February.

George's first job after we got back was to build a small float to put his boom winch on. He would then be able to push or tow the winch around to where he needed it—mainly for pulling boats out of the water or tightening cables on our standing boom. It was small enough that it wasn't too much work to cable together. Just as he finished tightening the

Me and George with a nice spring salmon. There weren't very many guests that first summer, so we had plenty of time for fishing.

last cable, he received a call to work on the floats again for the Francis Millard Company. This time he towed the float to Finn Bay and proudly used his own winch to do the work. We were always looking for ways to make more money.

Must Make More Money

September 1977 and our second fishing season was over, our last guests had left, and we had winterized everything and packed all the summer equipment and boats away. We had quite a few more guests in our second season and had hired two young fellows to help with the work on the dock. The crew were gone and we were planning to head to Edmonton to stay with my sister June and her family while we worked and saved money for next year. We both found jobs easily when we got there and worked for the next three months—some of which were the coldest on record.

George's first job was on an outdoor building site. He had never experienced such cold weather in his life and quickly found a cushier, indoor job renovating an office. I worked for the city hall and at a drug store. The best part of this winter was staying with my sister and having fun every single day!

While we were there, George sent in a quote for a contract with the federal Fisheries Department to modify the A-frame building that Fisheries personnel used every summer at Dawsons. With George's design experience, he produced drawings that showed how the building could accommodate more people. He won the contract, so we were excited about having more work when we returned to the inlet.

We bought an old station wagon to drive ourselves, and all the stuff that we had accumulated over the winter, back to Vancouver. On our way out of town, George pulled off the highway just outside of Edmonton and drove along a country road for a few miles then turned into a farm. Several Rhodesian ridgebacks ran up the drive barking. George had seen an ad for puppies, and we bought one to take up to the lodge. Zak was a wonderful dog who loved sleeping in the sun yet looked and sounded scary enough that he would make me feel much more comfortable on my own in the middle of nowhere.

We got back to the inlet and immediately organized projects for ourselves. This included replenishing the wood supply that the caretaker had used up. He must have really liked to have the house warm all day and all night. Then George had to collect logs. We planned to build a second guest cabin and would need lots of logs for building the float for the cabin to sit on.

Our first guest cabin had three beds in each guestroom. This setup limited us if we booked couples, since we could only take two couples at a time instead of, say, six men. We were booking quite a few couples because our lodge had bathrooms in each guestroom, which was a major innovation at the time. Most fishing resorts had one bathroom down the hall for many guests to use, and women would have to run the gauntlet of poker-playing men late at night. Our rooms were large enough, but we needed more accommodation if we wanted to make more money.

George had been collecting logs in earnest since we arrived in Sleepy Bay in early 1976. Every time he went out in the boat, he kept his eyes peeled watching for logs. He made lots of beachcombing trips around

Me and a catch of rockfish. I could catch fish for dinner then put the head and guts in the crab trap to catch the next night's meal: crab—still my all-time favourite dinner—served with a loaf of French bread, a green salad and garlic butter with lemon balm from my garden.

the islands and all the way out to Addenbroke Island, always on beautiful sunny days with no wind. He could spend hours and hours just putt-putting along enjoying the scenery, watching for logs and daydreaming. If he did see a log on a beach, he would pull up beside it, hammer a metal staple with a rope attached called a dog-line into it and tie it up to a tree at the high-tide mark. The unwritten rule was that once there was a dog-line tied to shore, no one else could take the log. He would go back to limb the log at low tide and then head back at high tide when the log would be floating again and tow it home. Towing logs is a very slow process, so it was well worth waiting for a dry day or he could end up sitting in the rain for hours.

When a Girl Says No

I t was a beautiful blue-sky late winter day, cold and clear with almost no wind. We were just back from Edmonton and we needed more logs to build the next guesthouse float. Conditions were perfect for George to retrieve the logs that he had beached several miles from our bay. Zak and I stood at the front of our house and I waved to George as he left the bay. He promised he would be back by 2:30 PM, or I would go out looking for him, but there would have to be something terribly wrong if he wasn't back by then. It was now 9:30 AM and George would be collecting his logs and then slowly, very slowly, towing them home.

I walked into the house and left the door open to let the crisp morning air in. I popped a couple of pieces of wood into the kitchen stove and closed the oven door. It would be a good morning to do a little baking and I could get a head start on the stew for dinner.

I mixed the cookie dough by hand so I wouldn't have to start the noisy generator so early on such a lovely day. I love the peace and quiet when there is no chugging generator in the background. The sound of a varied thrush whistling carried through the open door. There were also a few seagulls fighting over a bit of compost and every once in a while I could hear bald eagles with their high-pitched bugling. I listened to CBC on the radio that we had hooked up to a car battery and an inge-nious compact soapbox antenna: inside the plastic soapbox, copper wire was wound around and around then clamped onto another wire that had been fed through a tiny hole in the window frame. Someone on the coast produced dozens of these boxes and sold them through local stores. The only channel that we could receive was the CBC, and I was thankful for it because otherwise I would be left talking to myself, which was something I did a lot of while I worked on my own when George was so often out and about in the boat.

I had pulled one pan of cookies out of the oven and was about to put another one in when I heard a low thrumming sound. It sounded like a boat was coming into the bay. I looked out and saw Zak standing at the edge of the float. As the engine sound got louder, Zak started to bark. He looked pretty scary when he was serious about something. He weighed about eighty-five pounds and his distinctive ridge of hair that stood straight up along his spine had the effect of making him look angry even when he was quite content. I caught a glimpse of the boat as it passed the shallow channel to our bay and headed for the wider and deeper entrance. It was the *Grizzly King*, the fishboat owned by Jack Rendle. I called him Uncle Jack—most people did. He had a tendency to show up right when baking was coming out of the oven. I don't know how he did it, but it was an uncanny skill.

Zak settled down when I told him it was okay, and Uncle Jack pulled his boat alongside the front of our float and I tied it up. Uncle Jack always stood holding onto the cabin door of his boat, chatting about anything that came up, just waiting for an invitation. Of course I invited him in for tea.

The delicious smell of fresh-baked cookies wafted out the door and Jack was delighted to see the rack of cookies and went over to sit on the bench behind the kitchen table. I started to put a few cookies on a plate and all of a sudden, Jack had grabbed my arm and was stretching his toothless, wobbly face toward mine trying to kiss me. He wouldn't let go of my arm and was grabbing at my head trying to pull it toward him. I managed to yank my arm away from him and ran around to the other side of the worktable. He lurched after me and I continued on around the table shouting, "No!" at him, then took a breath and whistled for Zak. Zak immediately appeared at the door and lunged, growling at Jack. Jack thumped back down on the bench behind the dinner table and whined, "Boy, when a girl says no like that ... she really means it!"

At this point, the kettle whistled and I made tea. Jack seemed to be safely tucked away behind the table and I stayed standing behind the worktable with Zak standing by my side. I realized that Jack, who I never called "Uncle" again, had seen George towing his logs and knew that he wouldn't be home for several hours.

I had trouble processing the information that this old man, who was a practicing Seventh-day Adventist, who we had known for the past two years, could be so gross and disgusting. Every Saturday he anchored his fishboat in a bay around the corner from us and supposedly spent his time there reading scripture. Hmm, I wonder.

Good thing there were two tables between us while we had our tea, and I was very glad that I had left the door open for the fresh air and my protective dog. This person was not who I thought he was and there was more trouble to come later when I would not be able to convince George that I didn't want to be alone with Jack on his fishboat and especially without my trusty Zak!

Boom Winch and Other Floats

When George had enough logs for the float, he started assembling them side by side in a tight row shaped like a rectangle in front of our house. Using rope and staples, he tied the logs together to keep them from moving while he used the come-along on the boom-winch float and hauled a smaller log up and crosswise at each end of the narrow sides of the rectangle. This top log would be the "lash log" that would permanently hold the float together once we tightened the cable around it and each log. He coiled one-inch cable around each log and over the lash log then under the next log and up and over the lash log again. This is a tedious job because one-inch cable is very hard to work with and doesn't bend easily. Next he would string the cable over the Gilchrist jack then lightly attach the cable with a five-inch steel staple. This is where I come in.

George straddled the log while hitting the cable with a heavy sledge-hammer, and I jumped up and down on the handle of the jack to pull the cable even tighter. After many hammer smashes and hops, the jack could be clicked one more notch. This would drag the cable tighter and tighter with each click until he could pound the staple deep into the wood, and that would hold the cable solidly at that point. Then we would start over at the next loop over the next log. The new float had ten huge logs in it so this process was painstakingly slow and required an incredible amount of energy. The float took two weeks of utterly exhausting effort. Jack and fellow commercial fisherman Ken Moore stopped by at the same time one day, and while we chatted in front of the house, they both walked over and kicked at the cable lashings to check whether they were tight enough.

I was constantly afraid of slipping off the Gilchrist jack and splashing overboard. We usually did everything we could to not fall overboard, since the water is so cold, and it's just not nice to land unannounced in the water fully clothed. I ended up over the years wrenching my back, pulling hamstrings and damaging ribs in various efforts to not fall in, when often, just letting go and landing in the water would probably have been much easier to deal with.

George had enough logs left to build a float that would be capable of carrying a large amount of boat gas. He did the calculations over and over and checked with others to make sure that he would have enough flotation to carry the three thousand gallons that the tank could hold. The tank hadn't arrived on the freight boat yet, but he needed to have the float ready to receive it when it did arrive.

It was near the end of February and time for George to do a little business in town and start getting supplies lined up for the Fisheries contract. Before he left, he checked the water tanks and the water line, made sure the batteries were all topped up with water and the generator diesel tank was full. He also filled two day-tanks with gas for my speedboat and made sure the connections on the boat battery were all functioning. He didn't want me to be stranded somewhere when he wasn't in the inlet. I would have contact with our neighbours on the VHF radio, and there was VHF on the boat, but it was nice to have all motors and equipment in tip-top shape before he left me alone in the middle of nowhere.

He worked right up until we heard the plane fly over the house, then he ran in to shower and change. I grabbed his already-packed bag and threw it in the back of the boat. A few minutes later, I could see the plane, a Beaver, taxiing up to our airplane float. I started the motor and untied both ropes but held onto the stern line. Moments later, George jogged out of the house, jumped into the boat and I jumped in after him with the rope. We zipped out of the bay and then slowly approached the airport so we wouldn't rock the airplane with the boat wash. We tied up the boat just as the pilot climbed out of his plane and tied it up with the one rope that he used in the middle of the pontoon.

I put on my brave face as George folded me in his arms and I finally had to let go knowing that I was soon going to be so alone. The pilot took George's bag from him and tossed it into the back of the plane then stepped aside for George to climb the two steps up and in. There was no one else in the plane, so George eagerly worked his way up into the front co-pilot seat. The pilot untied his rope and climbed in, then I pushed on the wing to move the plane away from our float. When they were a few feet away, the pilot started the engine and off they went, with a thunderous roar, taxiing out of the bay and lifting off the water, then disappearing around the corner of the island and behind the trees. I stood on the dock watching until I couldn't see or hear them any longer, and the quiet closed in and draped over me.

I carefully climbed back into the boat, mindful that I was by myself now and started the engine. It sputtered to life with no problem and I leaned over and untied the stern line. I felt much better when I pulled up to the float and Zak was there to greet me. He was very good company, but it felt strange to suddenly be the only human for miles around. George was going to be away for a whole week. I would have to get used to the quiet, which actually felt very heavy and made me feel tired even though it was only 1:30 PM, and he'd only been gone five minutes.

I would have to get busy or I would go crazy here all by myself. But for now, I just wanted to sit down and read. I had a pile of books that I would finally have time to work through, and after making myself a nice cup of tea I sat down and started on the first one, *Shōgun* by James Clavell. Once I got involved in the story I knew I was going to have trouble doing anything else until I finished the book. I had the most amazing feeling of freedom: no one was there to tell me I was reading too much or for too long or wasting time. I read through the afternoon and until it was too dark to see the words on the page, and finally I lit a lamp so I could continue reading. I eventually went to bed when my eyes couldn't take it any longer.

When I woke up the next morning, I decided that I needed to accomplish something before I would allow myself to read like that again. I wandered around outside and noticed that the boom-winch float was tied up in front of the guesthouse. There was no boom winch on it at this moment. It had been used to pull our guest boats out of the water for the winter and then when we built the new guesthouse float, but George had since put the winch away in the workshop. The empty float was about ten by twelve feet and looked like it needed something on it. I had wanted a greenhouse for a while now and thought it would be such a good idea to build one while I had the chance and the time.

We didn't have a lot of extra wood around so I took an axe over to my garden and chopped down some small saplings. Each one was about six feet high and only about two inches at the thickest part. I would need at least two poles for each upright and a few extra to lash the two sides together to form a U-shape that I could cover with plastic. I tromped around on the island for hours picking out just the right sized trees and chopped them down.

Then I limbed them and hauled them down to the work skiff, all the while keeping a close eye on the boat so it didn't get hung up on the shore as the tide went out. I didn't want to get stuck for hours on the island while it got dark, waiting for the tide to come back in to lift the boat off the rocks. I was ultra careful about the boat and extra careful when I used the axe. I placed my steps cautiously on the uneven ground—I didn't want to sprain my ankle. I couldn't rely on getting help for myself, so I had to rely on not making any mistakes. At least I felt safe enough on my island since the only wild animal we had seen on it was a deer. No bears or cougars or wolves yet! I would not have felt safe climbing around on the big island behind the lodge because there were always wild-animal prints and sounds of them howling or crashing through the bush.

I nailed the bottom of the poles to the float logs along both sides, with enough room to walk on either side of the float. Then I lashed the poles together with rope to form the uprights and also lashed branches along the middle to keep the structure rigid. We had a good-sized roll of plastic that was left over from covering *The Page*. I found the plastic and rolled it out and cut enough to cover the structure. I had already been working on my greenhouse construction for a couple of days and I didn't want to start covering it until I had a whole day in front of me, so I left the plastic in the shop and made a quick supper so I could sit with my book again.

The next morning, I loaded the heavy-duty stapler and tied a string to it with a loop to go over my wrist in case I dropped it. I then covered the poles. For an entrance, I knotted the end flap so that I could lift it and walk in. Now I just had to put some plants into it. Again I went over to the island and, this time, I dug up several ferns and some wildflowers and planted them in large cans and a couple of wooden boxes from the workshop. Then I stood back and admired my work. I have to say, it was a thing of beauty.

I knew that the mail plane had been to Dawsons so while I still had lots of daylight left, I headed up to the store in *The Page* to pick up supplies and mail. Partway up Darby Channel, where there is an open area about two hundred yards across, I could see two humpback whales leaping out of the water. I zipped along quite close to shore until I was in line with where they had last leaped and crashed back into the water. I shut the engine off, drifted and watched a spectacular display. It was almost like they knew I was there and were putting on a show for me. Then I saw the flukes of both whales and knew they were diving deep. I floated along for a couple more minutes, then feeling a little trepidation that they could quite easily come up under or over my boat, I started the engine and took off toward the store.

Seconds later, the cabin of my boat filled with a roar that boomed and deafened me and I thought I was being swallowed by one of the giant whales. My breath caught and my heart raced as I sped away hoping to outrun the monster that I couldn't see. Suddenly, a shadow passed over the front of my boat and, as my vision cleared, I could see a fishing-resort owner's airplane zoom in front of me, not more than ten feet above my boat. I continued on my way and there was the plane, tied to the dock in front of the store. I pulled in, tied up my boat and stormed into the store. I could see the fellow was still laughing with Lucky but I was so full of the fear-fuelled adrenaline rush that I marched up to him and roared, "You asshole!" right in his face. He was gobsmacked and lost his stupid grin. They didn't call me "Don't-Mess-With-Me Ardley" for nothing.

I had one day left before George would be back and I spent the time reading and relaxing. I was quite pleased with my work on the greenhouse and looked forward to showing it off. I had not actually had much time to think about how quiet it was or how much I missed having George there with me. Once I was safely tucked away in bed, I didn't worry that something bad might happen, and as long as I didn't have to go out in the dark to turn the generator off, I was perfectly happy to use an Aladdin lamp to read by. I didn't need power for anything else.

George arrived home in a new-to-us, but used-by-others speedboat. It had a deep V-shaped hull so it would be more comfortable than our flat-bottomed speedboat in choppy water. We cleverly named this boat *Sportspage*. George immediately noticed the new structure. He was most concerned that he might need the boom-winch float to actually use the boom winch. I told him that he would have to build me a greenhouse then, because I was very happy to be able to potter about with plants and looked forward to getting vegetable seeds started in the spring. I told him, "Don't leave me alone if you don't like what I do while you're gone."

Brass Balls

The new guesthouse float was finished and plans were starting to take shape for the Fisheries building in Dawsons Landing, but we needed money and more supplies for our new guesthouse as well as the A-frame. We hired a new caretaker and we left the inlet hoping things would still be all right when we got back. We had one week to spend in Vancouver and we had to make every minute count. We would visit friends and family, shop for supplies and work with our travel agent and friend, Nigel, to put together a marketing plan. We had given up on the travel agent from Vancouver Island as someone who was too far from the epicenter of fishing traffic. We went to our bank to ask for money to build the new guest cabin. We had been with CIBC for a few years now and thought our proposal was quite good. We could show them that we already had the contract with Fisheries. That should count for something! The loans officer told us that we would not be getting any money from them, we weren't solid enough—and we were floating for God's sake! George was so mad that he reached over the desk and plucked our bank file from the fellow's hand and—while the man was still blubbering, "You can't take that!"—we walked out of his office.

Then we tried the Bank of BC. We met with a nice fellow who listened politely and took our information and told us to come back in a few days. We went back to George's sister's house where we were staying, feeling uncertain about the outcome of that meeting. We returned two days later and the nice bank fellow told us, "Sorry, but we can't see your lodge and therefore we don't feel that we can lend you the money." We were ushered out of his office but before we left, I used the washroom down the hall. When I came out, George and I found ourselves waiting for the elevator with the same nice bank fellow. As we rode silently down to the main floor, I turned to him and said, "You call yourselves the Bank of BC but you should be called the Bank of Georgia and Granville Streets. I have heard that to be a successful business you need two things: a strong capital base and brass balls. Well, we have half of the requirements and I think you should trust us enough to lend us the money!"

Thanks to my quick wit and the brass fireplace decoration sitting on our bedroom shelf, the next day we received a phone call telling us that we were approved for the loan.

Building the A-Frame

It was now the end of February and we were running out of time. We had to get back up to the inlet. We ran in all directions at once and picked up and delivered as many supplies as we could collect. We had to come up with a serious timeline to do the work on the Fisheries A-frame building by March 31 so we could build our guesthouse and finish the rest of the lodge work before the summer fishing season.

There were building supplies that George could order over the VHF phone but the phone system was not 100 percent reliable and sometimes didn't work for days at a time. I had fun shopping for groceries that would last through several months, new rain gear to replace the not quite adequate gear that we had been using for months and a few bits of cloth to make myself some warm work shirts. Meanwhile, George ordered the rest of the equipment and supplies that we would need to add on to the Fisheries cabin and everything would be shipped from Vancouver to Dawsons Landing on the freight boat.

We flew back into the inlet on a beautiful sunny day. Flying over the waters of Queen Charlotte Sound but close to shore most of the way, we could see great kelp beds and incredible swirling turquoise water as it broke over rocky islets and crashed onto the long sandy stretch of beach in Blunden Bay just north of Cape Caution. The beach is mostly inaccessible except for the odd helicopter, intrepid kayaker and the commercial Cessna that once foolishly landed there.

We flew over our buildings to signal to the caretaker that we were back. The Beaver landed in Darby Channel, taxied into the main bay and was tied to our airplane float. We had time to unload all the supplies before a sheepish-looking caretaker finally pulled up slowly to the dock in our work skiff. He wasn't supposed to use *Sportspage*, our new speedboat, because there was something wrong with the starter and it sometimes wouldn't start, which could potentially leave him stranded somewhere if he used it. While he was slowly driving out to pick us up, he must have been trying to come up with a good excuse for why *Sportspage* was on the other side of the inlet. Next we heard that Zak had knocked him overboard three times as he bent to tie up boats. After we heard that, we were actually feeling pretty good that we had a place to come back to. What else might he have done if we had been away longer? We sent him on his way and wandered around touching everything and enjoying being home on our own again.

George drove our work skiff over to a fellow's handlogging camp in Draney Inlet where *Sportspage* had been abandoned and towed it home.

He had the parts to fix the starter, but he wanted to work on it at home where he could use his own tools.

We needed the covered speedboat to use when we drove to Dawsons to work on the A-frame. It would be too cold to have to make the twenty-minute run in the open skiff every morning and then back home at the end of a tiring day. He worked on it all afternoon and finally, I heard the engine start and purr along nicely. Hooray, I wouldn't freeze on the way to work!

We headed up to Dawsons to start work on the ground around the cabin. The freight would be arriving in five or six days and we needed to clear a place to pile everything. There was thick slush on the water all the way up Darby Channel, which really slowed us down, but we could easily make out any logs or floating debris as there was a fresh coating of white snow on them in sharp contrast to the grey slushy water. Everything at Dawsons was coated with snow and ice so there wasn't much we could do at the cabin except check on the tarps and move a few supplies around.

We headed back home to get our cold-weather chores done: chopping wood and kindling and filling both wood boxes, trimming the wicks and filling kerosene lamps for later, and shovelling as much snow off the floats as possible. The weight of the snow made our floats sink lower into the water and lower still if it started raining and the snow soaked it up. So much time was spent on chores just to keep comfortable in the winter.

I kept seeing moths flying around the kitchen. Then I saw the odd one flying crookedly in the living room. Something was wrong. I remember cleaning out the whole linen cupboard at our home in Winnipeg when I was young. Everything went in hot water in the washing machine because my mom would not allow moths in her house. I started a search, checking every drawer, cupboard and shelf. I finally saw a moth flying from the attic. I poked my head past the trapdoor and flashed the light around. I climbed into the attic and crawled across our funny-looking carpet that we had rolled up and stored there because it was too strange to use in our house. (More about this carpet later.) There was also a round cheese crate in the attic full of raw wool that George's dad had brought for me to card and spin.

When I turned the flashlight onto the crate, my flesh crawled. The wool had been eaten into a hollow cone shape and was covered with squirming, wriggling larvae. Obviously, I was only seeing the ones downstairs that the bats didn't eat! I couldn't get out of there fast enough. I called to George that I had an emergency, and he came running into the kitchen. He took a large green garbage bag up and gingerly placed the whole crate in it while I ran to get the work skiff, a bucket of used diesel oil and a blowtorch. I pulled up in front of the house. George lowered the package onto the bench seat, and then he took the container to my garden island, poured diesel all over it and set it on fire. Sadly, without realizing it, he burned the mess right over my stunning poppy-plant roots. They produced beautiful huge red poppies that could be seen from passing boats out in Darby Channel, but they would never bloom again.

The weather along the coast can change very quickly, and the days warmed up and melted the snow and ice. We headed back up to Dawsons and started working in earnest. George had already put in the footings for the two new corners but hadn't backfilled them yet, which was what I did all that day. I collected huge boulders from the shore far below the cabin. I lifted each one up onto the lowest part of the wharf, hoisted them into a wheelbarrow, then pushed the wheelbarrow up the wood-plank walkway. The wheelbarrow would be so heavy that it tipped over almost every time I came to the same turn in the wooden boardwalk, no matter how I balanced the load. Maybe I tried to carry too much each time, but I was determined to push as much as I could at once to get it over with. Once I got to the cabin, I hand-carried the boulders one at a time down a set of rickety wooden stairs and dropped them where the new footings were. Then I collected many heavy buckets of shells and sand to pour in beside the boulders. These buckets full also took the laborious and circuitous trip from the beach up, up, up to the cabin.

Every day that we worked on the cabin, I brought a few bundles of shakes in the boat and, using a wheelbarrow, pushed them up to the cabin site. They weren't as hard to push but it was still awkward. Then I would wrestle the large, heavy bundles down the stairs and around the base of the cabin to pile them close to where I would be using them. When the freight boat arrived, we spent two days moving the lumber from the store float up to the cabin. All our supplies were landed at the store float this time because the ship had blown an engine and was not able to manoeuvre into some tight places like Sleepy Bay or to the Fisheries float at Dawsons. We were concerned that Lucky would be mad at us again for bringing groceries into Dawsons but, because of the special circumstances, he was friendly and just charged us a docking fee.

One item that arrived with our supplies but belonged to the Fisheries was a barrel with a one-hundred-foot length of three-quarter-inch chain. The barrel was eighteen inches in diameter and about two feet high. They had asked George if he would move it from the store float over to the Fisheries float. I can still hear them laughing. It was all George and Lucky could do to raise the barrel to the upright position onto Lucky's freight truck. Then Lucky suggested that it might be easier to move the chain outside of the barrel.

Our friend Richard had arrived to pick up his own supplies so George asked for his help, but while Richard was in the store, George thought just maybe he could move the chain on his own. A heavy chain doesn't react like rope does, so before he moved it, he tied one end to the edge of the lower float, just in case. He cracked open the barrel and pulled one end from the pile and lowered it about four-and-a-half feet from the store float down to the tie-up float. Unfortunately, there was a small gap between the higher and lower floats, so as soon as there was a few feet or so of chain hanging over the side, the weight of it pulled it straight down and all George could do was jump aside and let it go, while checking to make sure that neither the chain nor the rope was wrapped around his ankle. The chain just slid over the side and kept going until all one hundred feet was hanging in the water. The rope held though, but now George sheepishly had to figure out how to raise the chain.

Richard said they could try using his net drum on his gillnetter to spool the chain in, but he hadn't run it since last summer's commercial fishing, so they'd have to see if it would even operate. Once the engine was in gear, the drum made one revolution and abruptly stopped, so Richard jumped onto the foot pedal that operates it and the linkage cable broke. He managed to get enough slack in the cable to tie it back together and after another fifteen minutes was able to get the net drum to turn sporadically if he continually jumped up and down on the pedal. It was a big pedal that required all his body weight, so while Richard was frantically jumping up and down on one side of the boat, George was pulling with the drum on the other side. When George stopped pulling, the drum stopped turning, but Richard kept up his jackrabbit performance.

They finally got all of the chain onto the back of the boat, but they still had to unload it at the Fisheries dock, fifty feet away. When they got there, they found that while the chain had been doubling and tripling over the drum, it was getting wound up in a rope and it took them another hour to unwrap the tight mess. Then Richard turned to George with a silly grin and said, "This is what it's like each and every time I go fishing!" Minus the chain, of course.

When the weather wasn't good for working on the Fisheries cabin, I spent a lot of my time digging up my garden and piling seaweed and starfish into compost piles. I had abandoned the garden on the top hill. When I dumped the buckets of soil and compost over the ten-by-fifteen-foot area, I could see that even if I continued to do this for the next twenty years I would still not have enough real soil.

George used the inclement weather to cut lumber on my island from his beachcombed logs. Using his Stihl 090, with a forty-eight-inch bar, and an Alaskan sawmill attachment, he first squared the log and then cut planks. He was piling the lumber that he would use on the Fisheries cabin onto a small float he had just built. When he had piled enough on, he would tow the float to Dawsons and unload. When the days were really ugly, he worked inside on small wood projects like building shelves for our bedroom, a new kitchen table and finally cupboard doors for the kitchen. I sanded and painted the pieces. He set up a woodworking shop undercover on the woodshed float. His main shop, which was originally Axel's workshop, was for sharpening saws, repairing motors and for storing plumbing, electrical, motor and logging tools.

Another one of George's projects was to put four large truck inner tubes under the corner of our house float using a bicycle pump his dad sent. The float was low in the water with the weight of my little rowboat garden. He pushed the inner tubes under the logs with the valves just visible between the logs. After they were all in place, he used the bicycle pump and pumped them up and together they raised the front side of the float by almost two inches. He had quite a few more tubes that he would eventually use under the old guest cabin.

One day, we were sitting on a log in the sunshine taking a lunch break in front of the Fisheries cabin when a fellow we didn't recognize approached us. He wondered if we could rent rooms to his logging crew and cook three meals a day for about six weeks in April and May. I almost choked on my salmon-and-green-tomato-relish sandwich at the thought of making money before the fishing season even started. He said he would pay for the food and for the expense of shipping it in. George and I carefully exchanged glances, and after a few questions about boat use and fuel, we answered that, yes, we would be able to look after his crew. After we agreed on a price per day per man, the fellow left saying that he would be in touch. As soon as he was out of sight, George and I did a celebration dance and started making mental lists of supplies that we would send for. My other sister, Marcia, had just moved to Edmonton so I was also daydreaming about a trip to see both of my sisters. Now I could afford it.

We worked on the cabin for another six weeks where half of the time was spent wrangling heavy lumber and bundles of shakes up the damn hill. If only we could get the supplies straight up the hill from the water below, but the hillside was utterly impassable. So we either hand-carried the heavy boards from the float below or I put what I could in the wheelbarrow and pushed it up the walkway. After the walls were up and the shiplap boards were attached, I put my hand-split shakes on the outside while George finished the inside. We finished the cabin just before the end of March, right on schedule. We were now ready to look after the logging crew.

They arrived a few days later, and early the following day they headed out with a packed lunch and returned well before dark. They had been working for only two days when the boss showed up and told us that they would be leaving. Every time the fallers dropped a potential tree, it exploded into dust. The wood on his property was no good. Sometimes the inside of huge healthy-looking cedars can be completely rotten. We were just as disappointed as the boss man was. It was not easy to watch that money evaporate along with my trip to see my family. We just did what we would always do: we worked harder on our own projects. George cut a stockpile of lumber for the guesthouse and I worked on the gardens and built planter boxes to spruce up the lodge with flowers.

A Middle-of-the-Night Freight Boat

I was jolted awake from a deep sleep by the high-pitched blast of the freight boat *Tyee Princess* as it stopped in front of the main bay. In the semi-dark, I could see that George was still sound asleep. I used my elbow to wake him and shouted, "The freight boat!" He grunted and rolled out of bed and fumbled for his clothes. I jumped up and dressed in my warm pants and sweatshirt that I had laid out at bedtime. I pulled on my gumboots, grabbed flashlights and headed out the door wondering if the freight boat always tied up somewhere out of sight during the day?

The new guesthouse building supplies were on the boat and we had been running out of things we could do until they arrived. We had tried to stagger the freight between boat trips but with one order arriving late and the next order arriving early, there were going to be tons of supplies on this boat. The company tried to keep to a schedule but there were many circumstances that kept them from being on time. The wind could come up, they might have trouble unloading, and they might take extra time trying to find someone's last item of freight that somehow got lost in the bowels of the boat. So many variables. We had hoped they would arrive in daylight because of the amount of freight they had on board for us.

We now had a larger float to use as an airplane dock and for freight-loading and off-loading. The fire chief from Ocean Falls had helped us with a controlled burn of the *OM* after George finally gave up on his pipe dream of fixing up the old boat.

George used the work skiff to push the now empty *OM* float out to Darby Channel and signalled the skipper with a flashlight while I called them to say that he was slowly on his way. We would need the fridges and freezers to be on for the groceries so I turned on the generator then climbed into our workhorse speedboat, the original *Page*.

I swallowed my fear and headed out into the dark to help. It was hard to see the shoreline from inside *The Page,* and since the boat had a hardtop I couldn't stand up to see over the windshield. I pulled the side window open and drove with my head hanging out the side. If I squinted a little, I could just make out where the shoreline was and could follow it around my island and into the main bay. Then bright spotlights from the ship flooded the channel and I felt like I was working my way toward the Star of Bethlehem. George was just arriving with the float when I pulled up. I tied *The Page* to the lash log and climbed out.

The float was about eighteen by twelve feet and it didn't have planks in several places. I could see where to step in the bright ships' light but had to keep moving to stay away from the boom that was lowering the pallets of freight. There was lumber, plumbing parts, windows and thirty-pound boxes of nails strapped together in huge bundles. The float went lower and lower in the water as more freight was added. We only had half the supplies and I was already slogging around in water well past my ankles. This was my worst nightmare. I could so easily imagine a long tentacle sliding over the side of the float and wrapping around my leg to pull me screaming into the deep, black water. I steeled myself to remain calm and kept working, piling lumber from the sling onto the sinking float. As I very carefully dragged my boots along the planks to keep from falling through, I could smell barnyard. Manure was a funny thing to smell coming from the freight boat. Were they carrying cows to someone? Then they lowered a pallet loaded with car batteries and I had to concentrate again. We couldn't let them get wet.

George asked if I could take the boat back to the house and unload everything there. This seemed like the lesser of two evils to me, so we overloaded *The Page* with batteries, plywood, the boxes of nails and anything else that might be damaged by water. We finished loading with two rolls of carpet that we propped across the roof of the boat and over to the wheel well where the 115-horsepower motor sits. *The Page* was very low in the water as I inched my way back to the lodge, motoring so slowly that I wasn't worried about hitting a log or other floating debris. My main concern was sinking before I hauled some of the freight off. I finally pulled into the dock and clambered out between the rolls of carpet, jumped onto the float and spent the next forty-five minutes unloading the freight, one piece at a time because everything was so heavy.

I really wanted to stay home but knew that I had to get the boat back out to the ship in case there was more dry freight. I climbed back aboard *The Page* and was again overwhelmed with the smell of barnyard. I leaned down and sniffed closer to my gumboots and smelled the distinct aroma of manure. It was me! I had been tromping around in my compost piles during the day, using a pitchfork to turn the muck. No cows on the freight boat, just my own compost. My heart felt a little lighter as I chuckled and headed back out into the dark.

Once again I drove carefully out to the ship, but this time I tied the boat to the stack of two-by-fours because the entire float was underwater. You could only see part of the piles of lumber above the water. I stayed in the speedboat as George shuffled more dry goods to me. The last to be off-loaded was our order of groceries, which I gently piled on the seats. Hurray for fresh produce! We were finally finished and George untied the ropes from the ship and the crew hauled them aboard. The skipper told us to stay where we were until he was well away from us, and with my heart in my throat, we waited while the ship backed away, turned and as we watched in horror, headed in the wrong direction. The world was still pitch black but you could just make out the outline of the surrounding mountains against the sky. Seconds before we expected to hear crunching of the boat hull on rocks, we heard the engine roar into reverse thrust and the ship gradually came around and away from danger. Somehow the skipper must have forgotten where he was while we drifted and turned for three hours in the dark. He corrected his direction and we watched as the ship slowly headed safely on its way.

Freight boats and tugs and barges from various companies would continue to arrive almost exclusively in the dead of night for the next thirty-four years.

I gingerly drove back into the bay while George towed the float very, very slowly to the lodge. By this time, the tide had come up enough that he was able to bring the float through the shortcut, which shaved at least twenty minutes off his towing time. Then we spent the rest of the night unloading the freight and spreading the weight around the rest of our floats, afraid that we might not find anything in the morning if we didn't move it off the sunken float. It was early daylight by the time we finished moving all the freight, and I went in and, with shaking hands, stoked the kitchen stove to make breakfast. A good breakfast fry-up always lifted my spirits. Then I gratefully dropped back into bed.

Building the Second Guesthouse

We were ready to build our second guesthouse. The new float was built, our contract with Fisheries was finished and we had building supplies from the freight boat. We were not afraid of long hours, and the weather was warming up so we didn't have to spend so much time on winter maintenance. George had cut thousands of board feet of cedar planks that we would be using for stringers on the float that measured about thirty by fifty feet. That was the first job, levelling the two-by-twelve stringers across the logs.

Next, we took turns using the electric drill with an eighteen-inch bit to drill several holes in the two-by-twelves. Then one of us would drive a two-foot spike through the plank and into the log. These planks created the base for the building as well as tied the whole float together more securely. At this point George spent several days ripping two-by-twelves into two-by-fours for us to use on the building structure.

Once we had the stringers down on the logs, all level, even and braced, we were able to steam ahead. First we marked out the footprint of the building on top of the two-by-twelves, and then we loosely nailed old planks around the marks so we had a surface to walk on. The next step was the cabin floor joists. As soon as those were down, we practically threw the building together. We did all this with our tools tied to our belts. Hammers, sledgehammers, squares, levels, drills—everything seemed to have an affinity for the water, and if you dropped it, it was almost guaranteed to sink. We couldn't afford to lose any more equipment, even if it meant going overboard with it!

The exterior walls went up, the interior walls and room divider joists went up, then I put the cedar siding on the outside while George got the roof trusses in place. We were late. It was already April and we were running out of time. We worked morning, noon and into the night until we couldn't see the hammer and nails in our hands.

The building was almost closed in. George had put the wood stripping on one side of the roof and attached aluminum roofing. He needed to turn the float so he could get at the other side from a ladder propped on our float. He pushed the new float away from the dock and moved in between with the work skiff to turn it around. He manoeuvred it out and around and started pushing it back in toward our house. I had a long gaff in my hand and when the float came a little closer, I leaned over to snag the coil of rope that was piled on the corner of the log. As I leaned out, the tip, the very tippy-tip of the gaff caught in the log and jerked me off balance. I splashed into the water with the huge float heading right at me less than three feet away. George was on the other side of the building, unable to see what had happened. In panic, I turned toward the house

Aerial of Rivers Lodge, 1978, with two guesthouses on the far right floats. The second guesthouse was built when we realized two guestrooms were not going to bring in enough revenue. Our house/lodge is the building in the centre. To the left is the workshop with generator shed and a small boathouse.

float and kicked up so hard that I landed on the deck just as the giant float thumped into the side of the dock. It drifted back a little and there were my two socks, floating on the surface of the water, forced off my feet by my miraculous upward thrust.

George ran the skiff into our float, threw the weighted line over a log and jumped over to grab a tie-up line. I was already tying up the other side. He turned to me and burst out laughing when he saw me standing there in bare feet, soaking wet, with water dripping from my hair. Then the look on his face changed to horror when it dawned on him what had really happened and with a gasp he crushed me in a bear hug.

We closed in the four-bedroom guesthouse in twelve days from bare float to lock-up stage.

One morning while George was cutting lumber, I walked past the radiophone and overheard one side of a strange conversation. When making a VHF radiophone call, the speaker can ask for privacy. The operator can then blank out the radiophone side of the call but the town people can hear the person and all I would hear would be *beep, beep, beep*. But I would be able to hear the person on a landline in town. The landline caller who was speaking was being evasive and secretive so, of course, I stopped to listen. Something about "Logs … middle of the night … close the area … head of the inlet."

I ran to the front of the float and blew the tinned foghorn to catch George's attention. "Quick, come and listen, something strange is going on!" He lifted the saw up onto the pile of planks and jumped into the skiff. They were at the end of their cloak-and-dagger conversation, but George was able to pick up a few more hints and we guessed that there had been a major break from a log-boom site at the head of the inlet. George then made his own cagey call to our friend Richard to start heading up the inlet with as many dog-lines as he could grab and he would do the same with our speedboat. They would meet somewhere in the main channel. We both ran around collecting rope, dogs, axes, a can of spray paint and binoculars and put it all in the boat. George fuelled it while I threw a lunch together for him to take and off he sped to chase down the escaping logs. The valuable fir logs would be drifting out of the inlet and would be lost if not collected as quickly as possible.

George and Richard knew what they had to do and didn't waste time chatting. George raced from one log to the next, hammering a dog with a rope into each log and spraying a large "G" and "R" on the end of each one. Richard, in his slow fishboat, went from log to log collecting all the ropes until he had a long line of them that he then dragged over and attached to the shore. Then he would head out to collect more ropes and logs. At some point during the day, other people found out about the log break and also started collecting logs, so it was very important for George to mark every one he found with their initials. They spent the whole day chasing down logs and only stopped when it was too dark to see.

The next day, George and Richard collected all the long lines of logs into one spot so the logging company could pick them up all at once. They had acquired quite a large collection of them. We knew that the logging company would pay us a fee per board foot or per log for rescuing them from heading out to sea. We waited with great expectation to find out how much money "G and R's" logs were worth.

After two long days on the water, we got right back into full cabin-building mode. George finished the other side of the roof and I started sheathing the interior walls. Next on George's list was to run electrical wires through the attic. He climbed up into the small space and started running 120-volt and twelve-volt wires to carry generator electricity as well as battery power to each room for when the generator was turned off at night. I was attaching four-by-eight-foot sheets of medium-density fibreboard (MDF), to the wall studs. MDF is wood pressed with resin and glue to form a very hard, smooth finish. It is cheaper than plywood and is more suited to our moist climate than drywall.

Unfortunately, I was still using the ringed nails from the thirty-pound box that George bought years ago. The nails were thin and bent easily in the hard material, which was frustrating beyond measure. If I hit the nail slightly off-centre, it would bend. Once it bent, there was no fixing it, and you couldn't pull it out because of the rings. I started counting out loud as I snapped off bent nail after bent nail with the hammer. My voice got louder and angrier as I went. "Fifteen." *Smash.* "Sixteen." *Smash.* "Seventeen." *Smash.* By this time, I couldn't have hit one straight on to save my life. George called gently down from the attic, "Why don't you slow down?" "Eighteen." *Smash*. "Why don't you shut up? ... Nineteen." *Smash*. By the time I got to twenty-nine *smash*, I knew I had to get the hell out of there or before I knew it, my hammer would be aimed at George's head. He was keeping very quiet up in the attic since he was the one who had insisted that I had to use those nails.

I finally stormed off after thinking the better of kicking the ladder down from the attic. It would have been funny except that if he jumped down when the coast was clear, he would have landed in all my sharp, broken nails.

There was a super-low tide early the next morning and we could see the bottom of our bay very clearly behind the greenhouse float. There were crabs scampering across the silty bottom and lots of gem-coloured starfish clinging to the rocks near the tide line, huge sunstars barely moving along the seabed, and sea cucumbers. Yes, sea cucumbers. They were about a foot long, two inches thick and greenish with burgundy colouring and bumps all over—just like cucumbers! I had read that they were edible so we had to check it out. I scooped several up in a net and carried them to the cleaning table. In my hand, they felt like half-full water balloons. The moment I poked one with the tip of my knife, all its guts spewed out all over the table. *Eeesh!* It was so gross. Okay, so this was my worst experience with trying new seafood. But I persevered and cut down the length of the now empty skin. There are five muscles running head to—umm—toe. These are the most edible part. The guts are poisonous so I washed them away. There is not much meat in the five muscles so I poked, emptied and sliced the other two and had a little mound of slippery cucumber muscles. Fried in butter they tasted like ... butter—delicious sweet, salty butter with just a hint of a sea breeze.

It wasn't long before a cheque arrived for our two families to share. Collecting the logs was worth sixteen thousand dollars.

The Ugly Carpet and Other Stories

We finished the cabin and I spent the next week getting the rooms set up and ready for another summer fishing season. George did the wiring on the four new twelve-foot speedboats that had just arrived, which were a great improvement over our open skiffs. There was a top on each boat that covered the seats so our guests could stay out of the rain, and a steering wheel instead of the tiller arm at the back, making the fishing experience much more enjoyable. We were looking forward to a very good summer with more guests than ever before. We hired two teenagers to help with cleaning boats and salmon, fuelling and garbage and any other jobs that we would like to have help with.

The lodge that tied up in Finn Bay for the winter had a devastating chimney fire that quickly got out of hand. They lost several buildings as well as a couple of new boats and motors that were pulled up on the float. This inspired us to research insurance for the lodge. We were told that we would have to get a land survey done of the area first. We had held off as long as we could because we didn't have any reference pins for the surveyor to start from, and the extra cost involved in having the surveyor search for the pin or finding a reference point was prohibitive.

One day George headed to the store with the mail. On his way back, he followed the shore along the west side of the beach. He turned the corner past an island just half a mile from our bay and saw a yellow rope hanging high up in a tree. It was strange that he had never noticed it before. He beached the boat and went up to investigate, thinking that it must be marking something interesting. It was a perfectly good piece of poly rope about twenty feet long, so he coiled it up and headed back to the boat. As he stepped across from one slippery rock to another he looked down and, lo, hidden down in a crevice of the rocks there was a brass surveyor's mark about the size of a quarter, cemented to a huge boulder. It was like it had been placed there for him to find. Coincidence? I think not.

When George got back to our house, he was so excited that he ran the workboat up on the ramp attached to the side of our house. There were two long planks that projected out over the water that were attached to the float at one end and not attached to anything at the other end. George could nudge the bow of the skiff up to the planks then gun the motor and the skiff would ride up on the planks. We usually threw the heavy, weighted bow rope over the lash log and wound it around the cable. This time, he just threw the weight and ran in to tell me about the pin.

The wind picked up that night. Picked up the boat too. Picked it up and dumped it into the salt chuck, and since George had brilliantly taken the plug out of the bottom—it sank! Along with my twenty-horsepower Merc on it that he had taken off *Patty's Page*. As it happened, Richard and Sheila had stayed over that night, so in the morning they hooked onto the boat, and using Richard's fishboat, the *Red Witch*, they pulled the skiff up off the bottom. Richard towed it to the surface and with the bow high in the air, water sloshed out over the stern. George jumped into the front and bailed like mad, faster than it was coming in. The forward motion also helped push the water out the plughole. He was finally able to make his way to the stern and put the plug back in.

The surveyor arrived two weeks later and did his work so we could get proper insurance. While the fellow was with us, George pulled the old forge out of the workshop and cleaned it up nicely. Axel had used the forge to make his own logging staples and dogs. George got a wood fire going in the base of it and, using the bellows, cranked up the heat. I had a lovely salmon that I marinated in the afternoon, and after baking some foil-wrapped potatoes in the nice hot coals, I placed the salmon on a wire rack and draped it across the top. What a luxury that dinner was, with our surveyor there to enjoy it with us off our own forge barbecue. So luxurious that I felt I should "dress" up my usual work outfit featuring my new pretty hanky. My sister Marcia had sent it to me for my birthday. Her husband, Murray, had laughed and said, "What on earth does Pat need a lace hanky for?" To which Marcia replied, "Every lady needs a handkerchief."

So here is the description of this lady's outfit, straight off the Rivers Inlet Runway:

Here comes Pat, wearing a dashing purple and grey toque cleverly folded twice, creating the impression that it might dip down to modestly cover the eyes. A trim blue turtleneck covered by a warm pale pink and white long-sleeved wool bodice Stanfield's-style undershirt, followed by a red and black plaid cotton work shirt. Together they combine to form the new charming layered look, very "in" this season, with the second layer surprisingly longer than the first and third layers, which is a very thrilling revelation. On the bottom, a pair of corduroy pants, extremely worn-in—so extreme that the fabric is near see-through in spots and of the faintest blue with just the hint of red long johns peeking about the knees and ankles, where one should note the thickly layered grey wool socks, which are jammed into tall, dark-brown, compost-slicked boots with a one inch heel and startlingly playful decorations in the tread. The pièce de résistance is the dainty white cotton and lace hanky, minutely embroidered with tiny white daisies, being held aloft with quiet nonchalance between thumb and forefinger of the as-yet un-smudged right hand.

That's what Pat needs the hanky for, Murray!

Our fishing season started with a bang. Literally. Our newly acquired second-hand fifteen-kilowatt generator flashed and banged when George started it one morning, so we had to send it to Vancouver for repair. We had been running the auxiliary five-kilowatt gas generator all through the spring, which had about one-fifth the power of the diesel one, and we hoped that it would last until the diesel motor could be returned. Because of this, I was left to choreograph power all summer. This can run, that can't run, these need freezing, those need chilling, heat that up, cool that down, wash those, dry these. I felt like I might go mad. And then the washing machine broke down.

We had a stockpile of parts to make sure the five-kilowatt generator kept producing power, so the only thing that could go wrong with it would be if the motor straight up and died, which we thought was unlikely to happen. Well, the motor died and we were reduced to using our 2.5-kilowatt portable generator that struggles to keep the freezers freezing. I was washing dishes by hand, running out of fresh towels, and had to let the guests know that they wouldn't be able to blow dry their hair until the new motor arrived, hopefully on our flight later that day.

And on top of that, we hadn't had rain for weeks and weeks and I had to be so careful with how much water I used in the kitchen.

The fuel barge was scheduled to arrive in about an hour, but it was far too large to enter our bay. George pushed the new float with the new three-thousand-gallon gas tank out to meet it as it floated around in the channel. They lowered the hose down to George and he placed the nozzle end in the open pipe on the top of the tank. He left one of our crewmembers holding the hose and climbed into the speedboat to put pressure on the float, pushing it toward the barge so it wouldn't be able to drift away. The crewmember climbed on top of the tank for a better hold of the hose, and after the gas had been pumping for about twenty minutes he suddenly shouted to George that the tank was tipping. George shouted to the guys on deck and they quickly made the hose suck out gas instead of pumping it in. Well, that was a disaster averted. A quick response on everyone's part and maybe a horseshoe in George's back pocket. George slowly pushed the fuel float into the bay and spent the next several afternoons adding outriggers to the float to stop that from ever happening again.

It had been a complicated summer, but on the plus side, Fisheries needed a guardian with a speedboat to patrol the inlet during that fishing season. George got the contract and bought a great, newish boat enclosed with a hardtop and lots of glass windows all around from our Merc dealer and called in a friend to drive it for the summer. The money from the contract would pay for the boat, which was interesting, and possibly a bit of a conflict of interest because this friend of ours would sometimes be patrolling commercial fishing, but also patrolled sport-fishing boundaries. Luckily, that didn't come up in the negotiations. We had to install a single-sideband phone on the boat, as per Fisheries instruction, but we would be able to continue to use it at the lodge after the summer.

Partway through that hectic summer, we were expecting a large order of fishing rods to be delivered to the inlet. George gave the fellow who sold them the address of our freight boat and told him exactly when they should be delivered. I picked up a call from a passing tug and barge—not our freight boat—saying they had our rods on board but would not be able to stop, so please send someone out to grab them as they passed by. George had his friend, Chas, jump in the speedboat with him, and they raced out as the tug passed in front of our bay. There was a man standing at the back of the barge. They could see a few long bundles at his feet. George had to cautiously run the boat up to the back of the barge, careful not to go too fast or too slow while Chas climbed onto the very front of the boat, reached up on his tiptoes and grabbed the bundles one at a time from the barge man and leaned them over the windshield for George to balance. Why was there never an easy way to receive freight?

One of our guests gave me a pile of magazines, one of which was *ArtReview*. I thumbed through it and saw pictures of Persian rugs that in 1965 were worth about five hundred dollars but in the then-current market could fetch as much as five or ten thousand. George had acquired a carpet from a friend when he worked for a moving company in his teens. He had used it on his floor at university, had mad parties on it, dropped food on it and hauled it around to the various apartments he had rented, dragging it up and down stairs. We had it rolled up in the dusty attic because it was very strange and off-putting with faces all around the perimeter that corresponded to a story on the border. There was Jesus, Buddha, Lord Nelson, Confucius, a pope and many others we couldn't name.

I knew the man who'd given me the magazine was interested in collecting carpets, so I asked him if he would like to see the one that we had (the one that had barely escaped the lamb's wool moth colony incident). One look at it and the man's eyes started to glow. He said it definitely had 350 hand-tied knots per square inch and was a blend of wool and silk. He also said it was probably worth at least six thousand dollars. He told me that there was a Persian carpet show coming to Vancouver and we could probably sell it there.

More crazy busy days. A plane buzzed the house and I had to run and change my outfit so I could take a boat out to the airplane dock. It was a man from Tourism BC coming to check the place out. I entertained him and the pilot for as long as I could, but George didn't come back from fishing for an hour, so they left. They were impressed with the quality of our resort and we soon received a Tourism BC–approved placard in the mail. After they left, I ran around in all directions to get the rooms cleaned for the guests who were staying with us, then another plane buzzed the house. I zipped out to find two unexpected guests. They had been here already this summer and just really wanted to come back. I had a big pot of soup and fresh bread that I could feed everyone with, and I frantically tried to keep ahead of the dishes, which I was still washing by hand because of a lack of electricity with the tiny generator that we were using.

Everyone went out fishing again, and by the time the kitchen was clean, it was time to start dinner. I started the fire, raced over to the island to pick vegetables and whipped up dinner for eight guests with four courses. I had nearly finished cleaning up, and the guests had all left for bed, when suddenly there was no water. They had each taken a shower before bed and ran the damn dam dry, causing an airlock in the line.

I was up again at 4:30 AM to get the fire going to start breakfast for our eager fishermen. I leaned on the bathroom counter and stared at myself in the mirror wondering if I could find a clue in my eyes or in my expression that explained how I had ended up here. *"Kill me now, Jesus!"* is all I could think. I didn't know how long I could keep this up. How long could I go without a proper sleep? *"Let me sleep, Jesus!"*

I had to wait until it was light out before George could get the airlock out of the water line. The new motor for the five-kilowatt generator had arrived but when George tried to remove the old motor, he found that he couldn't separate it from the generator, so he left with both the generator and new motor to see if the mechanic at the fish company could help. I couldn't get a nap in because a few of the guests stayed in bed and would want a late breakfast. How very relaxing for them! They finally headed out fishing and the two men who were leaving that day came back, so instead of catching up on chores or catching up on rest I had to entertain them until their flight arrived.

George finally returned with a tiny generator that would only run one freezer at a time. At least that's something. We ran both small generators at the same time and just plugged a freezer straight into the borrowed one. He had left our generator with the mechanic, who was an alcoholic and who said it will be ready tonight or tomorrow, but I wondered about that.

I accidentally smashed the fridge door into my face, which caused my nose to swell, and I could hardly see. My sinuses were affected and my eyes keep watering, my nose kept watering and every few minutes I sneezed. Not to mention the pain. I finally took an antihistamine, which helped my sinuses but was putting me to sleep—and the dishes just keep piling higher. Ah yes, then it was time for the Fisheries officer and his wife to visit. My legs and hands keep twitching as I thought of all the things that I needed to be doing instead of trying to be polite over tea.

They soon left and I rushed to prepare lunch. I sighed, thinking, *if only they would all use the same butter knife and use their hands instead of bread-and-butter plates.* George had finally hooked up the water, and I got a fire going to heat some for the dishes. By now I was so tired I could hardly stand up but there was an impossible mess to deal with. I finally washed ten things and lay down for a few minutes, washed ten more things and again lay down for a few minutes. This was the only way I could finally finish the dishes throughout the afternoon and eventually start getting dinner going with a pork roast in the oven.

I took a call from the Vancouver company rep, who was repairing our diesel generator. The fellow told me that the generator was fixed and would be on the freight boat that was leaving in three days. That meant that we would have our, what I liked to call, "city power" generator back at the lodge in about a week. Just in time for the end of our fishing season.

I had a full forty-five-minute nap and this carried me through dinner. George had picked up the repaired five-kilowatt generator from the mechanic at the fish camp and after putting oil in it, he started it and, miracle of miracles, it ran! Even though our water supply was low, I ran the dishwasher, justifying it because I was sure someone, somewhere once said that dishwashers used much less water than handwashing and I was going to believe it. Just before I closed my eyes, I heard rain start to patter on the roof and I smiled.

Halloween

We went to a party and then we went to a funeral. Everyone who lived at the mouth of the inlet was invited to a Halloween party at Lucky's home at Dawsons Landing. There were commercial fishermen, sport fishermen, handloggers, beachcombers and a couple of ladies who could do all of the above as well as knit! The costumes were very inventive given that there wasn't a craft store or department store where one could buy actual costumes. We used what we had and embellished by adding papier mâché, glitter, ribbons, funny hats and in my case—laundry!

I went as a laundry basket. I trimmed handles into a large cardboard box and drew a wicker pattern around the box with a black felt pen. Of course we would be staying overnight at Dawsons so when we dressed to leave, I stepped into the large hole in the bottom of the basket and then piled the clothes all around me that I would wear home the next day. I put a toque on and pinned the rest of the clothes that George wanted all over the surface so laundry hung down over my head and shoulders. I was feeling rather proud of my costume and pleased that I didn't need to pack an overnight bag.

The party started early so people could arrive while it was still daylight. Only gentle, elderly Olaf Slayback didn't make it to the party. He lived right across the bay from Dawsons Landing, but he wasn't feeling quite up to the noise and excitement. Everyone brought food and liquor, and the drinking and dancing was well underway, long before it was dark. There is nothing like a costume to bring out the best in people—we seem to lose our inhibitions. And when you throw in hard-to-come-by alcohol, you have a dynamite combination. We still didn't have a liquor store in the inlet, so people had been saving bottles of wine, rum and rye for just such an occasion. The food was fantastic: fresh bread and buns, several salads, salmon patties, pickled halibut, clam chowder, thin slices of abalone, fresh mussels, cracked crab and fried cod. My favourite item was a mixing bowl full of just-caught, cooked and peeled jumbo prawns. Warren and John had pulled their prawn traps on their way to the party and cooked them on the tugboat stove then peeled them as they drove up Darby Channel to Dawsons.

We danced and danced, sang our way through a stack of cassette tapes of the Beatles, the Rolling Stones, the Who, Queen, Fleetwood Mac and everyone's favourite dancing group, ABBA. I stood to the side at one point to catch my breath and watched as young and old danced together and age didn't matter. The only time I had seen this kind of mix-and-match dancing was at a wedding with a room full of relatives. It felt so good to be part of this very diverse group of people all having a wonderful time together.

As the evening was approaching midnight, Eric and Steve, two of Lucky's sons, thought it would be a good idea to set off some fireworks and outdated flares. They had the presence of mind to contact the Coast Guard to let them know that they were sending up half a dozen flares at midnight and not to worry, it was just for show and that everyone would be safe. We all stood on the lower dock while Eric lined their planter boxes with burning schoolhouses, bottle rockets, Roman candles and other impressive pyrotechnics and set them off with a propane torch.

The night was perfect, with a huge clear dark sky like a blank canvas, and we oohed and aahed at the sparkling light show. Then Eric handed out the flares and we pulled them one at a time and lit the sky all around the bay and made it look like it was daytime. The flares soared three-hundred feet into the dark sky and exploded into brilliant light that could be seen for miles.

We then had to go back in and dance off some of the adrenaline rush from such excitement. More ABBA and Beatles tunes, more food and drinks all around. An older couple, John and Edith Moore, who lived on the other side of Dawsons Landing, were the first to leave. We saw them off, waving as they rowed their little boat out into the dark. Then we headed back to the dance floor. We were shocked, though, to see John walk back through the door thirty minutes later. With a solemn face he informed us that old Olaf Slayback was dead in his bed. Silence crashed in on us as we all felt the burden of having just killed him with our fireworks display! Eric's face was ashen with the implication that his lights and noise had been too much for our dear old Olaf. Well, that was the end of the party. We all slinked off to our borrowed beds, and sleep was in short supply the rest of that night.

The police arrived the next morning to confirm Olaf's passing while we huddled in groups over coffee and biscuits. It was a very different scene than the happy, devil-may-care Halloween night that we were all now regretting. After a short visit to Olaf's home, the police came back across to Dawsons Landing and their waiting float plane. One of the constables came over to our table and informed us that Olaf had died between 6 PM and 10 PM the previous evening. There was a collective sigh of relief as we realized that our fireworks display hadn't killed the dear old gentleman after all! But we were still a rather subdued group of people as we climbed into our boats to head home and get back to our regular lives.

Olaf's funeral was on Friday, November 3, 1978. He was eighty-six years old when he died and had been living in the inlet since 1922, hand-logging and fishing for most of those years. It was overcast and drizzly, and the little inlet cemetery looked ever so forlorn. It's situated on a flat patch of grass far above the high-tide line, is surrounded by huge cedars and is in a tiny cove called Taylor Bay, off the main inlet. The minister from the *Thomas Crosby V* officiated, and most of the people who had been at the Halloween party were in attendance. Fishboats, a tugboat, a rowboat and several speedboats were anchored and bobbing on the swell in the bay.

The collection of bare-headed individuals were dressed in their finest rain gear and surrounded by towering West Coast cedars dripping great drops of rain. The little cemetery already had six wooden crosses, all with a good view of the pretty cove where the boats were floating. "Old Peg-Leg Pete" was written on one cross. He was known for stomping around on his wooden leg on the deck of his fishboat. Also buried here: Mrs. Perry, who before passing on at eighty-one was still chasing loggers and bears with a broom. Old-timer Jack Rendle was the unofficial care-taker of the cemetery and visited the site regularly during the year to cut the grass and keep the area from being reclaimed by the forest. Before the funeral for his old friend, Olaf, Jack had scythed the grass, put sand on the slippery cedar steps leading up from the beach and helped dig the grave.

Olaf's coffin was on the back of a tugboat and all hands were on deck to lower it into Jack's skiff before he rowed his old buddy to shore. Several people put wreaths on the new grave—plastic wreaths that they had at home just in case. There would not have been time to order a real flower wreath. Where in the world was I that people kept a wreath in their linen cupboard in case someone dies?

Setting the Hook in Twelve Inches of Water

The morning started out to be so lovely. It was all sunshiny and warm with lots of birdies chirping. We were looking after the BC Tel station for our friends, Andy and Nell, who had left for their six-week vacation. The station was on the north end of Calvert Island and there was a lovely house for Andy and Nell where we were staying. It was on a flat grassy area just above a little bay that had a tidal flat that goes dry for several hundred feet out from shore. Because of that, the dock was on the other side of the spit of land about half a mile away. There was a rocky, rutted and rolling road between the dock and house, then it wound from the house up about two thousand feet to the top of the hill where the telephone and repeater equipment were also housed.

George leaped out of bed to make coffee and breakfast. He was in a hurry to leave in the boat to go to Dawsons Landing for the mail and to check on our house and lodge. The weather had to be good because the round trip now took about five hours, and he had to cross Fitz Hugh Sound, which can get very rough very quickly.

Needless to say I was surprised when George returned in the truck less than fifteen minutes later. George's workboat was missing and he had hurriedly tried to start the speedboat so he could search for it, but the battery was dead. The extra battery, the backup system, was also dead. The master switch had been dutifully turned off, but the ignition key was left turned on, so power must have leaked out all night long. George had come back to grab some jumper cables, and he couldn't wait for my help since I didn't have shoes on.

I quickly threw my shoes and cap on, called Zak and jogged down and up, and down and up, and up and down to the dock. George was having trouble getting a good connection. It took thirty minutes of fiddling and scraping and jerry-rigging to get the engine started. We hauled the rubber dinghy in the back, called Zak again and cast off. We started off by scouting the bay around the dock as far in as we could go. The bay narrows in one back corner and then opens wide but shallow into another bay. This bay is totally dry at low tide. We couldn't see anything, so we took off quickly while I scanned the shores with the binoculars. We angled to the left outside of the bay and headed up the channel that becomes a dead end about two miles away. This is where we would normally anchor our boat and head across the island for beach adventures. In the other direction, Kwakshua Channel is about four miles long and opens into Fitz Hugh Sound.

Meanwhile, we were both thinking about the large boat that we had seen pass by in the channel the previous evening. We had thought it was the *Thomas Crosby V* coming for a visit, but no one came to the house. So we just figured they would come over in the morning. The boat wasn't there the next day, and it would be unlike the crew of the *Thomas Crosby V* to not drop in for a visit. We didn't know what to think.

The missing workboat had my twenty-horsepower Merc on it as well as an auxiliary seven-and-half-horsepower Merc lying on the bottom with lots of ropes, axes, dogs and wedges. A lot of money's worth to lose, not to mention how indispensable the workboat was. Also, the boat had a leak in it, which meant if it wasn't found within two high tides, or twenty-four hours, it would probably have sunk, never to be found. We were hoping that it simply got hung up on the shore somewhere.

We got to the end of Kwakshua Channel, and George nosed the boat as far into shore as he dared so we could see into the bay that opened in the corner just like the one near our dock. He was getting too close to the weeds, and by throwing the engine hard into reverse, stalled it. It would not start again. The wind was pushing us into shore so we scrambled to get the anchor out and George leaned over and set the anchor into twelve inches of water. He had already pushed the dinghy out of the boat and we quickly searched for the pump. The dinghy was only about three-quarters inflated and we couldn't find the pump. George climbed into the mushy dinghy and started towing the boat off the beach while I hauled up the anchor and we dropped it again in deeper water. George tried a few things with the battery to see if he could get the motor to start, but nothing worked. I put a life jacket on, got the dog in the bow of the dinghy and climbed in.

We started the long row back to the dock, against the wind and tide. When we were about three-quarters of the way back and ninety minutes later, I spied a boat coming up Kwakshua from Fitz Hugh. "Ah, for a distraction to keep my mind from murderous thoughts," I mumbled under my breath. We finally decided it was the *Thomas Crosby V* coming back, maybe even with our boat. It seemed to take it forever to get closer to us, while George kept rowing. It started to turn into our dock so I waved my fluorescent life jacket and they turned and bore down on us. The eighty-foot ship towered over us as they lowered a ladder so I could clamber on board. George offered to row Zak the rest of the way back to the dock since it wouldn't be easy to lift him onto the deck. I think he felt it was his penance due.

I was quickly warmed by a cup of coffee, but just as quickly shattered by the news that, no, they hadn't anchored in our bay last night and, no, they hadn't seen our errant skiff. They offered to run us back to our speedboat and, no, George didn't need to get a battery—they had one that we could use. The skipper, who is also the minister, nudged the huge bow up to the dock, and after securing Zak inside the truck cab to keep him safe from the wolves that were probably watching us at that moment, George climbed up and over on to the boat deck. Then we motored back to the anchored speedboat, about ten minutes' worth of chugging along as the ship goes quite a bit slower than our speedboat, though quite a bit faster than a half-deflated rubber dingy.

They anchored in deep water and put a small boat over the side to use to tow our speedboat alongside. George and the engineer then spent a full hour trying to get the motor started but for some reason they still couldn't get the right connection. They finally decided to try another battery, so George and I and two deckhands took their small boat back to the dock again to get the battery out of the truck. George went up to the truck, which now had a flat tire.

Using the hand pump from the back of the truck, I re-inflated the dinghy. I then took it, along with Zak and one of the deckhands, and rowed as far as we could into the back corner of the bay to see if our skiff had floated in there during the night. By this time, the sun was almost down. We rowed a long way into the bay, most of the time in only about ten inches of water. After twenty minutes of rowing we finally had to pull over to the shore and secure the boat to a branch and walk the rest of the way through mucky tidal flats.

Suddenly, I saw our skiff—hallelujah! My heart skipped a beat. I was so sure we would never see it again because we were so close to the open Pacific here. It was high and dry on the rocky shore and wouldn't be floating again for quite a while. I tied it up to a tree, and then we headed back to the dinghy. We had to take a different route because the tide was coming in so fast it was filling the huge bay as if it were a little bathtub. Fortunately I had tied up the dinghy high on a thick tree branch.

George had arrived back with the speedboat by that time. He put a seven-and-half-horsepower engine on the BC Tel skiff, started it and the gearshift fell off in his hand. It was just as well since there was no gas in the skiff's tank. We were about halfway back when I called to him and said that I would trade a good used boat for a tow back to the dock. After all, I had tied the skiff up, which gave me salvage rights. He promptly came out for us in our speedboat, as the batteries seemed to have recovered. We got back to the dock and piled out of the dinghy when I noticed Zak chewing on his paw. He had picked up a treble hook between the pads. By this point, I was looking for a patch of sand to bury my head in.

I straightened up from helping Zak and overheard George talking to the minister on the radiophone, saying that we would like to invite everyone over for supper. I must have looked stunned because he leaned over to me and said, "It's the least *we* can do!"

The sun was on its way down so that meant that suppertime shouldn't be too far off. I immediately started jogging back to the house, trying to count the number of people on the boat. *He thinks I'm a wizard already*, I was thinking. *An instant dinner for ten adults and two kids, after spending the day searching for our boat on the high seas?* As it turned out, the minister called and said, "Only four people will be over for supper, the rest are Indians and they like to keep away from Whites." It was an ill-spoken comment from a man of the church that I have never forgotten.

I made a big pot of chili, baked a shortcake, tossed a salad, heated bread, thawed strawberries, set the table and was just in the process of whipping the cream when the other half of "we" drove up with the dinner guests. The skiff was already back, floating and securely tied to the dock with two ropes instead of one. We were quite giddy throughout dinner

The *Thomas Crosby V* came to our rescue when we lost our skiff at Calvert Island.

as we laughed and counted all the things that had gone wrong that day. But as I climbed into my cozy bed later, I counted all the things that had gone right.

Chickens and Ducks

Our "ugly carpet" was auctioned off at the Sotheby's Parke-Bernet public auction at the Bayshore Inn in Vancouver at the end of the next summer. It was 1980 and it sold for $13,500. My dad had recently bought a revenue one-and-a-half-storey house and property in Winnipeg for $13,500. My cousin had been at the carpet auction and was breathless with excitement as she told us the final price. We thanked our lucky stars and the God of Moths for protecting the carpet from larvae damage. Then we did a Snoopy dance while we both imagined what we would love to do with all of that money. We settled on buying two more speedboats and motors. Not very romantic but very worthwhile. Now we had accommodation for twelve guests and six fourteen-foot speedboats for them to fish from.

We spent time the next winter building a new float with a thirty-foot greenhouse on the south side and two more crew rooms on the north side. I was very happy to spend time collecting soil for the deep boxes in preparation for the fresh herbs, edible flowers, and squash and tomato plants that I would eventually plant.

The following spring, I needed a dentist. I had bitten down on something hard and hadn't just chipped a tooth, I cracked a big piece off the side, big enough to loosen the filling, which fell out. I was having trouble eating and couldn't wait much longer before I would have to get the tooth fixed. We also really needed some supplies and fresh produce, so I booked a flight out to Port Hardy. I would go to George's dentist who lived in Lake Cowichan, where I could stay with George's mom and dad, Irene and Ernie. It was always so much fun to stay with them, and they still had tea and toast every night just before bedtime. Sometimes we dunked the butter-slathered toast into canned fruit swimming in sweet juice. It was such a great tradition.

My first dental appointment was the next morning, and it would take a couple more appointments to properly fix the tooth. In the meantime, Ernie, Irene and I went out shopping for items on my wish list. We had replaced the old wood stove, which had two propane burners on the side, for a much better new wood stove. But I found that I really missed the instant heat of the propane burners, so we looked for something to replace them. We drove back to Duncan, and Ernie took us all over town so I could find counter tiles, hinges for my new kitchen cupboard doors and a two-burner portable propane stove. George was building a shelf beside the wood stove for the burners and running a gas line into the kitchen from the hundred-pound tank outside. While I was trying to decide on the right tiles, George's dad went next door to a second-hand shop. He came back grinning from ear to ear holding a tiny chainsaw just for me.

My tooth was fixed and I had bought as much as I could carry, so after we enjoyed an ice cream cone from the Dairy Queen in Duncan, another great tradition, Irene and Ernie dropped me at the bus station.

I took the bus to Campbell River where our new friends Rick and Kris Hackinen met me, and we took the ferry to Quadra Island and drove to their place. They had ten acres with a tiny cabin as well as chickens, goats and a couple of horses. I felt completely at home feeding the chickens and moving heavy bales of hay for the horses. Rick loved fishing so we had fresh fish and lovely fresh produce from their garden. Somewhere around the third or fourth glass of wine, Kris and I cooked up a plan to find some chickens for me to take back to the lodge so we could have fresh eggs.

The next morning we headed out in Kris's Volkswagen Bug on an adventure, with the island's newspaper open to the for-sale section. The road on Quadra is up and down and around and around, so I was getting quite carsick. I was still used to driving on the Prairies where you can see miles and miles of straight, flat highway in front of you. We stopped at a little farm with a sign that told us they had chickens for sale. The tall white chickens were in a very large fenced area and we were expected to catch them ourselves if we wanted them. Chickens don't like to be caught, so we had to be quick and smart. Chickens are quick, but not smart. After a little running, tricking, flapping and laughing, we had three chickens stuffed in a cardboard box. Next, we headed out to find some raspberry canes to plant.

On the way to the nursery, we passed a sign that announced ducks for sale. Kris made a quick U-turn, and we went in for a look. They had Muscovy ducks, which are large and white and lay very large eggs. These ducks were running around loose in a big yard. We had to be even trickier to catch these ones. The owner helped as we herded a bunch into a little side yard where we could grab them one at a time. Shortly we had three Muscovy ducks also stuffed in a cardboard box. We headed out again for the raspberry canes. We were having so much fun, that I didn't think about what I was going to do with the birds when I got back home. I also gave very little thought to actually getting them home! We finally found the nursery, where I bought six raspberry canes for my garden, and then we headed back to Rick and Kris's so I could pack my bags. Kris and I then drove to the ferry, and she dropped me off at the bus depot in Campbell River. All my parcels fit nicely on the big comfortable bus, including the boxes with the live chickens and ducks. But the driver took one look at my belongings and yelled, "This isn't a moving van ya know!"

The bus arrived in Port Hardy at about 6:30 PM so I would have to stay overnight and fly into the inlet the next day. I walked into the bus depot and asked the woman in charge if I could leave my extra parcels, including the two boxes with chickens and ducks in them. She said, "sure, no problem," without even batting an eye, and told me I could pick everything up on my way to the airport in the morning. I left my stuff, crossed my fingers and checked into the Seagate Hotel. The next morning I had a leisurely breakfast before I arranged for the airport shuttle to pick me up at the bus depot and headed there when it was time to leave. I walked into the building and found the woman in charge in a panic on top of her desk. She shrieked at me as I entered, "Help, there's rats in here!" I could hear the scratching noises were coming from the cardboard boxes. Poor lady, she had thought I was leaving two cartons of *frozen* chickens and ducks. I thanked her profusely and started carting my belongings out to the shuttle.

There were no other passengers on this flight so there was no problem loading all my freight into the back of the Beaver. The weather wasn't the best for flying but I trusted that the pilot also wanted to get home that day. And I was missing George terribly, so all I could think of was getting back to him. We had a bit of a bumpy flight with the plane lifting and dropping and careening about—we rarely flew a straight line. I let my mind drift to my safe place, and after forty minutes of being bounced around we were finally flying over Sleepy Bay, and there was George waving from in front of our house. I could see smoke whipping away from the chimney and thought about how the house would be so warm and cozy. I waved back at George as the plane tilted a little to my side, and then the pilot started turning the plane in a wide circle. We bounced and dropped and jerked around violently as we turned, and I could see whitecaps being blown off the waves in Darby Channel where we were supposed to land.

The pilot did indeed want to get home safely that day. I didn't even have a chance to wave goodbye to George since I was now on the wrong side of the plane to be able to see him. Of course we couldn't land safely on the water in this wind, so, suddenly we were headed back to Port Hardy. Bouncing and dropping so hard I could see the airplane wings flapping like those of a large bird. Oh, how much pressure could the wings take before they snapped off? We banged and rattled, swayed and knocked our way with the engine groaning and thrusting each time we dropped. I was so busy grabbing for handholds that I didn't have a chance to do my silent singing, all I could manage was a low growly hum that reminded me to breathe. *Breathe in … growl out … breathe in … growl out.* And there was the airport finally coming into view. The wind was relaxing a little and the pilot made a huge sweep around the runways and came in from a different direction than usual, but he made a perfect landing. As we taxied to the terminal building, there were a few blasts of wind that I felt almost flip the airplane, but we pulled up safely and came to a stop.

I walked with wobbly legs into the terminal and sat down with a sigh of relief. The realization hit me that I would have to do that all over again tomorrow. I'm still looking for the skyhook! Hopefully they would check the weather better before we took off. This time I felt so bad for George, who I knew had the fire stoked, the house all cozy and somewhat clean and a fresh pot of coffee ready for my homecoming. We should've been together and chatting heartily over coffee by now, not just me sitting here wondering if I would ever get back home safely. Oh!—and the chickens! I got up and raced over to the airline counter to let the people know that there were live chickens and ducks in the boxes. We had a good laugh when we saw the look on the face of the baggage handler as he wheeled the moving boxes into the back. The airline had travel cages for dogs, so we carefully let the chickens go in one and the ducks in another. I had a bag of feed with me and fed and watered them before I headed to the hotel for another night. The airline staff was fine with having the chickens and ducks there. Just pay them and they will store and carry anything and everything, anywhere you want.

The wind blew for hours, but I noticed when it started to settle down in the middle of the night. The Seagate Hotel is right on the shore, next to the government wharf, and I could hear the rigging clanging and banging on the fishboats tied there. As the wind died down, the jangling of equipment also settled down. I was finally able to sleep.

The next morning I eagerly headed out to the airport because the sun was shining and I could barely detect any wind. They were loading the airplane again as I arrived, and after I helped get the chickens and ducks back into the boxes, we were all set to go. The weather was perfect for flying, and I actually enjoyed the flight. I was so happy when we safely touched down on the water just outside of our bay. George came out to the airplane float and we whooped and hugged and I had trouble letting go. I was holding on for dear life, holding on to dear life!

It was so good to be home. George was so happy to see me after watching the airplane bouncing its way back over the bay that he didn't even get annoyed that I had arrived with six large, live birds in cardboard boxes.

We let them go in my lovely new greenhouse that George and I had built the previous spring. Now we had to come up with a plan for a chicken coop that would keep the birds safe from otters, mink, cougars, wolves, eagles and hawks. Well, there was the boom-winch float that we weren't using at the moment. George wanted nothing to do with the darn birds, so using the chainsaw Ernie bought for me, I built a little

Rivers Lodge in 1980. The two guest cabins are on the right. The main lodge/dining room is in the centre. Attached to the main lodge are our small bedroom and bathroom. The building on the left is the workshop and generator shed, and the big greenhouse with crew rooms is behind.

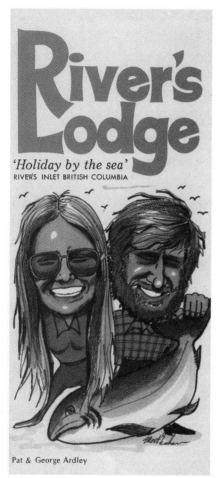

River's Lodge

'Holiday by the sea'
RIVER'S INLET BRITISH COLUMBIA

Pat & George Ardley

For this brochure, we thought the caricature of George and me would stand out and help people remember our lodge.

house with lumber and scraps that we kept on hand for spur-of-the-moment projects. I laid chicken wire down completely covering the surface of the float. There was a natural dip between the two middle logs that I draped the wire into, creating a safe pond for the ducks. Then I built the frame around the edges of the float and attached the chicken wire to it and moved the house across one end. I also covered the top of the cage completely with chicken wire. On one corner I wrapped wire around a two-by-two at the bottom and put nails into the upright so I could secure the wire but open the cage if I wanted to go in. I wasn't going to go in very often and muck around in the poop, so I put hinges on the roof of the little house so I could lift the lid and reach in for eggs. I used cedar shavings to line boxes for the hens to use as nests. I collected plenty of greenery along the shore to throw in for the birds. They soon felt safe and comfortable and the ducks happily splashed in their pond. Then they all started laying eggs. Duck eggs are amazing, with huge orange-yellow yolks—very creamy and delicious. I made gorgeous duck-egg noodles with them, and was always experimenting to find interesting things to make for our fishing guests.

One day I was sitting on the edge of our float dangling my legs over the side. Mist was rising from the wet planks all around me as the sun rose over the trees and warmed them. There was complete silence.

George was out in the boat, no generator was running—it was just me and the fishes. I was splashing my feet in the water when suddenly there was a loud thrumming sound, getting louder, and then sounding like a train was heading right at me. I looked up just in time to duck my head as an eagle swooped above me—so close that it ruffled my hair—with its talons extended, intent on the chicken coop. It aborted its dive awkwardly at the last second when it saw the chicken wire across the top and rose, skimming the roof of the woodshed by mere inches. It was a close call for all of us.

I loved having the chickens and ducks. I enjoyed watching them, feeding them and collecting the eggs. George simply enjoyed eating the eggs. Once in a while I would scoop out the valuable chicken manure into buckets and carry it to my garden. After it had composted for a few months, it would be an amazing fertilizer for my vegetables.

Sockeye Fishing with a Kidnapper

Jack Rendle wasn't just toothless. At that time he was at least seventy-eight years old. His back was bent over with osteoporosis, age and hard work. His head wobbled uncontrollably, and he was as skinny as a starved chicken. His jaw stuck out, his hair—of which he had very little—was always greasy hair, his face and neck were deeply wrinkled and saggy and there were many spots on his wretched hands that seemed to be permanently bandaged.

Jack was anchored in our main bay when we got back from the store one day. George pulled up to the side of his fishboat and chatted with him for a few minutes. Jack invited me on board to have a cup of tea, which I declined but George accepted on my behalf. I thought I might look mean if I continued to say no, so I let George help me climb up and onto the damn *Grizzly King*. George continued on into our house, and I sat on the side of Jack's boat. He boiled a kettle on his oil stove and made a pot of tea, then handed a cup to me with a strange look on his face.

The sockeye run was going to be huge this year and there was a commercial opening starting that evening at 6 PM. Jack was almost ready to set out his net and asked me if I would like to fish with him that evening. "No," I told him. "I have to make supper for George." He laughed and said George would be able to take care of himself. Then he pretended to reach for my empty teacup and grabbed my wrist instead. He leaned over and tried to kiss me, with the promise of more to come later in his eyes. I wrenched my hand away and stood up. "Please take me home," I said, again trying not to sound bad tempered. Jack laughed and said he wanted me to come fishing with him, but he begrudgingly started the engine and drove me home.

George came out of the house all smiles and helped tie the boat up. I jumped off the boat and headed straight for the house while Jack explained that he would like to take me fishing so I could see how it was done. George came into the house. "Hurry and get your rain gear," he told me. "Jack wants to take you fishing." I blustered, "He tried to kiss me!"

George said something like, "pshaw," grabbed my rain gear off the hook in the back hall and started pushing me out the door. I insisted, "No, he tried to kiss me!" To this George said, "This is an incredible opportunity for you to see firsthand what it's like to put the nets out and catch sockeye. I would love to go. You're so lucky—you can't miss this!" There were already hundreds of commercial boats in the inlet just waiting for the 6 PM signal to announce the fishery opening. I conceded that it might indeed be the only time in my life that I would be invited onto a working commercial boat fishing for the world-renowned Rivers Inlet sockeye run. Somehow, George cajoled me out of the house and onto Jack's boat. Then Jack threw the engine into reverse and quickly pulled away from the dock, just in time for the start of the opening.

We immediately headed out of the bay into Darby Channel and within fifty feet of the entrance of our main bay, Jack threw a bright orange Scotchman overboard to mark the start of his fishnet and, using the steering at the back of his boat, played out the net as he headed across Darby Channel toward Stevens Rocks. I stood in the cabin and watched out the front window as boats all around us were also setting their nets. Jack didn't settle for long and, after about half an hour, called for my help as he started to haul the net back in. We pulled it as it came over the back of the net drum and every few feet, Jack stopped the winch and we picked kelp or twigs and sometimes fish out. By the time we had the whole net in the boat, there were twenty bright silver and blue sockeye in the ice-filled hold.

He put the *Grizzly King* in gear and headed a short distance away from Sleepy Bay. Then, without coming into the cabin, he again threw the Scotchman overboard and let the net slide over the back of the boat as he slowly and carefully chugged along between other nets. This time he left the net down for about forty-five minutes before he started hauling it back into the boat. There were forty more wriggling sockeye added to the hold. He put the engine in gear and again moved farther away from Sleepy Bay. I came out on deck and asked him to take me home now, before he put the net out again. Jack just looked at me and smiled.

"I can't stop fishing now," he said. "I have to put the net out." He threw the Scotchman over the back, pushed the throttle forward and the net dragged off the boat again. He then came into the cabin and put a pot of stew on the stove. "I'll leave the net out while we have supper," he said.

"Take me home," I repeated. "I don't want supper here, I want to go home."

"Well I can't take you home while my net is out, so you might as well eat," he said. "I made it myself."

I was sitting on the bench that ran along one side of the cabin. There was a table attached to the floor in front of the bench. Jack sat down beside me on the bench and stared at me with googly eyes. I picked up a magazine and started reading it. He leaned over, reached for my toque and tried to yank it off my head. I reached up and jammed the toque farther down onto my head.

"Take your hair out of prison, Kitten," he whined.

That was too much. I whirled on him and hissed, "My hat stays on and I am nobody's kitten!" At that moment, Jack's eyes widened— he jumped up from the bench, bounded up the two steps and out the door. It was getting dark and had begun to rain, and as I glanced out the window I could see tree branches reaching through the rigging of the boat. I watched for a minute or two and then went to look out the door, slightly curious.

Jack was leaning overboard and frantically sawing through his fishnet with a knife. It was indeed an emergency for him to cut his net, as the current had sucked the net through a channel, and was pulling his boat onto the rocky shore. I wasn't concerned for my safety at the time, because we were surrounded by boats, and I knew that any one of them could drop the end of their net to rescue us. But Jack was very concerned about his boat getting dragged onto the rocks. I could not muster any sympathy, as I watched him getting soaked in the rain while he cut and sliced his very expensive sockeye net. He should have been paying more attention to his net and not staring doe-eyed at me. The smell of scorched stew filled the small cabin.

I thought that would be the end of the fishing adventure. But no, he managed to cut the net that was hooked on the rocks, put the engine into reverse and free the rigging from the trees. He then motored another 150 feet toward open water and away from Sleepy Bay. Then he reattached the Scotchman to the tattered end of his net and played it back out over the end of his boat. He was making another set! I couldn't believe my eyes.

At this point in the evening, I was so angry that I could have tossed him overboard. I was not at any moment worried about my life or my virtue. I was slightly worried about how it would look if I dumped an old man out of his boat while he was leaning over the side reaching for his net, but he would have been a very sorry man if he tried to approach me again. The nice and heavy cast iron pan on the side of his stove would do the trick.

When he was satisfied that his net was once again safely set, he stomped into the cabin. He was soaked from head to toe and rather disgruntled. He went forward and climbed down the set of four steps into the forward bunk area where he peeled off his wet clothes. Suddenly he was dancing about in front of the steps calling in a singsong voice, "Don't look now ... I have nothing on!" I grabbed the nearest magazine and held it up in front of my face. There wasn't a chance in hell that I would want to look at that old wrinkled scrawny bobbling body. I did not put the magazine down until I was certain that he had finally put dry clothes back on.

I told him he had to take me home. I was sure that George just thought that Jack would put out his net once or twice and then bring me back in. It was fully dark now, and I knew that George would be anxious. Jack just pretended to not hear me and went back out to pull in his net. Once again there were beautiful bright sockeye caught in his half-shredded net. He moved his boat another few hundred yards away from Sleepy Bay and put his net out yet again. He came into the cabin and wouldn't look at me. Ha—as if he was mad at me!

"Please take me home," I repeated. "George is probably really upset by now."

"No, no," he said. "We're going to have breakfast in Namu."

"Oh no we're not. There is no way that I am going to Namu with you." Namu is about forty miles from Sleepy Bay.

"Oh yes," he said. "We are having breakfast in Namu, and you'll love it."

I argued that I didn't want to go to Namu, that I didn't want to be on the boat with him for another minute, that I knew by this time that George would be getting really annoyed. Jack just laughed and went out to check on his net. I was furious and didn't want to be anywhere near him. I stayed in the cabin and picked random books and magazines off the shelf behind the bench and read through the night. At one point I stood up and looked out the windows that were all around the sides of the cabin and saw lights from boats and net markers in all directions. It was a beautiful scene with all the fishboats twinkling around us. There were roughly a thousand commercial boats in the inlet for the sockeye opening, with several hundred fishing here in Darby Channel. Rivers Inlet was sometimes called "The River of Lights," and it was a magical sight. Then I saw Jack working away at the back of his boat, and with a low growl, I thumped myself back down on the bench.

Jack continued to set his net then pull it in, always with sockeye to throw into the hold. Then he would nose his boat skilfully between the other nets and boats to set it again, always farther from Sleepy Bay and out toward Fitz Hugh Sound. He came back into the cabin to grab his rain jacket off the hook when it started pouring rain again. I didn't look at him, I was seething with rage, but bided my time until the sky started to lighten and I could see other fishermen working away at the back of their boats. When Jack had pulled his net in again, I went out on deck and told him that he had to take me back home. He started to sputter out arguments about how much fun we would have.

"See that fellow at the back of his fishboat a mere fifty feet away?" I said. "I wouldn't even have to raise my voice to let him know that you have kidnapped me and that my husband has been looking for me all night. Turn the boat around—and take me home now!"

He knew he was defeated. He was very angry and turned the boat so hard that I had to grab at a rigging pole to keep myself from toppling overboard. He weaved in and out of the nets, one Scotchman on the right, the next one on the left, waving hello to the working fishermen. There were so many sockeye still being caught, they must have thought he was crazy. I certainly did. I *knew* he was crazy. A crazy, ancient, decrepit old coot. We finally turned into Sleepy Bay and rounded the little island. A dishevelled George was already standing at the edge of the dock. Jack reduced the *Grizzly King*'s speed and turned it sideways to our dock, slowed down further but didn't actually stop. I jumped onto the float and George steadied me and gave me a big hug. Then he glanced up with a quizzical look as Jack and his boat made a hasty retreat from our bay.

I told George about my commercial-fishing experience. His mouth dropped open and his eyes got bigger partway into the story, and stayed that way until I finished. He had become concerned when I wasn't home by 8 PM, and then 9 PM, and finally he thought something must have happened. So he headed out in our speedboat to look for us. He spent three hours weaving in and out of boats and nets in the dark before he finally decided that he wasn't going to find us and talked himself out of the concern that he was feeling. Then he went home to bed and finally fell asleep until he heard Jack's boat coming into the main bay. I walked into the house, stepped out of my rain gear and sank into bed.

The following week, we went to visit our friends, the Coopers, on the other side of the inlet and ended up staying overnight with them. During the next afternoon, the wind picked up and kept getting stronger.

We headed home anyway after George convinced me that it probably wouldn't be that bad on the inlet. As we passed Duncanby Landing, where Jack was the caretaker, we could see that the wind on the inlet had started to blow like stink. We wouldn't be able to head home after all, and heading back to the Coopers was impossible by now because of the hundred-foot walls of water that were rising and flowing up to the head of the bay. I swallowed my disgust as George pulled into the Duncanby Landing dock and we tied up safely out of the wind. Jack welcomed us, and of course he said we could stay overnight in one of the extra rooms. But during the night, I could hardly sleep, remembering my experience with him on his boat and expecting him to come dancing into the room naked with a rose between his teeth. Fortunately nothing happened, and we made it home safely the next day.

Footings for the Fisheries House

We needed gravel. We had another contract with Fisheries. This time we were building a house for them at Dawsons Landing, so we couldn't just dig up gravel from the side of the local rivers. There was a huge pile of gravel at Addenbroke, left over from a big building project that was now finished. Since lighthouses and fisheries are both managed by the federal government, we got the okay to go and pick up as much as we needed. We had a light twenty-one-foot speedboat that would not easily tow a heavy barge, so we asked our friends Richard and Sheila if they would come with us and tow the barge back with Richard's fishboat, the *Red Witch*.

We waited for good calm weather and when we were sure there would be several days without much wind, we headed up the coast in our speedboat to Addenbroke. Richard and Sheila left shortly after we did, towing the Fisheries sea truck, a heavy, thirty-foot, flat-bottomed aluminum boat with no motor. We arrived well ahead of them and circled around in front of the lighthouse until we caught the attention of one of the children on the island. Then we anchored our boat in the bay where the wharf is. We had a quick visit with the lightkeepers who had replaced the Salo family and showed them the letter that authorized us to help ourselves to the gravel. Then George and I started piling the thick black plastic bags of gravel onto the freight wagon. It was gruelling work. Every bag weighed at least fifty pounds, and the stack was below the raised walkway and not easy to reach. We used the tractor to haul the gravel down to the wharf, and we had enough time to get several wagonloads piled on pallets on the wharf, before Richard and Sheila arrived.

The water was calm when they pulled into the bay and anchored the *Red Witch*. Unbeknownst to George, Richard dropped the anchor line for the sea truck straight down behind it. They climbed into the lighthouse skiff, and the keeper rowed them to shore. We worked for another hour, and after piling a third pallet with the heavy bags, George decided that we had enough. It was late afternoon by this time and the lighthouse keeper helped us use the crane to swing the heavy pallets down into the aluminum barge.

We watched the three boats floating peacefully, bobbing on the swell as it rolled gently into the bay. We were running out of daylight but the boats looked just fine, so we decided to stay the night and have a little party with the lighthouse people. We knew from experience that lightkeepers love to have company and company equals a good excuse for a party. The boats looked completely safe, the weather forecast was good and we needed the break as well. We had brought a bottle of rum just in case, the Coopers brought wine, and the lightkeepers had beer so we all had a fine time into the wee hours of the morning.

At some point in the night, the wind picked up a little, and there was a rough chop coming into the bay when we arrived at the wharf in the morning. We figured it shouldn't be a problem. We all clambered down to the beach while the lightkeeper lowered the rowboat with the crane. He dropped me and George off at our boat and then went back for Richard and Sheila. George started to pull our anchor line and immediately ran into a problem. Since the sea truck's anchor line had been dropped straight down and all the boats had been swinging with the wind, all the anchor lines had been twisting around each other all night.

We waited until Richard was on his boat and ready to pull his anchor, and we tried again to pull ours. The wind was getting a little stronger as we tried unsuccessfully to untangle the lines. George shouted for me to start the engine just in case, and I could see the puff of diesel fumes that showed that Richard had started his boat. George was leaning over the back of the boat and shouting instructions to me to put on a little throttle. "Turn the wheel … turn it harder … turn it that way … more throttle!" My heart was in my throat. I was afraid of doing the wrong thing and having George tumble off the back.

The tide was about halfway toward low, and there were several feet of rocks jutting out of the water that we were quickly approaching. Our anchor was off the bottom and we were now drifting but not loose from the unyielding anchor of the sea truck. Then George climbed down onto the platform at the back of the boat trying desperately to separate the lines as we rocked harder and harder in the growing waves. The boat floated closer and closer to the shore while George was busy at the back. Then a huge swell rolled into the bay, and as the boat rose up, I knew it was going to crash down on the rocks. George was bent over out of sight and wrangling with the anchor lines. Without thinking about anything but saving the boat, I suddenly leaped overboard onto the rocks, beautiful wool Holt Renfrew coat and all!

I momentarily teetered on the uneven rocks then turned to see the boat looming above me as it rose up on the swell, frigid water swirled past my waist and I pushed against the boat with all my strength. I braced my feet against the rocks and the rising boat and heaved and pushed as the swell washed back out and the boat slid crunching and grinding back down with it. Another swell rose up and almost knocked me over, the water was so deep that this time I was up to my neck in it, but still pushing on the boat, as it again crunched down across the rocks. George was shouting something but I couldn't hear him over the crashing waves and engine noise. Another wave and swell lifted the boat and I looked up at it, pushed with all my might as once again the ice water was up to my neck. This time, as it crunched down the rocks, I could see George reaching for me over the side of the boat. When the boat was at the bottom of the swell, and just before another one arrived, I pushed again as hard as I could, grabbed George's hand and made a mighty leap to drop unceremoniously in a heap on the floor of the boat. George had already turned to the steering wheel and, ramming the motor in reverse, blasted us away from the shore.

Every muscle and every nerve in my body was vibrating. I was chilled to the bone and wrapped in a soaking wet full-length coat. We weren't finished yet, but George made me lie down in the cabin and covered me with any extra jackets and life jackets to keep some warmth in. At this point, Richard untangled his boat from the sea truck, and they finally managed to pull the third anchor line. He hooked a line onto the sea truck and started towing it out of the bay. Freed from the lines, George quickly turned our boat out of the bay and headed home as fast as he could go. I spent the whole thirty-minute trip trembling with mind-numbing, teeth-chattering cold.

The boat was barely tied to our dock before George was sprinting into the house to run a warm bath for me. *Ahhhhh!* I was so cold that my bath started out little better than lukewarm. George kept bringing kettles of boiling water to add to it as I warmed up very slowly. He brought me a hot, sweet cup of tea, and just as I was finally starting to feel a little better he brought me the most delicious meal I have ever eaten. A platter of bacon and eggs, baked beans, slices of tomatoes and hash browns. This had been one of George's signature dishes, and our go-to meal at the end of a fun day at the beach, a late night with the freight boat or other frightening escapades. And by the way, his other signature dish was fried-egg sandwiches. No one could make them quite like George could.

Richard and Sheila arrived while I was still warming up in the bath. They tied the barge full of gravel to our house float and headed home. We all had more than enough adventure for one day, and the minute I was out of the bath I headed straight to bed. But a cold had crept into my bones.

We stoked the fires all night and through the next day to keep the house cozy but I was still wracked with a cough and stuffed head. Around dinner time the next day, the living room fireplace started roaring. We had a chimney fire. George sat up with it till midnight to make sure it had burned itself out. Now I was growing paranoid about a chimney fire in the kitchen stove, so we stopped piling wood into it. It's hard to keep a warm kitchen with a cool fire, so a little dancing was in order to help heat the house. I cranked up Buddy Holly on the radio and danced about while George cleaned the chimneys. He cleaned both chimneys and designated me to clean up the spilled soot. He climbed ladders and I swept floors.

God's Pocket

When we travelled to Vancouver by boat, it was usually late fall or winter. Never the best weather to be travelling in. Every trip that we took had elements of danger. The weather might be all right when we started out, but winter weather on the coast can change in a matter of minutes. We would sometimes suddenly be surrounded by heavy winds, dense fog, snow that piled up on the windshield, or even freezing spray from the waves building up on the windows, making it impossible to see as the windshield wipers became virtually useless. There were times that I steered the boat while George squeezed himself out the window to scrape away the ice so we could see well enough to avoid logs and other debris. If I didn't actually have to do something to help keep us moving forward, I would sit on the floor of the boat and do my deep-breathing to keep myself from panicking, which would not do either of us any good.

It was November of 1980 when we made a trip to Vancouver to do some shopping and to allow me to fly to Edmonton to visit my sisters before we started our next big building project for the Fisheries. We travelled down the coast, with Zak in the boat with us, without too much trouble. We were travelling in *Sportspage*. We had sold the boat that we bought specifically for the summer Fisheries charter because it had too many windows all around, making it too delicate for George's purposes. When we arrived in Vancouver, we tied up at the docks under the Burrard Street Bridge. I used the pay phone in the parking lot to call the airport and made a reservation to fly to Edmonton in two hours. I grabbed my suitcase and left George and Zak standing on the dock and then ran back to the pay phone to call for a cab.

George rented a car and drove around doing a few business things, like going to the bank and stopping to see our friend and travel agent, Nigel. He helped us with our bookings for years, before we were eventually able to put in a proper satellite telephone. George parked the car every time he passed a grassy spot and took the dog for a walk so he wouldn't be too antsy to sit in the car while George was busy. At one stop, George had been in the bank for about fifteen minutes, and when he came back out, the inside of the car had been ripped and torn apart. Zak had gone into a frenzy, tearing the upholstery from the seats, then the gearshift handle, and finished with the panels on the doors. The inside of the car was unrecognizable. It was very uncomfortable to sit in the car to drive, so, very reluctantly, George took it back to the dealership. They didn't believe him when he tried to convince them that it was a wolverine that attacked the car in Manning Park in the BC interior. He had only had the car for a couple of hours, which was nowhere near the time that it would have taken him to drive there and back. But three hundred dollars later, he was given another car and went straight to a kennel to drop Zak off.

I had a lovely time visiting my sisters. We shopped and drank coffee, went out for lunches and dinners, had our nails done, and we talked non-stop the entire time. When I heard about the car, I decided that I should be able to spend three hundred dollars too and found a lovely red trench coat that reminded me of the rental car's interior upholstery. I came back to Vancouver a week later ready to get down to the serious business of shopping in preparation for another winter in the inlet. George and I shopped together for the dry goods at the Woodward's Food Floor and picked up books and craft supplies, and George ordered building materials. Most of the supplies would be boxed up and taken out to the freight boat and would arrive at the lodge after we did. We had several goodbye parties with family and friends and then loaded up the boat and headed back up the coast.

We had a very heavy load of groceries, plants, diving equipment, tools and hardware, plus the dog. The trip was comfortable but slow. We got as far as Powell River when the engine suddenly seemed to fade, then picked up again, faded, and then was okay. George decided to head into the dock at Pender Harbour instead of trying to get as far as Lund before dark, so we turned around and tied up there. It was Sunday of the Remembrance Day weekend and our Merc dealer and mechanic just happened to be staying at his cabin in Pender Harbour, so he came down to look at our motor the next morning. It turned out to be a major problem and would need to be worked on in a proper shop. He had his own boat trailer there so that evening we headed back to Vancouver. While waiting for and riding on the Langdale to Horseshoe Bay ferry, George and the mechanic tore the engine apart so that very first thing in the morning, it could be taken in to be rebuilt. They worked on it on Tuesday and Wednesday and we were able to leave Vancouver a second time, very early on Thursday morning.

We travelled faster this time thanks to the much-improved engine. We refuelled at Kelsey Bay on northern Vancouver Island, and then continued on to Sointula on Malcolm Island, where we tied up to the dock. We were going to visit our lighthouse friends Ray and Ruth Salo, who had moved to Sointula from Addenbroke Island. I folded my big black winter coat onto the floor of the boat to make a bed for Zak and told him to stay there. He always stayed when we asked him to. He would curl up in a tight little eighty-five-pound ball and sleep until we called him. George and I zipped up the back cover of the boat and walked up the road toward Ray and Ruth's house. We had tea and a happy visit with our friends, and walked back in the dark to the boat. When we got there, Zak wasn't on board. We ran in all directions at once, calling and calling him. We went up to the road where we had just walked and headed back toward the houses. I felt sick. Zak had never gone on his own adventure before.

We knocked on doors and asked people in the pub. No one knew anything. We headed back to the docks and passed a small, creepy-looking shed-like building. George looked inside and came out looking ashen. There was a huge blood spatter in the corner but no dog. We had a terrible sleep, and then got an early start the next morning. We headed out again just in case we had assumed wrong. Our suspicions were confirmed when we talked to a woman in the store who said she had heard that some kids had been driving along the road and hit a dog. He was badly injured, she said, so they shot him and dumped him. I felt like such a traitor. I hadn't looked after our dear friend and now he was dead. I decided that I would never have kids if this was how much it hurt to lose a dog. I wouldn't be able to stand the pain if my children were hurt. And it was a long time before I could think about having another dog. We couldn't get away from Sointula fast enough.

We headed to Port Hardy where we picked up fresh produce, fuelled the boat and stayed overnight so we could get a very early start Saturday morning. It's always best to leave at first light, as the wind wouldn't have had a chance to build yet. We could cross Queen Charlotte Sound in about three hours if the water was right, but there had been a storm blowing for the last couple of days and there would be a large swell. We left the relative safety of Goletas Channel and Christie Pass and only made it as far as Pine Island before we turned back because of the heavy slop. We listened to the forecast, which wasn't good, and the sky looked most foreboding. Once again, we headed back to Port Hardy to fill our fuel tanks.

Sunday morning we attempted the trip again. George had the idea that we would wait out at the entrance to the sound and tuck in behind the BC Ferry that was leaving Hardy Bay and heading up to Prince Rupert. When we got out to the entrance to Christie Pass, which is about twelve miles from Port Hardy, we could see that the sound was pretty wild. We would not attempt to cross with such a gale blowing. Instead of going back to Port Hardy, we decided to pull into a little bay on Hurst Island, off the east side of Vancouver Island, called God's Pocket, where there were two can buoys anchored for boats to tie to. We tied onto the outside buoy and settled in for the night.

The next day, the wind had picked up yet more, and now it was even too rough to get back to Port Hardy. With all our expensive radio equipment on board, we couldn't get a marine weather forecast. But we could get Vancouver and Port Hardy radio stations on our portable AM radio. From Port Hardy we heard that the gale warning was being upgraded to a storm warning with winds of fifty to sixty-five knots plus higher gusts. This was not good news. We untied from the outside buoy, and I carefully nosed the boat in to the shore so George could climb off the bow to refill our water bottles from a freshwater stream. Then we tied on to the inside buoy and ran a stern line to the outside buoy to stop our boat from swinging too much.

The wind seemed to blow harder after it got dark. Then it blew harder and harder again. Around 11 PM, a large halibut boat came in to the bay and tied to the outside buoy. I felt a little better knowing that we weren't alone, but it also meant that their heavy boat was putting a lot of pressure on our stern line. We were being tight-lined every time a gust hit. Because our lines were so tight, we didn't simply rock with the waves, rather, the night was full of sudden and violent jerks with every gust of wind. We didn't get much sleep Monday night in God's Pocket.

On Tuesday, the wind picked up considerably, so George put some extra ropes on the boat to the stern can buoy. Everywhere you looked the water was a white seething mass. The winds did not build up large waves in God's Pocket because it's a small bay, but there was a huge swell coming in from the sound and from Goletas Channel. That night it seemed to blow even more until we thought it couldn't blow any harder, and then it would blast us with an even worse gust. We were in a closed boat, but I could feel the gusts reaching through and blowing in my face.

The whole time we were in God's Pocket, I was grateful that we could run a heater and had a two-burner stove to cook on. I had a nice warm down jacket and a big bag of books, so at the beginning of the storm I nestled into a corner and surrounded myself with reading material. As the storm got worse and worse, I spent a lot of time wrapped in a sleeping bag and the action of the boat kept me from reading. George made our coffee and all the meals because I had trouble looking down when I was in a boat. We had now been stuck in our little boat for three days and it was feeling very cramped.

On Wednesday, the wind was driving walls of rain and ocean water at us. The wind had not dropped; it had only increased, but the forecast from Port Hardy radio called for the winds to drop to around gale force that night. Thirty to forty-seven knots would normally scare the wits out of me, but now we heaved a sigh of relief. A little too soon, though.

The wind howled all day, and when it became dark it was still blowing. We noticed that the boat was starting to swing much more than it should have been. The stern line had broken. George collected our last good length of rope and climbed out the hatch onto the front of the boat while I ran the engine all the way to half throttle to take slack off our existing ropes to allow George to tie on to the front can buoy. He looped the rope several times. We would just have to swing wildly the rest of the night.

If what was left of our lines broke during the night, our only recourse would be to run the boat on to the shore and hope to be able to scramble on to the rocks and not get pulled into the surging swell and waves, then—perish the thought—wait out the storm huddled on land while our boat broke up on the rocks. In the meantime, the wind and waves kept pounding us, and I felt that it was never going to end.

Around 10 PM the wind finally started to die down slightly, and we were thankfully able to get a little sleep. Thursday morning seemed to have very little wind, but there was another gale warning so we decided to scoot back to Port Hardy if there wasn't too much swell in Goletas Channel. We untied all our ropes and went back to the halibut boat. It was the first time we could talk to the crew, and they said they were also heading back to Port Hardy so if it was too rough, we could tuck in behind them. It wasn't too bad, and in thirty minutes we were back in Port Hardy, mercifully tied to the dock. We had trouble negotiating the stable dock and staying on our feet after having been thrown around for so long on the boat. It was like being seasick, but we were on land. I leaned on every lamppost we passed in order to keep from throwing up.

We immediately checked into a hotel for a nice hot bath and a good long sleep. Later in the afternoon, while picking up some new fresh produce to replace our first batch, we ran into a friend. When we told him that we had just spent the last few days stuck in God's Pocket, he exclaimed "So you're the ones. Wow! Did you know that it was blowing ninety miles an hour and gusting at Scarlett Point?!" Scarlett Point was the light station about a mile and a half from God's Pocket. George was often referred to as Hurricane Ardley after that.

The next morning, the forecast was for southeast winds of twenty-five or thirty knots, but we figured that we could follow the *Queen of Prince Rupert* when it left at 10 AM. We didn't realize how terrible the trip would actually be following the big ferry. George had to fight the throttle the whole time just to stay in the right spot behind the boat.

The seas were still so rough that we had to stay within forty feet of the back of the boat or the sea would've closed in and we wouldn't have been able to catch up. The ferry was so big that it wasn't terribly affected by the thirty-knot wind and was able to travel very fast. We were surfing on the wave right behind the boat and people on the ferry were holding up life rings and taking artistic photos of us through them. George had to concentrate completely for the entire three-and-a-half-hour trip to keep us on that one wave while avoiding kelp and driftwood and whirlpools from their prop wash. We pulled away from the ferry wake when we were just off the entrance to Darby Channel, and bobbed and bounced our way through the slop to the quiet channel.

To say that we were glad to be home is such an understatement. We barely had the strength left to unload the supplies and then tumbled into our cold and damp bed without even lighting a fire. Just before falling asleep, I was able to get George to agree that if we ever travelled to Vancouver in November again, we would definitely fly.

Building the House at Dawsons— Part One

The house we would be building for the new assistant Fisheries officer at Dawsons was on property owned by the government, just past the A-frame and the existing Fisheries officer's bungalow. At the moment, there was a twenty-four-foot trailer sitting on blocks while the rest of the property was wildly overgrown with salal, small alder, hemlock trees, blackberry, salmonberry and thimbleberry bushes.

Before we started the project, we took my mom and aunt to Hawaii. Both ladies lived in Winnipeg so it was a wonderful change for them from the cold and snow. For me, it was a wonderful change from the life in the inlet, because there we were always working at something. Taking apart, putting together, pulling down, building up. We never sat still. George thought just sitting and reading in the afternoon was a waste of time, which unfortunately is one of my favourite things to do. In Hawaii, you could sit guilt free by the pool or on the beach and read to your heart's content. George went scuba diving while the rest of us just relaxed.

We came back from our two-week trip in the sun feeling soft and out of shape. We had hoped that a lot of the brush-clearing at the new building site would have been done by the caretaker at our lodge, especially since George had left instructions for him to do the work and told him that he would be paid extra for everything he did. He did nothing. We never did figure out what he did for the whole two weeks he was at the lodge on his own. Oh well, we saved money—but it put us behind schedule.

Before we could start clearing, the freight boat arrived with our massive load of concrete in sixty-six-pound bags. We had to move the bags off the store float and cover them properly so the contents didn't harden before we could use it. The bags were very awkward and very heavy. George and I strategically loaded the wheelbarrow with four bags at a time, with more weight toward the front. We made a harness out of rope that I stepped into, then I pulled, like a hitched-up donkey, while George pushed. I was wearing my version of cork boots—golf shoes that George's dad found for me at a garage sale. We hauled load after load of concrete up the wharf ramp and along three hundred yards of plank walkway to the worksite. It was exhausting work. My vacation-relaxed muscles were screaming long before we were a quarter of the way through the pile. Lucky was watching the whole time. He was eager for us to move the extra weight off his floats as soon as possible.

Because of the size of the hill behind the property, the sun slipped out of view by around three in the afternoon, leaving the bay dark and cold. I didn't mind having a somewhat short workday when the work was such a physical challenge. When we got home, I had to get the kitchen fire going to start supper, because we would be ravenous and I couldn't get dinner on the table fast enough.

Several days of moving concrete and we could finally start clearing brush. I worked with a machete chopping the bushes while George used a chainsaw to cut down the small trees. We kept a fire going and burned the branches for days as we cleared the site. The trailer had seemed smallish when it was surrounded by all the growth, but once the hillside was cleared it stood high and towered over us. That was our next job—moving the trailer.

It sat right in the spot where the house was to be built. When all the brush was burned, we brought our two Gilchrist jacks to the site and used them to lift the trailer, so we could drive skids under it and slide it off to the side and out of the way. This job took several days and it made me think about the big picture: How long was this whole project really going to take? We would have to be finished well before our next fishing season to give us time to prepare for the arrival of guests.

One afternoon I walked down the hill to the store after the plane had been in to deliver the mail. There was a letter from our friends Rick and Kris from Quadra Island. They had been married back east in the summer and had finally had time to unwrap their wedding gifts. After stuffing the scraps of wrapping paper into the old wood stove to burn, they decided to go for a dip at a beach just minutes from their cabin. While they were enjoying a nice swim, the sky got darker and darker. Rick decided to head back to their house to call and find out if there was a forest fire nearby, only to be met by the utter destruction of their cabin and its entire contents. They were still reeling from the loss when Rick wrote the letter. Neighbours rallied and helped build them a simple A-frame house that would provide a home for the short term. And the Salvation Army opened their doors and said, "Take whatever you need." It's incredible how a community pulls together when one of their own needs help. Rick didn't want to mention to their new friends that their firewood supply had also burned, but he mentioned it to us in his letter. They were not prepared for winter, which was fast approaching.

George cooked up a plan and asked me what I thought of inviting Rick and Kris to join us in building the Fisheries house. They would have a warm place to stay, lots of food and would be paid for their work. I thought the plan was brilliant. I loved them both and thought we could work well together. They also loved the idea. They could help for two-and-a-half months after which Rick would start a job on Quadra that he hoped would be ongoing for many years. We told them to bring good rain gear because the worksite had become a mud field after the brush was removed and it had rained non-stop for ten days.

A few days later, while we were waiting for the plane to arrive with Rick and Kris, Jack came into the bay. After I tied up the *Grizzly King,* he climbed off his boat and turned to hand me a lovely wild rose! Where on earth would he have found a wild rose flowering on the 8th of November in Rivers Inlet? At least it wasn't between his teeth, and he kept his pants on.

Part of the design plan was to excavate for a crawl space. We had started work on it, but the Fisheries officer who would be living in the house pleaded with the powers that be to put in a full basement. A crawl space would not be good for anything but the furnace and hot-water tank. This brought the price up and added a load of work for us, having to dig out tons more soil with shovels and wheelbarrows. We ran into bedrock in the southwest corner and decided it would have to become part of the full basement.

It rained and rained, and we slipped and slid on the two-by-twelve boards that were laid out end to end running to the edge of the steep cliff as a path for dumping wheelbarrow loads of fill. George and I worked for two days to dislodge a huge old cedar stump, until Rick joined us and we all chainsawed, chopped and dug the gigantic stump free from the soil. We finally had all the pieces off that could be removed and used the come-along to haul what was left to the edge. We then used peaveys to launch it over the cliff. We celebrated our success with lunch in the trailer and planned our next step. We had one more major obstacle: a boulder the size of a small truck. This was moved using both jacks and the come-along in combination with bloody knuckles and red faces. As soon as it was moved off the footprint of the house, we left it and from then on worked around it. Too much time had already been spent clearing the damn property.

One evening during dinner after a particularly stressful and gruelling day, Rick looked at me, raised himself off his chair and said, "I don't think I should do this but"... and hurled a handful of mashed potatoes at our new ridgeback pup, Blazer, who was comfortably sleeping not far from the table. I looked at him in surprise trying to process whether he thought he shouldn't feed the dog, or shouldn't throw food from the table? With no answer at hand, I grabbed a handful of potatoes and also threw them at the dog. Then George and Kris were throwing potatoes. Poor Rick was trying to stop us but we were not to be stopped until all the potatoes were mounded around a very bewildered dog. We laughed like we were punch drunk—with that kind of laugh that bubbles up from your belly and you have no control over—while Rick tried to explain his reasoning. Nothing could stop us until we had wrung out the last speck of energy and collapsed in a heap on the table. Apparently Rick didn't like the lumps in the mashed potatoes, but Blazer thought he had won the lottery.

One morning *Sportspage* wouldn't start, so we headed to work at Dawsons in our two small, open fishing skiffs. We had sold our original tank of a boat, *The Page*, when we bought *Sportspage*. The drive took a little longer but the weather was good, so I enjoyed the trip with the wind in my face at the front of the open boat. That night when we headed home the competitive streak in both George and Rick came out, and we raced all the way home. Our boat had a little more weight with the large tool box and chainsaw but the two boats were quite even until we turned into the bay. George cut the corner behind the little island then cut the turn into the home bay. He turned so hard the skiff was on its side and I was holding on for dear life knowing that George would dump me out before he would lose a race in his own boat and in his own bay! Seriously! What is it with the men around here almost pitching me out of their boats?

We left Dawsons at the end of another hard day, in the speedboat that was ostensibly working again. We got partway home, though, and the engine quit. George radioed the fellows on the *Falcon Rock* who were tied to the dock at Dawsons. They came out to tow us home, where George could tinker with the engine again. We were about a mile from our home bay when the Fisheries boat suddenly died. George jumped back into our speedboat to see if it would start, and surprisingly it did. They moved the ropes from bow to stern and from stern to bow and George started towing the Fisheries! We pulled their boat, which was five times the size of ours, all the way back to Dawsons. Then we headed back home in the last bit of light, hoping against hope that the engine would make it all the way and … it did. In the soft twilight, George motored slowly into the bay and partway across, put the engine in neutral. Ripples flowed out from the boat and made the reflection of the lodge buildings quiver and dance.

We took a few days off for a Christmas break and showed Kris's sister, Beth, around the inlet. We also made what had become our traditional Boxing Day trip to Clam Beach, which is part of the Penrose Island Marine Provincial Park on the north side of the mouth of Rivers Inlet. It's a pretty little shell beach sheltered on one side and open to the swells of Fitz Hugh Sound on the other. On a perfect Boxing Day, the sun would be shining and we would wander along the rocks looking for shells and interesting bits of driftwood. We would light a fire for the hot dogs and marshmallows, then have a game of kelp baseball. George would perch on a rock facing the waves and contemplate life. I would sit and chitter-chatter with my friends. On a not so perfect Boxing Day, it would be raining and cold. We would still do all of the above but head home dripping wet and frozen. This particular Boxing Day was a Christmas miracle because it was sunny and warm all day.

Next up was New Year's Eve at Calvert Island. The four of us climbed in our speedboat and headed over for a visit with Andy and Nell at the BC Tel station. I went for a walk with Blazer out to the tidal flats in front of their house. I quickly noticed a wolf chasing geese in the distance. He noticed us and decided Blazer was more interesting than geese and headed over toward him. I called Blazer back but he pretended not to hear me and kept wandering farther away. I yelled for him to come. Then I screeched his name so loud that they both stopped, and three seagulls seemed to do somersaults through the reverberations. Twice, Blazer turned to look at me and both times the wolf advanced a little closer. It was like in a macabre game of Mother May I. I had to get Blazer back to me, but I was becoming more and more stuck in the deep tidal-flat gumbo that my boots were slowly sinking into. I anxiously extricated my boots and in a loud voice carried on a one-sided conversation with Blazer as I floundered carefully through the slop toward him. He finally turned and walked back to me. I grabbed his collar and, holding on tight, advanced toward the wolf. He sprinted away and then loped up into the bush, where I was sure the rest of his pack was inspecting us. I decided to get the heck out of there before he brought his friends back and surrounded us with a ring of glowing eyes with saliva dripping from their jaws.

We celebrated New Year's Eve in style with lots of dancing, lots of food and lots of laughs, but the elastic band of responsibility was pulling us back home, and though we did stay overnight we didn't stay long the next day. So much work, so little time!

When we got back we had a bit of time to catch up on chores: chop and pile more firewood, fill the Aladdin lamps, pump oil for the generator and the oil stove in our backroom and the cabin Rick and Kris were staying in. George pumped gas into all the day-tanks we had, fuelled *Sportspage*, sharpened the chainsaws and checked the water tank and pipes to make sure everything was in good order. I did laundry, a little cleaning, baked bread and made soup for the coming week's lunches. There was never a break from upkeep. Life would quickly grind to a halt if we didn't keep up with the lowly chores.

Happy New Year 1982! Now back on your head!

Building the House at Dawsons—
Part Two

We were well rested after our Christmas break and eager to get back to work on the Fisheries house. The freight boat was due to arrive a few days into the new year, and we had a lot of building supplies on it that would need to be moved again. This time George arranged for some of the freight to be dropped onto the Fisheries float so we wouldn't have to move it right away. We also had eight bundles of locally milled two-by-twelves towed to Dawsons and tied to the Fisheries float. We weren't able to talk Lucky into opening his log boom, which meant George wouldn't be able to push the bundles of lumber straight to the bottom of the hill in front of the building site. Instead, we had to break the straps holding the bundles together, unload the two-by-twelves, board by board, and haul them up the walkway two pieces at a time, one board precariously balanced under each arm. Have I mentioned back-breaking, exhausting work? Each load seemed heavier than the last, each load I looked over and cursed Lucky for not allowing us access to the bottom of the hill.

After several days of hauling wood up the ramp and slogging up the walkway, Lucky relented and said he would open his log boom. We now had enough wood to create a ramp from the building site to the bottom of the cliff. After spending a day of us gouging a path up the hill, George nailed two-by-twelves together in a ninety-foot-long ramp and attached the come-along at the top. While Lucky had the boom opened, George untied a bundle of lumber from the dock, pushed it through the logs with the skiff and tied it to the bottom of the hill. Then he quickly headed back to push another bundle through. I spent that time putting extra nails into the ramp so it would hold the heavy bundles.

The newly milled lumber was quite green so the wood was extra heavy. After hauling the cable down the ramp, George hooked it to the first bundle and turned the wood so it just rested on the bottom of the ramp. Up at the top of the hill again, he tried cranking on the come-along but there was no way that the bundle would move. I added my muscle to the handle, and we were just barely able to get the wood to move onto the ramp. George slipped a three-foot-long pipe over the come-along handle and poured oil on the ramp, and then when we both pushed and pulled at the end of the handle, the bundle started to jerk its way inch by inch up the ramp. It was arduous, gut-busting work that left me panting for breath and for a sunny lounge chair, a good book and bonbons.

There was so much mud to move out of the way for the basement. We had been slipping and sliding off the boards that were supposed to keep us out of the mud. It was treacherous, balancing a wheelbarrow full of mud and pushing it downhill. Many loads tipped as we lost our footing on the mud-greased planks. We were all wearing rain cuffs that covered our work gloves and went up to our elbows under the sleeves or our raincoats. We still ended up covered with mud inside the gear and out. We had to hose our gear off at the end of the day, as George wouldn't let us in his boat until we no longer dripped mud.

The weather warmed in the middle of January. I straightened up from a task as I felt a waft of a Hawaiian breeze gently ruffle my hair. I glanced over and saw a look of wonder on George's face. I could almost taste a tall cold piña colada. We worked in shirt sleeves for the next several days before the weather changed back to winter temperatures. While the warm weather held, we were able to get the basement walls poured. This required all of us pouring the dry cement mix into the portable cement mixer, mixing in the water, then wheeling the heavy mixture over and feeding the wet cement into the forms we had built before Christmas. Why is everything so heavy? The weather held and we had the walls poured by the end of the third day. There was much celebrating when we got home that day. We still had the basement floor to pour but not right away. Now we could get the stringers attached, get out of the mud and start working on the main floor.

My heart felt light finally working above the muck. We finished the stringers quickly and put down the plywood floor, and then we started on the walls. George and I had developed a system over our years of working on building projects together. We were able to argue while we knocked a wall of studs and headers together. Rick and Kris, on the other hand, would start to argue, slam down their hammers and not get anything done until they had either come to an agreement or shut up. George and I often disagreed. I had the habit of looking at the big picture and George often expected me to just do as he said. Often he wanted me to do one thing that I knew I would later have to undo or redo to set something up for the next stage. That afternoon we were able to frame an entire wall with a door and two windows and put braces in place while we argued. Meanwhile, Rick and Kris were still arguing about how they should nail the studs and "How exactly do you expect me to frame this window?" Ah, newlyweds!

Once the walls were up, we started work on the roof. Buying lumber that had been milled in the inlet was one of the reasons that we won the contract. The lumber was a little green, but George made up for that by insisting we use more large nails than we really needed. This was in case the wood cracked or checked as it dried, so the structure would still have integrity. We finished pouring the cement slab in the basement, and finished the roof before Rick and Kris had to head back to Quadra Island. It was a sad day. I loved their company and appreciated all the work that they had done. I also knew that all the big jobs yet to be done would have to be finished by either George or me.

One Sunday George went scuba diving with a Fisheries officer, Mike. Diving in the inlet in the winter is amazing. The water is gin clear and the sea life is varied, exciting and colourful. I waited above while George and

Mike were in the water. There was no way that *I* would go down into the scary depths of the ocean. When they finally surfaced, Mike checked for his knife and it wasn't on his belt, although he was sure he had slipped it into its sheath. They had already used up their dive time so they couldn't go back down to look for it, and a few days later Mike left the inlet.

George wanted to do another dive in the same spot. He had picked up a bag full of lead from commercial fishing nets and wanted more to melt down to make weights for our sport fishermen. We drove over to the same general area. There was a series of rocks that snagged the fishermen's nets, tearing big chunks out of them and the lead line. George dove while I watched nervously from the boat. When he hauled himself out of the water and into the boat, he had a bag of weights and Mike's knife. A week later I flew to Winnipeg to see my parents. I took the knife with me, packed it up nicely and mailed it to Mike at Dawsons Landing from Winnipeg. We laughed for years about the look on Mike's face when he walked into the Fisheries house at Dawsons with the package open in his hand and showed us his knife. He didn't know that I had been to Winnipeg and couldn't figure out how the knife could have possibly got there! It was definitely his knife—he knew the marks on it. He walked out with the same quizzical look on his face.

George was working on finishing the inside of the house while I put the siding on the outside. For a very short time I could attach boards from the ground, but then I needed a small ladder. And then a really big ladder. One side of the house faced onto the south side of the very steep hill so as soon as I couldn't reach to attach a board, I had to start climbing a ladder that was many times higher than the side of the building because the bottom of the ladder was way down the hill. I had to carry the board, which was usually at least three feet long, a hammer, nails and pieces of tin to attach behind any knots in the wood to keep the wall dry. Often I would get to the top only to drop the hammer or the tin, and sometimes I would lose my grip on the siding. Climb back down, climb back up, climb back down, climb back up to the full extension of the super-high-extension ladder. From the top of the ladder I could only reach to nail one board at a time. Then I would climb back down, collect another board, more tin, make sure I had nails and my hammer and climb back up.

I worked on that side of the house for days. At one point, I went down to the store to collect our mail. Lucky's wife was doing a little dusting on the top shelves when I arrived, and she complained to me how tiring it was to climb up her two-step stool to reach the top shelf. I just nodded and agreed that it must indeed be tiring to do all that climbing.

Once the siding was on, I worked with George to finish the inside, and the rest of the work went quite smoothly. The contract was only for the construction, so we didn't have to do any painting. Once we had hung the doors and cupboards, the last job was to build proper steps up to the main entrance, and we were finally finished. What started out to be a simple one-level cabin ended up being a lovely two-storey, three-bedroom house with a huge living room window looking out over the inlet and up to the snow-capped Coast Mountains. It was a tremendous feat to pull off without the aid of any heavy equipment. I still pat myself on the back for that one.

The house we built at Dawsons Landing for the Fisheries Department in the early 1980s. Back-breaking work.

Another Lost Boat

The wind was howling in our usually quiet little bay. We had walked around all of the floats during the day, putting anything away that wasn't tied down, and tying down anything that was too big for us to move. George checked all the ropes and cables that tied all of the floats and walkways together. He also checked the standing boom to make sure everything was still secure. Then we retied any boats that were not tight enough. We were hours from the worst part of the storm and we knew that the hardest winds would come in the middle of the night.

The floats were already groaning and knocking together. It had the spooky feeling and sound of a pirate ship from an old movie, and there was a sense of fear looming in the back of my mind. George and I settled down after rechecking everything and went in for supper. We are generally so sheltered here, all the way around the corner and in the back of the bay. There had been floats tied here when a tsunami caused by the 1964 Alaska earthquake rolled down the coast. At that time, the people living here noticed all of the floats rise several inches, all of the ropes tighten and then everything went back to normal. We weren't too concerned about the blow that was coming.

George went to check on things one last time before we went to bed. In spite of our superior knotting skills, one of our speedboats had worked itself loose and was gone. George couldn't see it anywhere near the floats, so it could have been on its way to Japan by that point. We could not afford to lose the boat, so George had to go out and find it before it went any farther. This would be a terribly risky trip in a small boat in this wind and the dark. I tried to talk him out of it. What would happen if he didn't come back? Would I then have to go out and look for him? Okay—now I have to tell you my little secret. I'm also afraid of the dark! It probably has something to do with my early childhood: me in my darkened room with my sister and brother crawling around my crib under a blanket, while I ran back and forth screaming. I pleaded with George to let the boat go or at least wait until it was light outside, but he was not to be persuaded. He said that the boat could have been miles away by then and we'd never find it.

I watched him bob and bounce out and around the corner and disappear into the pouring rain and howling wind, into the pitch black. He didn't use a flashlight, as even on the darkest night there was a little contrast between the water and the shore, and the light close to his face would only blind him. I made my way back into the house and turned on the overhead battery light. Fear was grinding in my chest and I could not distract my mind from thoughts about what could happen to George out there in the dark, rough water. My two worst fears! What on earth am I doing in this country—this wild and dangerous wilderness? And how am I still asking myself that question?

I paced from the living room to the kitchen and back again. I sat in the rocking chair. I stood on the porch trying to listen for the boat returning. Then I paced from the living room to the kitchen again. I knew that if George found the boat, he would have trouble getting a rope on it, and then it would be a slow process of towing it home. Knowing this didn't help, because I could imagine him falling out of the boat while he tried to get a line on the other one in the slop. It was a very long night, and finally the pitch black started to turn to dark grey and then to light grey, and then the oppressive feeling began to lift. I went out and chopped some wood in the half-light. It felt better to be doing something.

I stoked the fire in the kitchen stove and in the living room to make sure the house would be nice and warm when George got back. As I went out for my second armload of wood, I could just make out the intermittent sound of an outboard engine. Oh my God! He was safe! A few minutes later he came slowly around the corner, towing the errant boat behind him. He was finally able to find it miles from home because even in the dark of the storm, the white sides of the boat were visible as if they had their own light shining from within. And his propensity for boating in bad weather added more fuel to his Hurricane Ardley nickname.

Starting a Family

We headed into the 1982 fishing season feeling excited. Things were looking good. We had lots of bookings, and the summer season was taking shape very nicely. At the end of the last season, we sold the original twenty-one-foot *Sportspage* and replaced it with a used twenty-five-foot speedboat with a flying bridge, which we also named *Sportspage*. To house it, George designed a huge boathouse that we would build before the coming season. The roof would be high enough above the boat slip to accommodate *Sportspage* without having to put the antenna down. There would be a large woodworking shop at the back as well as storage space for several of the guest fishing boats and a second-floor level over the workshop with three more crew rooms. We were booking twelve guests at a time and we planned to hire more help for the summer season. We would have six crewmembers and they would each have their own room.

Anthony, our erstwhile part-time handyman who we hired from Port Hardy to help with some of our bigger projects, was staying with us and helping George build the boathouse float and structure. The roof trusses for the building were massive and required ingenuity and planning in order to raise them with just the two of them working together. By the time the roof was going on, I was felled by morning sickness. We had been feeling more settled and our coffee chats had often turned to discussing the logistics of having children to share our exciting life. I wasn't prepared to feel so terrible, though. We lived such a clean fresh-air life that I was taken by surprise that I could spend hours in the morning draped over the couch.

I hated not being involved in the building process, but all I had to do was lean over my chicken house to collect the eggs to be knocked flat by the smell. (I will carry the memory of that brutal combination of cedar shavings mixed with warm feathered bodies and chicken manure for the rest of my days!) I would be quite useless for the rest of the morning. It was more than I could bear to lean into the chicken-coop aroma to pick up the eggs. I was extremely affected by smells and I couldn't walk within fifty feet of the cage. Our solution: we gave the chickens and ducks to our friends the Coopers with the provision that when they were done with them, we would get the boom-winch float back. One day, George would be able to use it again.

One morning I heard a boat troll slowly into the bay and then George walking out to greet whomever it was. They carried on a conversation in low tones, which I wasn't able to catch because my head was in a bucket and the rest of me was again, draped over the couch. I found out later that the visitor was a police boat from Bella Bella, and the RCMP fellows on board were hoping I would make them lunch. George apparently explained to them where I was and what I was doing, and they beat a hasty retreat! I've always felt a little guilty about that. I do hope they eventually found lunch somewhere in the inlet.

There were rumblings in the global market that the world economy was not as rosy as it once seemed to be. Stocks were falling, oil prices were dropping and freight companies were losing business. What started out to be an amazing year suddenly wasn't looking so good. We lost quite a few bookings when large companies in the US and Canada had to lay off hundreds of employees. The perception would not be good if company executives were flying off for an expensive holiday when, at the same time, staff were losing their homes. We lowered our expectations and tightened our belts like most other successful companies were doing.

We had always had a large number of husbands and wives, or fathers and sons fishing with us. Many times guests who first came to us as part of a company group would book again with their wives. We had always had a washroom with a shower in each guestroom, so once the men saw that their wives would be comfortable at our place they happily booked more trips. This would be our saving grace when we could no longer rely on company-only business. Some women arrived expecting to lounge out on the deck, but they would get caught up in the excitement of catching such big beautiful fish and often became more avid than their partners, pushing for earlier wake-up calls and wanting to stay out through lunch.

We had a "good enough" season that year and went into the fall making plans to house a baby in our one-bedroom home.

But first ... we had a hunting trip to attend to. George had cooked up a plan to go moose hunting with our neighbours Lois and Floyd Casperson, who were caretaking at Duncanby Landing. They owned a fishboat, which was our transportation to Bella Coola, where they owned a home. From there we used their truck and drove up past the Rainbow Mountains, or "Rainbum Mountains"—so named because I was eight months pregnant at this point, and there were four of us crammed into the front seat of their truck. I sat sideways with my bottom pressed hard against the door, and I had to pee every few miles. It was initially a slip of the tongue but we continued to call them the Rainbum Mountains from then on.

We drove on and up toward the small community of Anahim Lake, about eighty miles east of Bella Coola. This road, Highway 20, which is called "Freedom Road," had way too many sharp hairpin turns with no possibility of seeing if another vehicle was coming around the corner. Some parts were so narrow that if you did meet another car, one of you had to back up to a wider space with the cliff going straight up beside your car on one side and straight down on the other. Some parts had an 18 percent grade and, at one time, we stood at the side of the cliff in a light cloud and could see three switchbacks below us before another cloud hid the rest of the road. After the most harrowing driving trip ever—there are t-shirts available, I survived the Anahim Hill—we arrived safely in Anahim Lake to stay overnight.

We flew in a tiny Cessna the next morning to Eliguk Lake, where the plane pulled up to a dock in front of the cabin we would use. The scenery was spectacular, with snow-covered mountains and glaciers in the distance. The four of us were staying in a large cabin that didn't have much in the way of amenities. Good thing I had an internal furnace because I might have frozen to death there. And, oh boy, what next?— an outhouse for my many trips to the toilet in the middle of the night. We had seen lots of grizzly and black bear on our way to Anahim, so I thought, probably correctly, that there would be plenty around here.

I started to feel uneasy when George went hunting with Floyd, and I was left behind with Lois—leaving me to sit and read, Lois to cast for fish off the dock. I squashed any pangs that I felt about being in the middle of

The new boatshed had room to house our new twenty-five-foot *Sportspage*, plus one of the guest speedboats, a woodworking shop, a mechanical workshop, crew rooms, storage and a winch for lifting motors. It was invaluable for its myriad uses over the years.

nowhere without a way of contacting the pilot. *I must be crazy*, I thought. I gave it up to pregnancy brain. What was George's excuse? Eight months pregnant, I should be sitting with my feet up eating bonbons and reading a good book. Oh, I was. But I wasn't supposed be in the Middle of Fuck Nowhere!

The men didn't end up shooting anything that morning—or any morning actually. They slogged around in the open bush and came home hungry and tired three days in a row. The guys had done the grocery shopping, and we were short of food. They thought we would be augmenting our meals with trout and moose steaks. It was harder to catch a fish than to sight a moose. When the plane finally appeared on the horizon, I started salivating. *I'm eating for two here!* I was starving!

We flew back to Anahim, drove back down to Bella Coola, and then took the slow boat to China back to Rivers Inlet. I think it will be a while before I am talked into a hunting trip again. It has been a while. Well, never. No, I'll never go hunting again.

Just two weeks later I flew to Edmonton to stay with my sister Marcia and brother-in-law Murray. For this I am truly grateful. I felt safe and cared for, and our dear son, Casey, was born just three weeks after that, at the end of December. My other sister, June, lived just a mile away, so there was much going back and forth between the two houses. My mom came from Winnipeg to stay with us and have some daughter-and-new-grandchild fun. We wore a rut in the road between the two houses.

Right after New Year's Eve, George flew home to the inlet from Edmonton while I stayed on with my sisters for more cherished cosseting. He planned to build a room for the baby at the lodge. It was a complicated build. Not just because it was on a float. But because he was joining three parts of the house with three different rooflines and none of the walls were straight and the floors were at different levels. But he was so proud of the sweet little room that he had added on behind the kitchen. It was perfect. He had also added a hallway and bathroom at the back of the room that joined with our bathtub room and the back of our bedroom. It must have been so frustrating, joining all those wacky sections. But I was happy because this meant I wouldn't

Our son, Casey, was born in December 1982.

have competition for the bathroom when we had summer female staff here.

Casey and I flew home to Rivers Inlet from Vancouver via Sandspit on Moresby Island. A circuitous route to be sure. Port Hardy was socked in with fog, so the jet flew right over it and headed up to the Queen Charlotte Islands and the Sandspit Airport. While waiting for the fog to clear, I met another mother with a very small baby. We started chatting and became fast friends. Bonnie Lunn was heading into Dawsons Landing, where her husband, Brian, was the new Fisheries officer. Eventually the fog cleared around Port Hardy, and we were flown back there to catch our float plane into the inlet.

George zoomed out to pick us up at the dock. He couldn't wait to show us the new baby room. Mmm, the smell of fresh coffee when we walked into the house. I could see that he had been working late nights to finish the construction. Everything was general chaos in the rest of the house but the baby room was immaculate. He had put together the crib and there was a changing table with diapers already piled on it. He hung up the tiny new outfits in the open closet and arranged stuffed toys on the shelves.

George walked Casey around his new digs and explained to him everything he was looking at. Then he carried him outside and walked him all around the floats and into the workshops explaining about all the tools and equipment and what he would one day be able to do with it all. They were an inseparable team from that day on.

You'd Better Have a Good Excuse

We were going to build a new float. We needed to collect the logs, either by stroke of luck—finding ones that had broken away from a log boom—or by a great amount of effort on George's part. There was still a public timber-cutting area about three miles from our bay, and we'd gotten float logs there before. George had marked several giant cedar trees for our use. He headed out in our work skiff at about 9:30 AM to cut one of the trees down. It was the beginning of February 1983, cold and dry, and the days were short with the sun going down behind the hills by 2 PM, leaving the channels and bays submerged in darkness and eerily still.

George would have to be back in our bay by 12:30 PM, or I would know that there had been a problem, and, worst-case scenario, I would need the extra daylight hours to help him. I pottered around in the house and after lunch put baby Casey down for a nap. After 12 PM, I started watching the clock, minute by minute ticking by. Usually, George would be home well before the cut-off time. At 12:15, I started to get anxious. By 12:25, I was getting mad. Did he really think I wanted to take our two-month-old out in a boat on a freezing-cold winter day to find out that he had simply forgotten to look at his watch?

I bundled Casey up with a little sense of urgency, strapped him into his life jacket and settled him in his car seat, which sat on the floor of the boat. We zipped out of the bay and pounded across the waves of Darby Channel and all the way to the farthest corner of Morgan Bay to where there was a tiny indent with no beach, just rock wall from the water to the trees.

I had the canvas top down on my speedboat, and I stood as I drove so I could better see over the windshield. As I rounded the last point at the entrance to the little bay, I immediately saw George standing on the rocks where a large creek tumbled into the ocean. I was flooded with relief and at the same time I furiously shouted, "You better have a bloody good excuse for being late!"

I slowed the boat down and as we trolled closer to the shore, I could see what George was pointing at. There was a tree, a tall alder with lots of branches, lying across his now submerged work skiff. George was standing sheepishly on a rock and his big Stihl 090 chainsaw was balanced across two other rocks about ten feet above him.

I nosed the speedboat carefully up to the rock so George could clamber on and gingerly climb over the windshield and into the boat. My anger had dissipated somewhat as soon as I saw that he did indeed have a good excuse. He was so lucky that the tree hadn't fallen on his head! He was also lucky that, in my relief in seeing him safe, I no longer felt the need to knock him over the head for sinking the engine, the extra chainsaw and all the other gear into the salt water.

The next day, George headed back over to rescue the boat and equipment. He used the Stihl to trim the branches off the alder that was holding the boat down. Then he bucked the tree into pieces that he could move one at a time on his own and rolled them over the side of the boat. At low tide he removed the motor and the gas tank and all of the tools, then bailed out as much water as he could. The boat floated when the tide came back in and other than the mess inside from the alder branches, you couldn't tell that a tree had recently smashed down on it. George towed the skiff home and ran fresh water through the engine to flush out the salt water and was able to get it running again for his next tree-felling exploits.

He promised me he would be more careful next time. He thought that he had put the undercut in the right place, but as he cut through the back side of the cedar tree it fell on a slight angle, and that made it knock over an alder, which knocked over two more alder, and the boat was tied to shore right under them. Never again did I have to wrap up a baby to head out on a rescue mission for him.

High Tides and Pike Poles

George loved scuba diving. He thought we might be able to extend our fishing season with diving charters. He already had the gear to wear in the water, and we had the accommodations. So he just needed a compressor to fill the air tanks. The compressor arrived on the flight with the two men he called to come and explore interesting diving sites with him. There were many old fish-cannery sites from the time when everyone just threw their garbage overboard. The areas beneath the docks of these old places would be ripe with interesting finds. They spent a fun week diving a different site every day and coming home with old beer bottles, ginger jars, opium bottles with the end snapped off and lots of old china, some of it dating as far back as 1885.

Also, the sea life in the cold northern water is vibrant and varied, more beautiful even than in warmer climates. But it would be a challenge to convince a couple who could fly to Hawaii and stay in a hotel for a week, scuba diving every day in warm water for the price of the airfare into Rivers Inlet from Vancouver. We tried to promote the lodge as a diving destination but after a few years decided it was not to be.

I had been spending so much time housebound with our wee Casey that when George suggested that just he and I could make a quick trip to our favourite beach on Calvert Island, I jumped at the chance. We had a beautiful calm day and on the way we dropped Casey off for a play-date with our friends. We anchored in Pruth Bay and walked across to the beach, full of anticipation because we hadn't been there for many months. As we approached the entrance to the beach through the salal bushes, we could hear the far-off rumbling of waves and taste the salt in the air. I leaped onto the log protecting the way and pushed through the bushes and then was suddenly racing down the beach, peeling clothes off as I ran. It was still winter but the sun was beating down on the white sand, and it was just so freeing to get rid of my heavy clothes. I turned and saw George running behind me throwing his clothes off as he ran. We ran past the winter-storm logs and piles of seaweed washed up in long lines and the grasses flattened by so many heavy rains. We ran past the craggy trees, the jagged cliffs and the windswept sand hills. Then we both slowed down and walked hand in hand to the far end of the beach. As we made our way back, there was the distinct sound of a helicopter.

Who is flying a helicopter near our wilderness beach in the winter? And there it was rising over the far-off treeline, shattering our peaceful day and heading along the beach. We dove behind a jumble of logs and crouched down hoping to hide from the intruders. As the helicopter flew slowly along the beach, the rush of air picked up our clothes and threw them every which way. This of course caught the pilot's attention and he lowered the helicopter, tilted it slightly and started following the line of footprints until he was hovering right over our bare bottoms! We were shocked to see the helicopter, and I'm sure they were shocked to see us. All we could do at that point was give them a wave and a sheepish smile and the men inside the cockpit appeared to snicker as they continued on their way and then disappeared in the distance.

We found out later that there were many helicopters in the area, chartered to land on their pontoons next to large herring fishboats. The herring-roe market had suddenly skyrocketed, and overseas buyers couldn't get enough. In order to be first on the scene as a boat pulled in its load of herring, the buyers were landing in a helicopter on the water beside a fishboat rather than using a boat to chase them down. It was like the Wild West on the fishing grounds, with buyers carrying green garbage bags full of cash and commercial fishermen shooting real bullets across the bow of another fishboat if it got too close. A lot of money was made in a very short season and I have not seen anything like it since.

We had another gorgeous sunny day after another storm passed a week later. We were having extremely low winter tides, so George thought we might be able to find abalones on some rocks closer to home where he had seen the tell-tale algae and seaweed that both abalones and rock scallops feed on. We again dropped Casey off with our friends for an hour and headed out in the open skiff with me sitting at the front, crashing down hard on the seat when we slipped off a large swell. George carefully approached the series of rocks, and as he got closer with me perched and ready at the prow, the boat rose up on the swell and George shouted, "Jump!" Of course I didn't jump. I wasn't quite ready. I have jumped at George's command so many times over the years but this was not going to be another one of those times. I was teetering at the front of the low-sided boat with no good place to hold on to. I could feel the power behind the swell as it pushed the boat up toward the rocks then sucked the boat away just as I was supposed to jump. The boat was rising on the swell and there was a split second as it reached its zenith, when I should've actually leaped. It took several more tries and more frustrated shouts of "Jump!" for me to finally launch myself at the sharp barnacle-covered rock without killing myself or landing in the frigid water.

I did indeed find a few abalones and rock scallops there but would never tell anyone where they were. Commercial tourist boats had essentially cleared out the abalone in the Hakai Pass area by using divers to collect them at any tide. Since 1990, abalone fishing has been closed all along the coast for conservation purposes because they are taking so long to recover from overfishing.

Another sea creature whose harvesting has been closed to local gatherers for decades is the wonderfully delicious clam. I had made many a delectable clam chowder, clam fritters and clams Rockefeller over the years. Suddenly one day in the early eighties there were Fisheries signs posted that said it was illegal to harvest all bivalves due to paralytic shellfish poisoning (PSP). The closure is still in effect today. Apparently, someone had recently died from eating clams about one hundred miles from us. Harvesting along the entire north and central coast had been closed. We had never seen the tell-tale areas of red colouring from PSP in the water, and we disputed the closure. We asked if someone from the Fisheries office at Dawsons could dig clams and send them in for testing. We were told that it was expensive; they would have to test the clams on rats, and the best clam tides were too early in the morning. I suggested that we would get up early and dig the clams, drive them directly to Dawsons to fly out on that day's plane to Port Hardy. And if all else fails, test them on Fisheries officers who simply wouldn't get out of bed in the morning. Too harsh?

Back at home, work continued. We needed more buoyancy under our woodshed float. It had a handy open-sided structure on it where we stored everything that needed to be under cover, and, as a result, the float had to carry more and more weight. Of course we had huge stacks of firewood but also old fire pumps, extra freezers, cleaning supplies, tools, plumbing and electrical supplies and a couple of speedboats overwintered inside.

Just ahead of one of the extreme winter high tides, George tied a huge cedar log on a loose line, and pushed it over to the far side of the bay where there is a straight rock wall. I scrambled up the hillside where I tied the other end to a huge tree. We headed back to the woodshed float, unhooked all the lines that were attaching it to the standing boom, and then George pushed the float over to the cedar log and I climbed up again, hauling cable behind me.

We wrapped the cable tightly around several massive cedars and back down to the float, so it was tightly held in place. The tide turned and was going toward a super-low tide, and we watched over the next six hours. The cables held the weight of the float as the tide dropped inch by inch. This made it possible for the log to roll underneath the suspended float. Then as the tide came back in, the float rested on the new log, making the float tippy in one direction. It was brilliant! The next day, he brought another nice straight log over, and we tied everything up again with the woodshed turned around. This time the log went under, and it straightened and levelled the float. The power of the tide in the wilderness is awe-inspiring!

That winter, George also built a sixteen-foot-long hot tub on a float. He built the float itself with a dozen good logs to carry the weight of the water in the swim spa. Our friend Richard had been a fibreglass instructor and helped George build the hot tub part. He also built a pool house on the end of the float to house the 450,000-BTU propane heater and did all the wiring and plumbing on his own. He hadn't counted on the amount of gas flowing to the heater when he hooked up two hundred-pound tanks of propane. The first time he turned the heater on, the gas rushed out so fast for the burner that the propane tanks froze on the outside, from the dials on top to a third of the way down the tanks. The water in the pool heated really fast! We were playing in the hot water within three hours of turning it on.

The hot tub was a popular place to relax after a day of fishing. We used it all winter.

We had a lovely day of rest at the beginning of May and before the fishing-season work started up again in earnest. We went to the nearby clamshell beach where we played catch with kelp bulbs and turned rocks over to show Casey all the sea life that scrambled away. We were on our way home in the afternoon and partway through Klaquaek Channel, when George noticed a disturbance on the surface of the water. He headed over, pulled alongside the bubbles and, lo, there was a halibut thrashing around just under the surface. With visions of many dinners-to-come dancing in our heads, we quickly looked around the boat but couldn't see anything even close to fishing gear. So George picked up our twelve-foot-long pike pole! He pulled closer to the halibut and standing up, drove the hook into the side of the biggest fish we had ever seen. It was easily wider than, and seemed almost as long as, the twelve-foot boat we were in. I may be using typical fishermen's exaggeration here, but it was big! He pulled hand-over-hand on the pole and the halibut slid closer to the boat where he hoped to get a rope through its gills. When it was almost within reach, a gigantic sea lion lifted out of the water and stared at George straight in the eye. George swore he heard it growl, "*Mine!*" I thought it was going to devour us. The sea lion leaned over and dropped across the halibut, dragging it off the hook and underwater, never to appear again. Drat—no halibut and chips for dinner every night for the next six months.

Back at the lodge, I started packing my bags to fly to Edmonton to be with my sisters. My suitcase was open on the bed and every time I put something into it, one-year-old Casey would toddle over and take something out. I was getting nowhere, so I took Casey into his room and suggested that if he could play there for a few minutes I would come and get him and make a snack for us. I finished packing in double-quick time and was so pleased that Casey had kept himself busy. I didn't like to disturb the quiet time but gently opened his door to call him for lunch. He stood proudly pointing at the windows. His room was quite bare. His windows were both flung wide open and he had been chucking everything out that he could pick up with his little hands. Books, train cars, stuffed toys, diapers, pillows, talcum powder. He had cleared every shelf that he could reach.

The back wall of his bedroom was within one log of the back of our house float. In front of and behind that log was ocean water. There was a gap of about two feet from the back of the float to the floating walkway that ran all along the back of the lodge buildings. There were a few books and toys scattered about on the walkway and a few random things on the log, but everything else was either floating in the water or had sunk into the depths of the bay. Well, that's one way to tidy up a room.

Our next big improvement that spring of 1984 was to build a walk-in flash freezer. There were twelve contact-freezing shelves, and each shelf could freeze a dozen vacuum-packed coho fillets in less than twenty minutes. We also put radiophones into all twelve of the boats. They weren't all guest boats: one was for the workboat, one was mine, one was for the fish master, a couple for the crew to use in their spare time, and there was one extra boat in case one broke down. They made it so much easier to keep track of the guests when they were out fishing. The guests could also get in touch with someone at the lodge if they decided to stay out instead of coming in for lunch. We would pack a basket with a lovely lunch with all the trimmings for delivery, making the guests feel very special. This was called the lunch run. Our fish master, George for many years, would make several trips out to check on the guests and make sure they were catching fish. He would deliver bait and extra snacks and sometimes a guest's fishing licence that had been left in their room. This one was called the bait run. And then there was the evening run that involved rounding up any guests who tried to stay out too late. An errant guest boat was one thing that got our usually unflappable George angry. Unless the guests had a monster-sized salmon on the end of their line, they'd better not try staying out until dark!

It wasn't a good idea to make George angry. One night a couple of men sat outside under the stars, talking and laughing so loud they kept the whole group of guests awake. In the morning, the two men didn't feel up to going fishing so George stood outside their now open bedroom window and started his chainsaw. The two bleary-eyed fellows got the rather broad hint and dragged themselves in for strong coffee and then headed out in their boat.

Another time, a couple of men—again—kept most of the guests awake with their boisterous conversation out on the deck. The following day, one of the fellows got up after George's wake-up knock on the door, but the other one stayed in bed and refused to budge. As everyone was getting ready to cast off the dock and head out fishing, George walked over to the sleeping guest's boat and slipped the key out of the ignition. He suggested to the fellow who did get up that the boat wasn't leaving until both he and his partner were in it. His friend showed up very soon after.

One night a guest boat came flying into the bay far too fast. The driver killed the engine partway across the bay and the boat drifted into the dock. The throttle had been stuck in full forward. It was still early in the evening and the guests had eaten dinner so I took them out fishing in my own boat. We came back in with the biggest fish of the night. A beautiful forty-eight-pound chinook. I never go fishing. Maybe I should.

The next group of fishermen were staying over the BC Day long weekend at the beginning of August. On Saturday afternoon, I opened the oven door of my new wood cook stove to put a roast in. The door spring cracked in my hand and the door was suddenly on the floor—snapped right off. This was an emergency. I had twelve guests to cook for and no oven in the kitchen. I grabbed the roast pan and ran down to the end guest cabin that had our old oil stove in the drying room. I cranked up the heat and threw the meat in the oven then ran back to the kitchen. Several times George tried calling the store in Vancouver where we bought the stove. Of course no one answered. It was not just the weekend, but the long weekend. Who would be around now? He then called his sister Gery and asked her to find an emergency number for the stove dealer and, if all else failed, to break one of the store's windows to get someone down there to investigate a break-in. She did finally connect with someone who then went into the store on the holiday Monday, took the door off their floor model and delivered it to the airport in time for our flight that day. George always brought out the best in people!

George had the respect of all of our guests, our staff and our suppliers. He treated everyone very well but wouldn't stand for anyone's nonsense. He loved taking guests on sightseeing tours in the afternoon when fishing could sometimes be slow. Some people would try to catch up on their sleep but there would always be a few who would happily go on a tour. With the warning "Do as I say, not as I do," he would flash between rocks that looked far too close together, fly around corners to catch wildlife doing what they do, and drift under low-hanging trees all while describing everything the guests were looking at: rocks, fish, moss, eagles, seals, sea lions, grizzly bears, the old sunken jail cell and distant mountain ranges. There was always something to see. One guest once suggested that when you've seen one mountain, you've seen them all. This did not sit well with George, and that particular guest was never invited back.

Big Plans

We had been running Rivers Lodge for eight years now and we made plans to increase the number of guests that we could accommodate at one time. We thought it would be great to eventually build a separate lodge building, but life was busy enough at the moment so we thought we could at least increase the seating capacity in our house/lodge and add more accommodation for this summer.

We had enough resources to build another guesthouse without borrowing money. Our helper Anthony arrived and with the three of us working, we knocked together another lovely four-room guesthouse with bathrooms in each room, in no time. I was much better at carpentry at this point and didn't spend as much time with injuries or swearing over bendy nails. Plus, we had finally moved on to ordering proper nails in a variety of sizes.

We retired the original guesthouse that had two bedrooms and used it instead for staff housing. We now had a fleet of eight guest boats as well as eight guestrooms for a total of sixteen guests at a time. Then George started work on our house so we could comfortably seat the sixteen guests.

One morning, George cranked up his chainsaw and started sawing through the front wall of our living room. The glass to put in a solarium-type window had just arrived on the freight boat. We could add an extra three feet of space to the crowded room by extending the wall out for the new window. We also took out the wonderful Jøtul brand fireplace to make room for a third couch and redid the carpet. The extra space added much-needed elbow room at the dining room tables as well.

The couch under the solarium window became my favourite place to sit with Casey in the dark. We could watch the night sky while cuddled up reading a bedtime story by flashlight. And in the daytime, it made the perfect perch from which to watch the ever-changing scene out in front of the lodge.

One morning, there was a commotion across the bay high up on the shore and under the low branches of a cedar tree. There was a skate lying on the rocks and a juvenile eagle with his wings spread wide, protecting his breakfast. Two other eagles, adults, thought they were in for a very decent meal, but the young one was ferocious in his flapping and pecking and seemed to have infinite patience to protect his food. A full hour later the two older ones finally gave up and flew away. The larger wingspan on a young bald eagle enables them to eat by increasing their ability to protect their food from older eagles.

The before picture: George cut through the front wall of the main lodge building (also our living room). We needed extra room added to the lounge area.

The after picture: George installed a solarium-type window that added an extra three feet of space to the crowded room. The couch under the solarium window became my favourite place to sit with Casey.

As we got closer to another fishing season, George made a quick buying trip to Port Hardy. He headed over early in the day and, not wanting to waste any time, then pounded through the westerly all the way back to the inlet in the afternoon, heavily loaded. That night as we were getting ready for bed, we could hear a boat motor, and it sounded like it was coming into our bay. There are not many boaters that drive around in the dark, but George thought he knew who it would be. He got dressed and headed out to the front. When he got there, the motor sound had disappeared. Figuring that the boater must be anchoring, he headed back in and once again climbed into bed. Then we distinctly heard a motor coming into the bay again. So George got up, got dressed and headed out the front. No motor sound.

He came back in, and while we were scratching our heads trying to figure out what was going on, we could once again hear the motor. This time George went out the back door, stood on the porch and breathed in gas fumes. Our new *Sportspage* was tied up quite close to our back door and in front of the generator shed. All was quiet for a few minutes and suddenly *Sportspage*'s engine kicked into full throttle! George leaped across the dock and jumped into the boat thinking someone must be trying to steal it. He flashed his light below and up top, and there was no one there. We found out later that all the pounding through the waves that afternoon had splashed so much salt water on the ignition up on the flybridge that it was arcing and starting the engine. I started calling the boat *Christine* after Stephen King's scary novel about a car that starts on its own and kills people. This added another notch to George's reputation.

Our first guests of the 1985 season were due to fly in with their own airplane. The fog was so thick we couldn't see to the other side of the bay. Out of nowhere we suddenly heard an airplane engine. Finally we could see the plane pulling up to our dock. They had landed on the water in the inlet just past Dawsons Landing where the sky was clear, and they step-taxied, or ran the float plane the whole four miles on the water, all the way up the channel to our bay. George went out to pick the guests up and as he arrived at the dock, a large sailboat turned into the bay. There was a woman sitting at the very front of the boat with her feet dangling over the prow. They didn't have the chart for the entrance to Rivers Inlet so the skipper had been driving as slow as he could while his wife sat up front watching for rocks. When they saw the airplane zoom into our bay the woman had shouted, "Follow that plane!" They came in and the husband took notes from our chart so they could continue on their way.

This season we had hired a cook to do a lot of the prep work for meals so I could have more time with Casey. One week there was a large group of men who had been fishing for three days and were ready and waiting for the airplane to come pick them up. They were whooping it up and roughhousing on the front deck when our cook went out and joined in the horseplay. Suddenly she pushed one of the guests overboard. He happened to be dressed in his town clothes, including his Rolex watch and Italian leather shoes. There just happened to be an extra seat on the plane and I was back to cooking full-time.

Family

Jessica Ardley was born in December of 1985. I wasn't as cavalier about birthing babies this time. No more hunting trips flying into even deeper wilderness a month before the baby was due. We stayed with my sister June and family in Edmonton for the last few weeks before Jess was born. Staying with my sisters before and after our children arrived was a joy beyond measure. Coming out of the wilderness and being wrapped in the loving arms of family for six weeks each time was an ideal way to bring a child into the world. Coming from the quiet solitude of the inlet to become the centre of attention was soul-satisfying. I'm surprised I didn't have more babies! Well—not really!

Our home in Rivers Inlet was full of kids' stuff. I couldn't picture how the summer would play out with guests and two children in our home/lodge. There were toys everywhere. Two little ones take up so much more space than one. They also take up more time.

We now had hired someone new to cook breakfast and do the baking, so we hired a woman who could do the lunch and dinner prep. Then I could breeze in, and put the finishing touches on the meals to ensure they were up to my standard. It didn't work as well as I planned, as

Jessy and Casey. We had to keep a close eye on Jessy. We were surrounded by water, and she headed out the door every time it was left open.

I found myself hiding with the two kids in the backroom trying to keep them quiet. Our guests didn't come to the lodge to hear small children.

By the time she was eight months old, I had to keep a constant eye on our adventurous Jess. Every chance she got, she dragged, then crawled her way to the door and the great expanse of water not far past it. By now, three-and-a-half-year-old Casey knew not to step out the door without his life jacket on. Jessy was sleeping in a crib, and Casey had the high bed from IKEA that was level with the window looking out over the back of the bay. Our watery backyard is very sheltered within the logs of the standing boom, and we spent many happy hours watching small schools of tiny fish, seals cavorting about, kingfishers diving for dinner, ducks swimming and the great blue heron feeding from the logs. We watched as the heron stood on the log and crouched lower and lower so slowly we could barely detect any movement. Suddenly, it would jab at the water and there would be a silver fish in its beak, squirming wildly to get away. Then the heron would flip it around so it could swallow the fish whole, and we could see the fish wriggling all the way down the long neck. We saw the heron catch an eel that was a foot long. The eel kept winding itself around the heron's beak. The heron flipped its head again and again, unwinding the eel until it eventually wore the eel out and was finally able to swallow it whole. One of Jessy's first words was "spots" because we watched a seal swimming upside down, and you could see black spots on its white belly. It was our own personal wilderness version of an aquarium.

Casey had a small rowboat that George tied to the dock with a long rope. He could row himself around a little and if he ran into trouble getting home, we could pull him back in. One day that summer, a guest misunderstood the reason for the rope and thought that Casey just couldn't get the knot undone. He helpfully undid the rope and off Casey went. The safety rope never limited him again. His new boundary was the front window of our house. If he couldn't see it, then I couldn't see him.

I relied more and more on my kitchen help, which was fine, but I didn't like the hiding with the kids part. By the end of the too-long summer, I told George that I wouldn't do that again. We would have to build a separate lodge, or I would be spending the next summer in town with the children.

What Time Is It?

We made a trip to Vancouver as soon as the lodge was put to bed after another fishing season. We met many times with our architect friend Chas. He and George designed a beautiful two-storey lodge with the second floor cantilevered out over the deck so people could take shelter from the rain underneath as they watched guests come back in to weigh their fish. The upstairs mezzanine would be a comfortable area for guests to get away from it all. There would be a separate upstairs area at the back of the building that had crew rooms, a washroom and an office with lots of storage space. The main floor had a huge living room and dining area, two more washrooms, a great kitchen that I designed, with a large pantry at the end of the kitchen and a laundry room next to it.

We borrowed money to start the building process, and George let our suppliers know that he would soon be ordering large quantities of building supplies. He just had to work out a timeline for early spring since we didn't have the floats on which to build yet. He had cut down massive cedar trees on public timber lands with permission from the BC Forestry Service. He had the licence on his desk when we received a snarky letter from a man in the Forestry office. He wrote, "Cease and desist cutting down trees on the public timber land until you have applied and paid for a licence to do the cutting." George wrote back with an ultra-polite letter to the man and suggested that he check the name on the signature line of his signed licence to cut. Of course it was the same man. Government officials!

George was able to slide some of the logs into the water himself. He got our friend with his tugboat to pull the others down the hillside and into the water. George collected quite a boomful, and we finally started putting them together. We worked all winter on building the new float for the lodge as well as a large float for another new guesthouse.

On Wednesday mornings we had our Montessori-style playschool sessions with all of the children who lived at our end of the inlet. There were four families with ten kids in total, and we moms met once a week at one of the four homes. There would be Tracy Nygaard, Bonnie Lunn, Jenny Salo and me, and we each worked with someone else's children throughout the morning and usually sent them off to play outside after lunch while we relaxed over our own lunch with coffee and plenty of chatting.

One Wednesday I heard the workboat engine zoom across the bay and, as it approached the house, George shouted, "What time is it?" I

The lodge boats were stored out of the water and wrapped for the winter. The structure and tarp covering took a lot of work, but the fibreglass was protected from sun damage over the years.

leaped up off the floor and plowed over two little kids as I raced to open the front window and shouted back, "Eight minutes after ten!" My heart was in my throat—I knew something was wrong. He shouldn't be there! One minute before, I had caught a glimpse of the new float loaded with the building supplies for the lodge, approaching the narrow entrance to the bay with George behind it, pushing with the work skiff. The float must have hung up on the shore on the now falling tide!

I ran back through the maze of kids and puzzle pieces and out the door, grabbing the tide book as I passed the kitchen counter. George had bellowed for Anthony, our helper from Port Hardy, to "grab the axe and get in my boat!" and he dropped him off on the end of the lodge float to help another crewmember push against the shore of the island with pike poles. I jumped into my speedboat and with my heart racing and silent words of encouragement to the engine, I pulled the starter cord while I untied the back end with the other hand. The lodge float had hung up on the sloping shore of the island, and the tide was going out. Seconds could make the difference now as the water drained from the bay and the barnacle-covered rocks reached out to seize the float in a catastrophic embrace.

The freight barge had just unloaded thousands of pounds of building materials onto the float tied up in deep water on the far side of the bay. There were: piles of two-by-fours six feet high, piles of plywood, boxes of nails, rows of windows, two-by-twelves, tar paper, cedar shingles, stacks of aluminum roofing. The tide was going to drop seventeen feet six inches, one of the highest tides of the year, and if we didn't get the float unstuck, we could lose everything while the float broke up on the shore and dropped all of the materials into the ocean. George pushed the metal teeth of the work skiff into one corner of the float and I pushed my boat into the log close to the skiff. With no teeth on my boat, it rode up onto the log. Fearing that my boat would swamp, I had to back up, letting water slosh over the transom, and I tried again. I drove it into a spot where there was a hump of a knot on the log. The boat stayed down and I gunned the engine. George had his engine full-throttle while he rocked his boat back and forth and back and forth and I did the same.

The float would pivot a little but it would not budge, and we were running out of time. George zoomed around and pushed from the other side with his engine's propeller coming within inches of the rocks and I snugged my boat into the right angle where the lash log meets the float log and went full steam ahead. It was not going to move. The water was receding almost two inches every minute and the shore was getting a better hold of the heavily laden float.

George pulled back and roared for Anthony. As he flew past the end of the float, Anthony dove into the skiff, clutching the axe. George zoomed over and dropped Anthony on the end of the fuel float, which was tied to our standing boom and shouted at him: "Cut the ropes!" All of the other floats that were attached to our standing boom were tied in with heavy cable and boom chains, but the fuel float was attached with ropes in case of an emergency, and we had to cut it loose quickly. Anthony is a big man, and with a few powerful chops, he cut through each of the heavy ropes holding the fuel float in place. At the same time, Bonnie and Jenny left all the kids with Tracy and jumped into their speedboats and were suddenly pushing beside me. Now the fuel float was loose. George worked the skiff in behind it and pushed it another forty-five feet away from the grounded lodge float. With no words exchanged, I knew what he was going to do. I joined him with my boat on the far side and, together, we pushed the fuel float—its tanks heavy with diesel and gas from the barge that morning—straight at the jammed lodge float. Just ahead of impact, we both pulled back on the throttles and let the float go. There was a moment right before the fuel float connected with the lodge float in which I felt the air being sucked out of the bay. As the one float rammed the other, we all held our breath and watched as the lodge float shuddered. There was an almost imperceptible *bump*, then a *bump, bump, bump*, and the lodge float settled free in the water, away from the shore.

Building the New Lodge

It was 1987 and we now had tons of supplies piled on the lodge float, and two more crew had arrived by plane shortly after the barge that delivered the goods had departed. There were now six of us to work on the building. My time was somewhat short as I had the two kids to look after—and sometimes more on playschool days. The rest of the crew was made up of Anthony, his friend Larry, who also had construction experience, and a couple who were very helpful at the beginning. He was a handyman who could do plumbing and electrical, and she cooked for all of us, so I had more time for kids and construction work. This couple liked to party, but the rest of us worked so hard and for so long that no one else had the energy to drink in the evening.

With three dedicated workers, as well as me and George at times, the building started to take shape quickly. George spent a lot of time on the phone organizing supplies to be delivered when we needed them, not before and not after. We didn't have extra storage space for all the wood that we required for such a huge two-storey building as well as a new four-room guesthouse—and the start of the new fishing season was looming. It was a delicate balance of delivery trucks and timelines, freight boats and barges that kept George hopping. He worked miracles with the suppliers who went out of their way to accommodate his urgent orders, sometimes delivering items within an hour of his call. We had amazing support from the suppliers, better even than if we had been building in town, I believe.

As we progressed with the building, George could see that we would not be able to finish in time with the small crew. He hired two more men. Then a week later, he hired yet two more. The building came together. The last of the windows went in within hours of arriving on a barge, and the finishing pieces were hammered on. George had been to town and bought a double fridge and a double-wide stove at an auction of Vancouver's Expo 86 kitchen equipment. The two pieces were so huge that I had to remove the door trim at the kitchen for them to fit through. Then it was all hands on deck to coax the enormous pieces up into the building and into place in the kitchen. The walls were painted, the carpet laid and the cedar boards applied to the ceiling. The pot lights in the dining area arrived and were too deep for the ceiling. George raced out to the workshop and created round doughnuts out of cedar to finish the lights, which gave them a porthole-like design feature that seemed intentional.

One afternoon, I was talking to George while he was up a ladder working with a metal square to mark sections of roofing gussets. He

Building the new two-storey lodge. The second floor was cantilevered out over the deck so people could be sheltered outside if it happened to be raining and watch as guests returned with their giant salmon and halibut.

turned to me and dropped the square. We both heard the *thhhp* as the two-foot-long tool slipped between the planks and disappeared into the water. We both stared, aghast that such a long tool could actually find its way between the planks of our walkway. Over the side, yes, but between the planks? Later that afternoon, George was again working up the ladder, and once again dropped a square. Unbelievably, the second square made that same *thhhp* noise and disappeared without a trace. What are the odds? He decided it might be prudent to stay off ladders for a while.

George hung the artwork that he had picked up on one of his buying trips. There was a huge triptych to fill one large wall, and there was his favourite: an E.J. Hughes painting of the entrance to the Nanaimo Harbour, with the little lighthouse on the island. This was the same lighthouse that he watched as a child every time he left Nanaimo on the ferry, which was the beginning of George's love of lighthouses and the very beginning of our excellent adventure.

I was hanging the towel rack over wet paint when I heard the airplane carrying our guests fly over the lodge. I left the towels folded on the

Guests relaxing inside the new lodge.

back of the sink, and ran home to change out of my work clothes. The construction crew flew out on the same plane that had brought our guests in.

We had started laying the stringers for the new buildings on April 12, 1987. Our first guests arrived on Friday, June 12. Two months from start to finish. One big beautiful lodge and a new guesthouse with four more guestrooms. My favourite new additions: a chef that we hired to cook lunch and dinner and a breakfast cook who would also do the baking. We now had a staff of ten including: the breakfast cook, the lunch and dinner chef, a manager to help George keep all the equipment and boats running smoothly, a housekeeper, and many dock staff to clean boats, clean fish, and perform the myriad jobs that needed to be done throughout the summer—garbage collecting and burning, fuelling boats, helping guests with anything and everything, vacuum-packing guests' fish, cleaning and fuelling boats again at lunch time, checking tackle boxes, looking after the guestrooms and laundry and watering my plants. And so much more. Okay, now we were on our way!

Well, not exactly. The chef we had hired seemed to have lots of experience but he just couldn't manage all the necessary little details of looking after a kitchen in the wilderness. Two weeks into our season, two weeks of me helping in the background, I sent the underqualified chef home. After organizing one of the dock crew to look after the kids, I took over cooking lunch and dinner. Then as the season progressed, drinking sent the alcoholic mechanic and his wife, the breakfast cook, home too. They were having parties in their room with the kids who were our dock crew and housekeeping staff. Every afternoon, the mechanic would be drunk and unavailable for emergencies by 5 PM. George pulled him aside one day and said he couldn't keep drinking like that. Otherwise something was bound to go wrong. Well, the fellow didn't like having someone question him about his drinking, so at about 3 AM, he stormed to our door and quit. Of course he took his alcoholic wife with him. So there I was: cooking breakfast, lunch and four-course dinners again, as well as preparing morning snacks, afternoon snacks and baking all the bread, cookies and desserts for twenty guests at a time.

Casey and Jessy on a pallet boat that Casey built with an IKEA blind sail and pallets from freight supplies that were delivered. The two of them sailed out of the main bay and out onto Darby Channel—with George following, of course.

That fall, I set up a schoolroom in the upstairs mezzanine area of the lodge. I moved most of the furniture out and lined the walls with plywood with lots of pushpins for attaching Casey's art and schoolwork. I had a sheet of Styrofoam so Jessy could attach her artwork too. Casey was a reluctant five-year-old kindergarten student. There were always many more interesting things to do outside. To make a distinction between home and school, he had to call me Mrs. Ardley when we were in the classroom. I spent a lot of time trying to get Casey to look at the board where I had written, "Lad runs." He would look everywhere but at the board. I think he felt that he simply couldn't be blamed for not knowing what it said if he actually never looked at the words.

We had sent away for correspondence courses from the BC Ministry of Education. The lessons came with lots of information for me about how to approach teaching. None of the lessons could compete with the fact that Casey would sometimes look out the "schoolroom" window and see a log drifting by into the bay and knew that he could get his dad to pay him two hundred dollars for it if he could just get out there and get it first! He was saving for a boat. George told him that when he could buy the boat, George would buy the engine for it.

My best tool for teaching Casey to read was not in any of the lesson plans. Bribery always worked. *Read to the end of this word and you will win three Smarties!* I am not above bribery. I am also very proud to say that against all odds, I did teach Casey to read—and he grew up to be a voracious reader! Jessy won Smarties if she could say the word for the picture on cards. She loved playing school. One time Casey had to write a story about a picture in his reader. There was a family crouched on the roof and holding onto the chimney of their house that had water up to the windows. Hovering above them was a helicopter, no doubt there to save them. In Casey's story, the house is sinking. This made sense to us since we lived on floats. I'm sure the kids in town all thought the water was rising because of a flood.

The Crew Sinks the Freight

It was June in 1988 and I had hired Peter, a wonderful chef, and we had a crew of nine others who were just getting the lodge and boats ready for a new season. I looked out the kitchen window and could just barely see something bobbing along on the surface of the water on the far side of the bay. No—there were *several* things bobbing along! It was too far away to make out what exactly I was looking at, but I knew that something wasn't right. I grabbed binoculars and looked again through the old wavy pane of glass. I could see a red gas tank and some cardboard boxes floating. The hairs on my neck stood straight up.

The freight boat had just left the bay, and I had asked two of the crew to make a few trips to the freight float to collect some of the goods and bring them back to the lodge. I raced out the door, yelled to Peter to come with me, and we both jumped in my boat and zoomed out toward the freight dock. As we got closer, I could see more boxes and bags and containers floating and making their way out of our main bay. We turned the corner and there were three—not two, but three—crew standing on the float, soaking wet, and I could just see the point of the prow of the work skiff poking out of the water.

As I swept up to the dock crew, their faces betrayed mixed emotions—guilt, fear, relief—but all I really saw was stupidity. I put my engine into neutral about fifteen feet from the float and yelled, "What the hell happened?"

"We loaded everything into the skiff," one of the crewmembers answered rather sheepishly. "And when the last person jumped into the front of the boat, water sloshed over the gunnel and it went down pretty fast."

Everything was: three brand-new twenty-five-horsepower outboard engines (which by themselves would have been enough of a load), a brand-new ice machine, three hundred pounds of frozen meat and another several hundred pounds of dry goods and fresh produce. Some of the cardboard boxes bobbing along would have the not-so-fresh produce. And we can't forget the twenty-five-horsepower engine on the back of the skiff, a full tank of gas and these three big guys, who had been, albeit momentarily, standing in the boat.

My mouth was hanging open in shock and disbelief. One of the guys called out, "Can we have a ride?" I snapped out of it and shouted, "FUCK YOU!" then turned and blasted away from them and back to the lodge. The chef kept muttering, "What the hell, what the hell?" Oh boy, what a lot of trouble this would cause. I called George with the bad news. He was in Vancouver getting a few things organized for the summer. He was stunned by the news but I could tell he went immediately into crisis mode and was working out what had to be done to rescue the equipment.

There was nothing we could do about the meat and groceries. They were ruined or gone. But George would have to dive to see if he could find the motors and the ice machine. I went right back out with a long rope with a weight on one end and a buoy on the other and dropped it down right where the skiff was. This would be a marker for George to help him locate the motors later. The rope went down about 125 feet, which was an extremely deep dive for him to have to make. I sent two dock crewmembers in two boats to pick up the idiots off the float with instructions to troll around and pick up anything they could get their hands on.

The skiff was underwater but not gone completely. The engine weighed down the back end, but we could reach the rope that was floating at the front of the boat. We towed it over to shore, tied it to a tree and then pumped the boat out as the tide went down. We seemed to be using the tide to empty boats far too often. Once the water was out of the boat, and the tide had lifted it, we towed it back to the lodge and took the engine off the back. A couple of the dock crew lowered the motor into a forty-five-gallon barrel of fresh water, then with a special hook-up for our hose, ran fresh water through it, hoping to minimize the saltwater damage. It was running when the boat sank so the electrics in it would be ruined, and the salt water would make a mess of the rest of the insides.

George flew back from Vancouver and started organizing his diving equipment. He filled a couple of air tanks, and sorted out all the other gear that he would need to hook on to the motors if he found them. Once again, time was running out as our first guests would be arriving in a few days, and three of our brand-new engines were lying on the bottom of the ocean.

After putting another engine on the back of the skiff, George loaded the boat with his diving equipment, and we headed over to the far side of the bay. He had shimmied his way into his wetsuit at home, but waited until we were anchored right beside the weighted rope before he put the rest of his awkward and heavy gear on. Then he dropped backwards off the side of the boat and, in seconds, sank into the depths, where I immediately lost sight of him. I hung over the edge of the boat with fear eating away at me. I knew the dive was extremely deep and that he would have very few minutes to stay at the bottom. I watched his bubbles break the surface, but knew that I was powerless to help if anything went wrong. He had followed the weighted rope to the bottom and would then swim carefully out from the rope in a small grid pattern. If he kicked his flippers too hard, the soft bottom silt would get churned up, making it difficult to see anything. Just before he was supposed to come back to the surface, he found one of the motors and clumsily tied a signal rope to it, then filled the small deep-water balloon from an attachment on his dive tank so the rope lifted to the surface before he did. Then he slowly began his ascent so that he wouldn't damage his lungs. With heart pounding, I watched as his bubbles started to rise in one spot and was so happy and relieved to see him pop out of the water. He had to do two more dives on the same spot over the next couple of days before he found the other two motors and the ice machine and attached floating ropes to each. We made the three crewmembers who had dumped them go over in the work skiff and hand-pull up each sunken item. One at a time of course.

Christmas at Rivers Lodge

Christmas Eve was always celebrated at our house in Sleepy Bay. We were situated on the route to Dawsons Landing, and our friends who lived in Sunshine Bay, Finn Bay and Goose Bay would head there on Christmas Eve to pick up their last mail, hopefully containing any packages they were expecting. On their way home, they stopped at our house to celebrate with rum and eggnog, or George's famous wassail, and a wonderfully delicious buffet dinner of delightful holiday dishes from my childhood.

Growing up in Winnipeg meant there was a heavy Ukrainian influence on some of my favourite meals. In early December, my friend Sheila Cooper came over and we made perogies together, which is a really time-consuming project that was much more fun to do with a friend. We put Christmas music on and danced around the kitchen mashing potatoes, grating cheese, rolling dough and cutting out the little crescent-shaped morsels. I also made cabbage rolls, or *holubtsi*, and another Ukrainian treat that we liked to call "beer rocks," which is sweet bread dough wrapped around a ground-meat, cabbage and onion filling. Also part of the buffet was a French Canadian tourtière with rhubarb relish and my mom's Icelandic vinarterta for dessert. We couldn't make everything in one afternoon, but I could put all the main dishes in the freezer as we produced them. Then on Christmas Eve, dinner was simply a case of popping everything in the oven and no one had to work.

In the middle of December we would head out in a boat with our friends the Coopers to find Christmas trees for our homes. What boat we used would depend on the weather. If it was a nice calm day, we would take our speedboat and tow a skiff that George and Richard could take

This is the Christmas card we sent out in 1988. There was a lot of fresh water near the surface in the bay that sometimes froze during the winter. George would keep a path open by running our work skiff, which had teeth along the prow to break up the ice so the ice didn't break up the boat. Commercial fishboats often had gum-wood along the prow. We found two gum-wood planks in the attic and George used them to make the best, strongest cutting-board table—it's still in use forty years later.

to shore when we spotted a good tree. If the weather was a bit nasty, we would head out in Richard's fishboat, also towing a skiff, so we could stay warm in the cabin until the last possible second before having to brave the elements and get to shore. We were looking for pine trees around six feet high. Most fir trees were way too big and the pretty little pine trees were few and far between. As luck would have it, the best trees were out near the mouth of Darby Channel and, even on a good day in December, there would be a large swell and sometimes some waves on top of the swell. There was one bay that we drove about half a mile into where it was sheltered and a little out of the wind. It would still be tough though, to get on shore with the rocky cliffs, the boat rising on the swell and either George or Richard having to leap onto a rock with a chainsaw in one hand.

George always made big thermoses of hot chocolate: one kind for the children and an adults-only version that warmed us from the inside out. We were never sure if our lips were numb from the liqueur in the cocoa or because we were chilled by the freezing wind.

One December, we had dreadful weather, and there was no end in sight. So we had to settle for harvesting a Christmas tree nearby. We chose a little hemlock from right in our bay. The poor thing could barely hold up even the lightest ornaments, but we decorated it anyway and had a lovely, tall, skinny tree with all the baubles knocking against the main trunk. Another year we had to settle for a less-than-ideal tree and cut down a six-foot spruce. The shape was lovely, but it hurt like hell to attach the lights and decorations to the prickly branches. Later in January, when I took the tree down, I had to crawl around on the floor picking hundreds of individual needles that had hooked themselves into the carpet so tightly the vacuum couldn't pull them out. Don't let them talk you into buying a spruce for a Christmas tree. Spruce should only be used in the direst of Christmas-tree situations.

The freight boat would arrive close to Christmas. Every year they tried to time it so they arrived with everyone's fresh produce and then they could get home to their own families for the holidays. We would receive fresh cream and sour cream and lettuce and tomatoes. There would be boxes of chocolates, maraschino cherries—the kind with the stem so it would stick out of the shortbread cherry balls—lots of nuts and candies, boxes of mandarin oranges (of course), extra pounds of butter, several dozen eggs, a variety of cheeses as well as a great big turkey. Opening the boxes of groceries that were ordered the week before was a highly anticipated event in our house. I always had plenty of vegetables still in the garden; Brussels sprouts, kale, Swiss chard, carrots, parsnips and the best turnips. I didn't think I would ever say "best" and "turnips" in the same sentence, but there was something about the soil in my garden that grew wonderful turnips that were sweet and crisp like apples.

One night we hosted a special "Christmas" party, of sorts. Our friends Warren and Tracy were Jehovah's Witnesses and we wanted them to have fun too, so we didn't include the word "Christmas" in our party invitations. It was snowing lightly, but we had the hot tub cranked up nice and toasty and the kids all played in the water for ages while the adults had drinks and got the party started. We dried the kids off, had dinner and then pushed the table against the wall, kicked up our heels and whooped it up. At one point during the festivities, George went into the backroom to get more ice from the freezer. I heard him head out the back door and come back a few minutes later. Then I heard the hand drill running. I went to see what was going on and saw water all over the backroom floor. George was drilling a few holes in the floor to let the water drain out. There is no basement in a float house, so he had turned the water off and would deal with the burst pipe in the light of day. We went back into the living room and continued dancing!

One Christmas Eve, we had the Coopers and our Fisheries friends, Brian and Bonnie, with us. After dinner, the kids put on a nativity play. Bonnie had made costumes for her boys, Craig and Jordie, and for Casey. They were the three wise men. Jessy and Jarrett, Bonnie and Brian's other son, were only one year old and just toddling around looking like drunk shepherds. I made a stable out of a large cardboard box covered with cedar boughs. We put stuffed animals around the stable and a baby doll in the manger. I read the story aloud from a Golden Book called *The Nativity*, while Bonnie prompted the three wise men when to enter the stage. Craig was to put a stick with a star on the top through a special hole on the roof of the stable. Before their entrance, Jessy and Jarrett discovered their toys in the stable and started throwing them over their shoulders and around the room. I was having trouble reading when the poor baby Jesus went flying past my head. Then Jessy and Jarrett decided to listen to the story and were suddenly hanging onto my lap staring up at my face. I could hear the "audience" stifling their laughter, and I tried to do the same. In the meantime the boys—I mean wise men—arrived and started collecting the animals and tossing them back into the stable. I sped up my reading, finished the story in double-quick time, and we all sang a rousing rendition of "Away in a Manger." Dinosaurs were big in 1987 and so was the dinosaur-shaped piñata. Each of the kids had a go at breaking into it with a baseball bat and suddenly there were toys and candies all over the floor and a room full of happy children. Meanwhile George wore large pieces of the dinosaur in a rather impolite way for his own delighted audience!

On another Christmas Eve, when Casey and Jessy were six and three, it was a bright and beautiful sunny day. There was crisp, blinding white snow everywhere, with a cerulean sky above. We shovelled enough snow to make a path out to the front of the float so we could help tie up our friend's boats. Partway through the afternoon, there was water dripping off the eaves and the air was fresh and sweet. We had our buffet dinner and then sat listening while George read *A Child's Christmas in Wales* by Dylan Thomas. When it was time to leave, we all headed out to help everyone into their boats. Everything was frozen again, and the snow crunched under our boots. The planks made a hard solid sound as if we were walking on concrete. George walked over and turned the generator off, thrusting the night into soothing silence.

The moon was up just over the treeline and the reflection glimmered and glowed across the water to our float. The entire bay was alive with twinkling light. Every surface of the buildings—the windows, the walls—every surface of the boats tied to the dock, and all the trees on the surrounding hills were sparkling. There were large shards of broken ice glistening along the shore as if someone had spilled the contents of a gigantic treasure chest. We all watched in wonder as each breath we puffed out drifted glittering in the air. It was magic. Christmas magic!

The tide was so low that John volunteered to leave first in his tugboat. He had the deepest draft so if he could make it, the other boats would too. He read his depth sounder as he drove slowly out the shallow entrance on the south side of my island. The other entrance was completely dry. When he had passed the trickiest part, he radioed back that it was safe for everyone else to leave, saying that he had "only scared a few barnacles on the way."

The Storm

One morning in late January 1988, George was supposed to fly out of Rivers Inlet. The wind had come up and we could hear it roaring through the trees. The sound of the building wind was coming from far away and there was a heaviness to the air that told us the wind would hit our quiet bay before long. The sky was a dull grey with high clouds scudding swiftly past. We knew the airplane would not be in to pick him up that day. We did not know that it couldn't fly into the inlet for five more days. George was scheduled to promote Rivers Lodge at a sports show in California the next weekend, but it was clear he would not make it. On one hand, I was happy that he couldn't leave, but on the other hand, I remained anxious about the coming weather. Big storms were always nerve-wracking and scary, and we were at the mercy of the wind gods. Would our tie-ups hold, would our roof hold, would we be safe and not risk our lives if there was an emergency while planes could not fly?

George's birthday was the very next day, February 1. We were thrilled that we could celebrate together. We spent the rest of the morning and afternoon making sure that everything that could possibly blow overboard was secured or put away. George checked all our shorelines again, even though he had already added extra lines and made sure the boom chains would hold while he was gone. I brought extra firewood into the kitchen box and piled big pieces of knotty fir by the living room fireplace. We had a forty-foot fir log that George had towed home one day. It was five-and-a-half feet thick at the butt and almost as thick at the other end. We burned that log for years! The oil stove in the backroom between our bedrooms chugged along putting out a constant low wave of heat. We would be warm and dry. George started the generator around 4:30 PM, and the kids played while I made supper. Ah yes, the calm before the storm.

During the evening, the temperature started to drop. The wind was howling around us but, strangely, there was ice forming on puddles and frost on the walls of the buildings. We put the kids to bed, and then George walked around with a big flashlight to check all the lines again. We climbed into bed with a feeling of trepidation. It may have been the drop in air pressure, but we could feel a strangeness to the storm. I was wakened often during the night by the bumping of our floats. They were tied very tightly together but the amount of strain on the lines could still push them around. At one point when I awoke, George was not beside me, and I knew he was outside looking around. I had to get up and check to make sure that he was okay. We both had a bad feeling and would not sleep well for days.

George was up first in the morning, got the kitchen fire going and opened up the living-room fire. We all huddled around the fireplace with extra layers on and had a special birthday breakfast. The temperature outside was now far below normal and, with no insulation in the walls or ceiling, we had to keep the fires cranked and blasting out heat to stay warm. The kitchen fire always died down during the night but George had stoked it several times when he was doing his rounds, and our Jøtul fireplace that we had re-installed in the fall acted like a furnace when it had a big knot in it and burned slowly all night. The wind was howling around the house and I could see the curtains in the kitchen blowing away from the windows. They didn't have any weather-stripping so the wind easily found its way in. I made a birthday cake with the kids, and we had a little celebration with a fancy dinner and treats.

We listened to the weather on our VHF radio and heard that there was no end in sight for the storm. We also talked to our neighbours on the local boat-to-boat channel to make sure everyone was all right. Over the next several days, that was our only contact with people since no one could get in a boat and travel, even across the bay because of the freezing wind. We could see walls of water, or "williwaws," as high as the trees, racing through our main bay. The temperature dropped to -12 degrees Fahrenheit, which was a record for all the years we have been in the inlet.

This is the forty-foot fir log that George towed home one day. We burned that log for years! And then we found out how much it was worth. Someone stole a fir log from a log dump on Vancouver Island, and the logging company it belonged to hired a helicopter and pilot to find it. Apparently the stolen log was worth sixty thousand dollars.

When I walked outside, the frozen planks popped and snapped because the water in the wood was frozen solid. I stepped very carefully to avoid slipping overboard and was only outside if I had to collect firewood or kerosene for emergency lamps. Otherwise, I was busy stoking the fires and keeping the children entertained. One old-timer told us that once there was ice on the water between Finn Bay and Dawsons Landing. At the time we thought he was making that up, but if the wind would die down for even a minute, I knew there would be ice on the way up to the store.

One family living in Finn Bay at the time was having a terrible go of it. They had an oil stove that stopped working the first day, when the oil froze in the line, and they only had heat from the oven of their electric stove for one more day. Then their generator wouldn't start so they no longer had heat and the fresh water they collected in their bathtub froze solid. They were wearing survival suits, wool hats and gloves to stay warm. Our fisherman friend Ray Reese came onto the radio and said, "I'm not going to so much as pick up a sharp knife until this blows over."

I collected quilts that had been wrapped at the lodge for winter storage and brought them back to our house. Using pushpins and the quilts, I covered all the exterior doors and some of the windows in the house to keep the wind from blowing in. We were getting along just fine, and then the oil stove behind our bedroom stopped working. George said that there must be ice crystals in the line. I closed the doors to the bedrooms so we wouldn't lose too much heat through them. They were going to be cold that night, but we had lots of quilts. *Phew*—we were warm, we had electricity. We were still doing well. I heated two cast iron frying pans in the oven and put them into Casey's bed to warm it before the kids climbed in. We had Casey sleep at one end and Jessy at the other to conserve their heat, and I piled on extra quilts. George and I were cozy because sleeping with George was always like sleeping with my own furnace.

It was strange to have so much wind blowing with clear, blue skies. And the colder it got, the more crystal clear the air became. The next day, the third day of the storm, George went out in the afternoon to start the generator and it wouldn't kick in. He brought the battery into the cabin and set it on a chair near the kitchen stove to thaw. Later when it started to get dark, I made dinner by the light of the overhead battery lights. After the generator battery warmed for a couple of hours, George tried again and the generator started and hummed along nicely. We had power for several hours and then the generator stopped, the lights went out and we were plunged into deep darkness. We curled up on the couch and watched the shimmering stars. Once again mom's old adage came to mind: What doesn't kill you outright, will only make you stronger. We were undeniably strong and were making the best of a dicey situation.

In the morning of the fourth day, George again brought the generator battery into the kitchen as well as a five-gallon drum of diesel oil and set them on chairs beside the stove to warm up. The only thing that I was accomplishing was keeping the house warm and cooking meals. I kept the wood boxes and our bellies full, and it seemed to take all day just to do these two chores.

George headed out in the early afternoon with the warm battery and oil and I was standing at the kitchen window when the generator chugged on. He came around the corner of the generator shed and we both did our special dance to celebrate that we would have power that night. He ducked back around the corner and a split second later the generator clunked off. I stood staring, shocked that it just died like that. Then George poked his head around the corner of the shed with a very large shit-eating grin on his face. He had come to tell me that, for some strange reason, he used the rag that was in his hand to wipe a spot of oil off the fan-belt cage and the rag got sucked into the fan belt, slamming the generator to a stop. He spent the next half-hour picking pieces of rag from the belt and housing and finally started the generator again. We were lucky that the oil and battery hadn't frozen in that time. Also, thankfully, he had started the process early enough in the afternoon so he still had daylight to work by.

The wind was still roaring around our buildings and the floats were creaking and groaning. Again George walked around checking lines and tie-ups and made sure any boats that were in the water were still tied up tight. We were not going to lose a boat; there was no way we could go after it in this storm. Everyone living at our end of the inlet was still in touch on the radiophone, and we talked with each other to buoy our spirits as well as theirs.

The northeast wind was still rushing down Darby Channel right past the entrance to our main bay and, two miles further on, straight into Finn Bay. It carried frigid water and slammed into a sixty-foot fishboat that was tied to a float in Finn Bay just twenty feet from the fisherman's family's house float. Later that day, the ice had built up so much on one side of the boat that the weight snapped the tie-up lines and the boat rolled over and sank. There was nothing they could do but watch it go.

The generator kept running and we had another evening of adventure with stories and hot chocolate by the fire. The wind was still blasting around the buildings, but by now we were quite used to the sound and the bumping floats. We heard that we were not the only ones being held hostage by the storm. People from Vancouver to Abbotsford were also suffering from the cold with power outages and trees down everywhere. New spring lambs were dying because there was no power to heat the barns. All in all, we were feeling pretty good about how we were coping with the freak storm. Sometime during the fourth night, the wind died down and both George and I woke up in the eerie quiet. No bumping floats, no howling wind, just quiet and dark. In the morning we were met by a bone-chillingly cold but sunny day with almost no wind.

I refused to think about how things might have gone if George had left the day before the storm. Timing is everything.

Midnight and Computers

I was sitting at the computer in our bedroom. It was about 11 PM. George was in Vancouver and the kids and I had been visiting friends in Sunshine Bay most of the day. We don't run the generator when we are not at home, so I was now trying to squeeze a little more time in with the generator to properly cool the freezers and fridges. Up until now, I had not spent any time just fooling around on the computer. It was either work or kids—no time for surfing the net. I thought I would see what the "internet" was all about. I typed "Martha Stewart" into the search line and a dialogue box came up asking me if I would like to receive her newsletter. The kids were sleeping at the time. So I put my information into the form, clicked next and, lo, I had a nice warm "Welcome to Martha Stewart" letter sent to me in less than one minute. There I was, sitting in my little house, surrounded by water that was surrounded by hills that were dark, dark, dark, surrounded by miles and miles of wilderness mountains and ocean and I had just received a welcoming letter from Martha from somewhere in Connecticut!

Years before, we had bought the new state-of-the-art single-sideband phone for our contract with Fisheries and we had it for our own use after that summer. The single-sideband had to have a better antenna or it didn't work at all. George constructed a tower that took the antenna up about thirty feet. The phone didn't always have the greatest reception, but some calls were perfect and both parties could hear each other. The best reception was at high tide when the whole lodge could be another fifteen feet higher than at low tide.

Our next single-sideband phone had fax capability! This was like magic. This new system required a big fat antenna to be attached to the side of our house. I had been phoning in grocery orders to various suppliers in Vancouver and Port Hardy that sometimes took half a day to complete. I would be ten items into the order and the phone reception would drop and I would have to call back numerous times to finally finish the list. It was always a challenge to get the shipping instructions through to someone in town who couldn't picture their truck delivering to a freight boat. "No! I mean deliver to the freight boat on Mitchell Island for furtherance to Rivers Lodge in Sleepy Bay, Rivers Inlet, and the mailing address is Dawsons Landing, BC ... Let me speak to your supervisor." The fax machine would eliminate these problems.

Then, miracle of miracles! In the mid-nineties satellite phones became widely available. We ordered a satellite system from BC Tel. It was to cost sixty thousand dollars to buy the equipment plus the cost of flying a technician in to the lodge and his time installing everything. Before the technician arrived, George had to construct a concrete base two feet high on the rock shore behind the lodge. This would be the base to which the eight-foot satellite dish would be attached. We had to pay for the dish and various boxes of equipment to be shipped on the freight boat. George also had to construct a little shed on the hill behind the lodge to house the equipment and batteries needed to keep the satellite working. Then there was all the wiring that had to be strung from the dish to the shed and down to the back of the wood-shed float and along the back of the buildings to the house. More posts and more wiring.

We bought the satellite system on a four-year term. We paid sixteen thousand dollars per year for the equipment plus the very high cost of each and every phone call, whether it was coming in or going out. At the end of the fourth year, I signed the final cheque and the ink wasn't even dry when BC Tel informed us that the satellite system was no longer viable, that the satellite was down, that we would have to get a new system! Telus had their sixty thousand dollars and we didn't have a phone.

In those four years though, the satellite companies had come a long way. The following summer, we bought a new system from Globalstar. This system could also have a pay phone attached to it. Finally we would have a private phone for guests to use. George built a little phone booth attached to the lodge. Guests could use their own credit card to access the phone line after I flipped a switch to make the pay phone work. The only drawback was that some groups of visitors that included busi-nessmen were wanting to use the phone so much that we were finding ourselves once again in line to make phone calls because there was only one line useable at a time—it was either at our house or at the pay phone. Sometimes I just closed my eyes and flipped the switch back to the house so I could make an important call. There was a large horn connected to the phone that was attached to the outside of the house, so wherever we were we could hear when the phone rang. We now seldom missed calls but were sometimes quite breathless by the time we ran the hundred-yard dash to answer. Then this satellite ran into trouble and we had to search for another system.

A few years later we found another company, Xplornet, with a trust-worthy satellite. The equipment was simpler, the wiring was simpler and the reception and internet capabilities were more reliable. A smaller dish, less than two feet across, was attached to the concrete base. We

It wasn't easy to communicate with the outside world from our remote location. We kept having to replace antennas and later satellite dishes.

had internet and telephone separate but in one system on one wire. By this time, the satellite systems cost much less to buy. This one cost about $2,400 in total, purchase price and set up, and was finally quite dependable.

Many years later, there was a fellow living in the inlet who was selling the newest satellite system from Galaxy. I bought the equipment, and he set it up for a total cost of about six hundred dollars. He helped our caretakers work out any kinks and was always available if they ran into any problems, which were few and far between. This system was on one small satellite and the telephone system worked off the internet, which was wireless and much more reliable. A letter from Martha Stewart would no longer be a surprise, as we have now joined the new age of communications. The only problem was that if the internet was down, then the phone didn't work either. This company has a Fair Access Policy (FAP) and if you used too much bandwidth, the company would FAP you, which meant shutting down your access to the internet for a full hour. With so many crew now bringing their laptops and guests often wanting to go online, there were quite a few times that the internet was down. We had to put controls in place that limited what the crew could do online. No more downloading movies and uploading photos to their Facebook pages. This smoothed out the works, and other than on very cloudy days or very rainy days or very sunny days, the internet worked just fine. We could contact equipment people, grocery suppliers, airlines and guests and generally run the business the way that it should've been run.

Relative Calm

It was now 1991, and we had built up our clientele to the point that we filled all twelve guestrooms with twenty-four guests who were arriving from all over the world. These visitors would be flown on two chartered Harbour Air Twin Otters straight from Vancouver. We had barrels of jet fuel on the dock so the Twin Otters could fuel up and would not have to stop to refuel on the trip back to Vancouver.

We had twelve staff plus me and George, and our kids were nine and six and were both great helpers. We had a new fleet of custom-built sixteen-foot speedboats with fifty-horsepower motors on each. The boats had smooth sides and gunnels so the large fishnets wouldn't have any points to get caught on while netting "the big one"—super-sized chinook and coho. Each boat had a top that easily snapped into place if it suddenly started to rain. Theoretically, each boat could hold four fishermen, but we had twelve plus two extras so we had one for every two guests.

We ordered golf shirts for our crew to wear when they were working. Each shirt had the person's name embroidered on the front. Little Jessy, honoured to be considered part of the crew, looked down in anticipation at her shirt and noticed that her life jacket covered up her name. There is a long-standing tradition for people living on floats that children have to wear a life jacket while they are outside. They are allowed to remove the jacket only when they are able to swim the full length of the floats, fully clothed, and climb out on their own. This was a very tall order because, by this time, our floats covered an extensive area, and it would be a long swim in drastically cold water. Casey had managed this swim a few years before. Jess had to have her name showing on her crew shirt, so she didn't hesitate as she stepped out of her life jacket and headed to the far end of the last guesthouse and jumped in. After gasping for breath for a minute or two, Jessy started swimming. George, Casey and I and several crew walked along with her, calling encouragement when she started to slow down. She finally approached the boathouse at the extreme opposite end of the lodge floats and, with a beatific grin on her face, hauled herself out onto the last lash log on the last float and triumphantly marched past the crowd amid a huge round of applause and went back to work on the dock.

We still had our wonderful chef, Peter, who cooked lunch and dinner for our guests for five summers. He worked for one of our guests' companies cooking in the oil fields of northern Alberta for the winter when we were closed. He loved coming back to cook for our fancy-schmancy guests who appreciated his fine food. In the oil fields, he had men hand broccoli soup back to him with the question, "What is this shit?"

One afternoon Peter was preparing racks of lamb. As he was working on the bones, Casey asked him what he was doing. Peter replied, "I'm getting the lamb ready to cook later." Casey was startled and asked with dismay, "Do you mean you kill lambs?" Peter took time to think carefully how to word his reply. "It's okay," he said, "we only kill the stupid ones." This seemed reasonable to Casey and he wandered away to drum up some business for his Wilderness Tours. On changeover days, Casey made a small fortune by towing guests in a separate rowboat while he rowed them around my island and sometimes into the back of the bay, all the while providing a running commentary about what the guests were seeing in the sky, on the land and along the shore. He also charged Peter one dollar for a handful of cedar branches to decorate the buffet table with. He made us so proud!

We also had a breakfast cook that summer who was up at 3 AM every morning to start getting breakfast ready and then baked bread, cookies and desserts after the guests headed out fishing. She prepared the snacks that went out on the boats with the guests in the morning and afternoon.

Things were going very well. They were going so well that George started feeling antsy. The crew worked like a well-oiled machine. There was a fellow hired to do most of the fish master job, but George still

Casey made a small fortune by towing guests in a separate rowboat while he rowed them around my island and sometimes into the back of the bay, all the while providing a running commentary about what the guests were seeing in the sky, on the land, along the shore and in the shallow water.

ran around in the boat when he wanted to give the fish master a break or when he took guests out in the afternoon for scenic tours. The fish master was in charge of bait runs and lunch runs and making sure that guests were catching fish. But with everything going so smoothly, George started thinking up new projects.

He said to the kids, "My God, aren't we lucky? We could be living in Lebanon. Instead, here we are in the middle of a huge forested, coastal wilderness area. We can construct our own laws up here. We can build our own business here. We live by doing what we think is right—there aren't many places like this left in the world."

He loved the adrenaline rush of having to race against time, and having to keep lots of balls in the air while the odds were stacked against him. I, on the other hand, enjoyed the well-oiled machine. I wanted to be able to take the time to be with the children. I thought that by now I should be able to sit and read a book in the quiet afternoon.

Given the large population of grizzly bears behind Addenbroke Island, George thought we could add grizzly watching to our list of activities. At the end of the summer season he chartered a float plane and packed it with a tent, sleeping bags, a small rowboat, shovels and a little food. He and Casey then flew to Elizabeth Lake, which was only accessible by air. They were dropped off at the edge of the lake, and the pilot was instructed to pick them up in four days. The small beach was covered with grizzly bear footprints—a fact that I was blissfully unaware of until much later. I didn't want any part of this excursion. I felt that I was far enough out in the wilderness without chartering a plane to take me even deeper into the hills. Jessy and I had our own lovely time. We spent hours in the garden and my new greenhouse. We went around visiting friends for tea and playtime. We had the playschool at our house. We cooked together and had fancy dinners at the dining room table. We also spent some deluxe afternoon time reading. First I would read to Jess and then we would each read on our own, or Jessy would draw to her heart's content, as she was developing a talent for everything artistic.

The grizzly-watching plan was put on hold. The cost of flying guests even farther into the middle of nowhere was going to be too high. The next plan was to offer painting retreats. We sold out five-day trips with four well-known artists, including Robert Genn and Mike Svob, who taught the workshops, and George and Jessy would run them around to the interesting canneries or beaches in the inlet. These retreats were a tremendous success. People who signed up were over the moon at the chance to work with such great painters in such a beautiful setting. But once again, it was the airfare that ended the workshops. Why would people pay such a huge cost to be flown to a workshop when there were ones that could be driven to? It was too bad, though, because these trips could help with the shoulder months of our fishing seasons. We needed the people whose eyes light up with anticipation when talking about flying to Rivers Lodge for the fishing.

In 1992 we built a new tackle shop on a float that jutted way out from the rest of the floats. It had plenty of room on it for a helicopter to land. Sometimes we brought helicopters in for adventures during the summer. The chef packed a beautiful basket with a delicious lunch, and the helicopter would fly guests up onto the glaciers at the head of the inlet. I put a red-and-white check tablecloth and napkins in the basket to create a

Sometimes we brought in helicopters. The chef would pack a picnic lunch and guests would be flown onto the glaciers at the head of the inlet. I flew with one group and felt that I had entered a prehistoric land.

Helicopter river fishing—George in the foreground. Some very wealthy companies and individuals loved river fishing away from it all. As it just so happened, they needed a fishing guide. George had to be with the guests every trip.

lovely visual contrast when the cloth was spread out on the snow at the edge of the ice. I went on one of these trips and felt like I had been teleported to a prehistoric land. I expected to see dinosaurs ambling over the next mountain peak.

Some groups also booked the helicopter to transport them to remote rivers for flyfishing that was even more "away from it all." One long-time guest, Adrien, booked a trip in the late spring to take him and his girlfriend out to the beautiful, long sandy beach on the west side of Calvert Island called Bolivar Beach. The beach would be all their own for the day since it was virtually inaccessible other than by helicopter. The pilot dropped them off with a basket of lunch and a bottle of champagne and flew back to the lodge. Adrien proposed to his girlfriend in this most romantic of settings and when they flew back later, she was wearing a stunning emerald engagement ring.

That same afternoon, George and I had walked across the stiff legs from behind the second guesthouse and over to shore to check on the big water tanks up the hill. The tanks sat on an area just out of sight, amongst the trees, so someone needed to check on them regularly. The odd time the water would stop running in the pipes, and we would find that a grizzly had chewed its way through one of the black lines. You could tell when it was a grizzly because of the size of the bite. One time George found one of our flotation barrels that once held forty-five gallons of apple juice concentrate with the bite mark of a grizzly. Its huge jaws squashed the side of the heavy plastic barrel.

Back to our romantic jaunt in the woods. We checked the lines and everything looked fine. We had to head back before the tide went out too far or the log we crossed would be too steep. My boots were not as secure as George's, and as we headed down and across the log he took my hand. He said, "Keep low," and a surge of warmth went through me for my darling who was being so considerate. Then he said, " 'cause if you start to fall, I'm letting go!"

The Next Big Step and Half of One

School was becoming more important. The correspondence teachers actually expected Casey to show good results with his work, and now Jessy was school age. Rivers Lodge was showing results for us as well. I was the one who did the accounting so I started actually paying George and myself real wages. All of my paycheques went into an account that would hopefully become a down payment on a house in town. We wanted to spend a little more time in Vancouver, so we rented an apartment on a short-term basis in the area we were most familiar with and where lots of our friends lived, which was West Vancouver. We knew where we wanted to live so I scouted out the nearby elementary schools to find the right fit. Casey was enrolled in one and attended for two months in the fall and again for two months in the spring. The following year, I wanted to spend a longer time in each place, Rivers Lodge and West Vancouver, because moving the office was so complicated. I needed to work on our accounts and George needed to keep in touch with guests, so there was always a lot of paperwork that kept us busy. We stayed four months, including right through the Christmas season that year. The next year we stayed for five months and we started looking for a house to buy.

We had watched as other couples raised their children in the inlet and then moved to town when they were school age. We had thought that we wouldn't do that because we were happy away from the city and schooling didn't seem, at that time, as if it could pose a problem. Funny how your life changes when you have kids. I was more than ready to have some fun city time, so the two situations meshed very well for me. Before we packed up for town that fall, our friends in Whistler let us know that the cabin next to them was for sale. We jumped at the chance to have a place in ski country. We were both avid skiers, and the kids enjoyed skiing, tobogganing and snowball fighting when we stayed with friends there. Being from the Prairies with those long, long, freezing-cold and snow-piled winters, I appreciated driving the hour and a half to enjoy some fun in the snow and then the short drive back to West Vancouver with its green grass. We bought the cabin and put the city house on hold for the moment. We liked to live by George's credo: Eat your dessert first.

Around 1995, George started to think that opening another fishing resort was a good idea. He found a piece of property just outside of Port Hardy that was perfect and then started on the paperwork. This was going to be very different from building a resort in Rivers Inlet. Nearly twenty years before when we started Rivers Lodge, we didn't need permits for anything. In Port Hardy, there were so many government offices to deal with, so many officials to meet with, so many permits to obtain that this project was going to take a massive amount of time and energy. He worked with my sister Marcia's husband, Murray, on a design for the main building that would blend in with the surrounding trees and hills. George applied for water rights to be able to use the fresh water that was on the property. He checked out what forms were necessary to use the foreshore for a dock. He was working his way through one layer after another of bureaucracy and getting bogged down in this new project close to civilization, where every step needed a stack of permits and licences.

After our second season of skiing whenever we wanted, George started to rethink the new project, which was to be called Silver Point Resort. Did he really want to put that much effort into filing all those permits, following all the new regulations, flying from the lodge to Port

Hardy and back throughout the year? We were having fun, and as Marcia always said, "Fun is the best thing to have!" All that work and back-and-forthing would cut into our Fun Time. We decided not to continue with the plans. We did, however, continue with the paperwork, started ten years earlier, for a foreshore lease for the property we were floating over in Sleepy Bay, including the area where our tie-up lines crossed over to shore. (Twelve years later, and long after we had abandoned the plan near Port Hardy, we received notice that our application for the water rights for Silver Point Resort was not approved.)

In the meantime, we had a whole lot of fun!

Boats Break Down

It was now 1996. I was invited to my nephew's wedding in Winnipeg on the BC Day long weekend in the middle of the summer. I replied, "not able to attend." There wasn't enough room to explain why.

Quinn and Jen, this is why! We had twenty-six people booked for the long weekend. We usually took twenty-four guests at a time but we could fit an extra bed into two of the rooms if necessary. The planes full of visitors arrived on Friday afternoon. Guests were shown to their rooms then came back to the lodge for a quick bite to eat while they filled out fishing licences. Then the new guests were given a tutorial on how to hook up bait and—very important—how to net a really big salmon. The crew had all of the boats ready, cleaned and fuelled, with snack in the front, bait and tackle box at the side. They helped the guests pick out their preferred fishing rod or they redid line on rods that guests brought with them. Then, after a quick lesson on running the boat, they headed out, following George to the fishing grounds.

At this time, the crew changed all the beds and cleaned all the bathrooms again. Earlier in the day, the rooms were cleaned but the bed linens would not be changed until the new guests arrived. There would be several hours that the guests would have to wait for their return flight while the crew looked after cleaning and fuelling the boats, boxing the guests' fish and moving the luggage out to the airport. The guests would have time for lunch before they left and, sometimes, guests would go back into their rooms for a nap. We found that changing the sheets after the new group arrived cut down on the number of beds that had to be changed twice. I helped put the fresh produce away that came in with the guests, and the chef started working on the evening's four-course dinner. I heard one of the guests calling the lodge to say their boat engine had stopped working. I called them back and let them know that Jessy, who was now eleven, would head out with another boat for them to use. It was a good thing we had a couple of extra boats and motors by then. Jess and the guests would change boats out on the water and leave Jess drifting in a broken-down boat. As I passed the VHF a few minutes later, I would hear another boat, then another calling to say their motor had stopped working. Casey, who was now fourteen years old, headed out towing another spare boat and helped one of the couples climb into it while George picked up the other two fishermen and helped them fish from *Sportspage*. They left the three boats drifting with Jessy in one of them. Are you confused yet?

I must interject: all of these motors were either brand new or had been meticulously worked over by a mechanic before they were carefully stored in town during the winter. We'd have them shipped back to the lodge, where George would hoist them back onto the speedboats, then test each one to make sure it was running like a fine watch.

Just before dark, the guests would start arriving back in the bay. At the head of the line came George in *Sportspage*, towing three boats. Riding with him were four guests, his two fishermen as well as the third man from two of the boats and, finally, Casey in his boat with Jessy, rescued at last.

During dinner, while George was working to find out what was wrong with the engines, the lights went out. One of the main breakers on our new fifty-kilowatt generator had flipped because we were over-loading it mercilessly with all the heavy equipment running at the same time. Casey and Jessy ran around turning off the pool jets, the vacuum packer, a couple of dryers and several heaters, while I raced out with a flashlight for George so he could get the lights back on and continue to work on the engines. He would have to fix the breaker later.

One of the boats had apparently sucked up some plastic into the impeller, which basically ruins the impeller. The other two engines were still a mystery, so George called, then left a message with the dealer. No call back. After dinner, one of the guests told me that there was no hot water in one of the guesthouses. I checked that out and found that someone had turned the water tank off. Who knows why? That was an easy one to fix.

There were twenty-four in for breakfast. Thankfully, one couple didn't want to get up early. We would have an extra spare engine on the freight boat, arriving in the inlet shortly. George headed across the inlet to rendezvous with the ship so he could have the motor twelve hours earlier than their scheduled stop at the lodge. The freight company had just fired the skipper and the "apprentice ship-driver guy" couldn't get the ship docked. He tried for an hour, and he just couldn't do it. Five feet forward and then he'd panic and gun it in reverse. George floated around impatiently glancing at his watch, wishing he could just clamber on board and hoist the damn thing off himself. It's a big ship and the new skipper is being careful, but seriously! "Sorry," new guy says. He couldn't get the engine off for George until he could dock the damn boat. Funny, because freight boats had smashed into our floats a number of times, breaking lines and crushing planks. He will practise on other docks in the inlet. Fine, we didn't want him practising on our anchored dock, so we'd meet him later in the afternoon, somewhere else in the inlet.

One of the guest boats called in. They were having trouble with the steering, so George headed back over to help Casey look after the boats. I was on the phone, calling everyone. Engine-part places, couriers, airlines, grocery stores, coffee suppliers. Oh yes! Some groceries didn't arrive the day before, and for the second time in a row the coffee didn't arrive from the coffee place. I would have to find a new, more reliable coffee supplier. Coffee is very important for our guests who are getting up at 5 AM. I ordered more from the Port Hardy grocery store to be sent to the airport and delivered to the inlet that afternoon. The grocery store sent the coffee order to the freight boat warehouse instead, which by that time was empty because the freight boat was already bumbling around in the inlet. Yes, the same slow boat to China with the skipper who can't dock the thing.

George and Casey enjoying life. Ah yes, they were always enjoying life!

Then there was another call: Who has some bandages? Casey ran back into the lodge with a guest who cut his finger and it wouldn't stop bleeding. Dr. Ardley to the rescue!

Are you still with me? This is still only 8:30 AM.

George was still away, running from one boat to the next helping people. He had stopped in momentarily to pick up the boat with the new impeller to tow out to trade with the people with a steering problem on their boat.

Casey fuelled up and headed back out with our patched-up guest. George returned, towing the boat that had the steering problem. Casey came back in and fixed the steering.

Meanwhile, I was back on the phone, still calling for parts and trying to coordinate deliveries and flights. George had managed to borrow four pounds of coffee from another lodge and buy four pounds from the convenience store at Duncanby.

Casey headed back out to help guests and hand out bait and pop, etc. Some guests requested lunch out on the water. Then another and another. I ran over to catch the waitress to stop her from setting tables and to start getting lunch coolers out. Nine boats decide to stay out on the water for lunch. The fishing is great, and they don't want to leave the fishing grounds. Four people came in for lunch, and I helped organize between cooler lunches and people who would be eating at the table.

George jumped into *Sportspage*, which by this point was full of lunch coolers, and zoomed out. Someone wanted Coors Light, but he didn't have any on board. So he called me to send Casey out with some. Then the chef suddenly realized that they'd sent our wonderful lunches complete with a bottle of wine, corkscrew—but no wineglasses. I called Casey, "Quick, come back and get wineglasses for everyone!" And as he headed out of the bay again, I called him back one more time to come and pick up some Diet 7UP. He was getting dizzy.

You would think this was our first rodeo! But it wasn't. More like a disorganized circus than a well-oiled machine. The guests barely noticed a thing because the fishing was so great and we were so good at conveying an air of effortlessness. Everyone was having a ball. Including George and Casey.

More Settled

After the 1996 season ended, I flew to town and looked at houses in West Vancouver with a real estate agent. The writing was on the wall: we definitely had to spend more time in town for the kids to go to school. Not just for the sake of the academics; I felt that it was really important for the socializing part too. We became well known at the school as the family who put their kids in school after Thanksgiving and took them out shortly after Easter. Casey and Jess were easily able to catch up on lessons in October, and, with our newfangled fax machine, they were able to finish the school year over the phone. By the time the kids graduated from high school, they had missed about four years of in-class time, but we always said that we didn't want schooling to get in the way of their education. And the teachers usually appreciated our kids' non-traditional view of life.

We bought a house in West Vancouver with an extra bedroom that became the office. I was still finding it difficult moving back and forth from the inlet to town. Not long after I felt organized with office work in one place, I would be packing up to move again. But we had the best of both worlds—three worlds really, since we spent every weekend throughout the winter at Whistler. Both kids moved through the levels of Ski Scamps and eventually they were both racing for the Whistler Ski Club. George did all the travelling with them when they had races away from Whistler, while I did more travelling with my sisters. An awesome trade-off for me. Casey would eventually become a beloved ski coach for the Whistler Ski Club. The kids he taught never wanted to advance to the next level because they would lose Casey as their coach. And Jessy developed a lifelong love of horses and show jumping.

We had a chef who had worked for us at the lodge for the previous three years. He was a very well-known name in food circles. I won't name him, as you will see why later. He was teaching in our off-season so the arrangement worked well for all of us. The food was wonderful, following in the path that I had set. We had a breakfast cook/baker and designated a couple of dock staff to help with food prep in the afternoons. I was comfortable enough with the kitchen staff's ability that I could sit and read in the afternoon. I was always out of sight of crew though, as I never ever felt that I could sit in one spot while there were people working for and around me.

Guests were catching lots of fish, and the summer was going very well when, again, boats started breaking down. George quickly determined that there was a spark-plug problem so he began zipping constantly from one boat to the next, changing the plugs, even though the boats could be miles apart. He finally started handing out spark plugs and a set of pliers to fishermen who he could trust to change the plugs without causing more of a problem. Whatever made me think that we could have a quiet summer with no drama?

One night when dinner was almost finished and dessert was about to be served, there was a huge window-rattling explosion from the lodge kitchen. I heard and felt it in my living room and raced over, colliding with George as he was leaping down the stairs from the office above. The fearful look on his face said that he thought someone might have been killed. "Everyone is all right!" the waitress quickly called out to us. Thank God everyone was all right, but there was lemon soufflé and sauerkraut all over the ceiling, dripping off the light fixtures and oozing down the walls. Our well-known chef had prepared soufflés for our twenty-four guests, but wanting the oven rack to be in just the right spot, he used four, twenty-eight-ounce cans of sauerkraut to raise the rack to the perfect level. *Unopened* cans. In a 450-degree oven.

The blast just about blew the door off its hinges and it has forever worn its buckled indent like a badge of war. Somehow, because it was cans of sauerkraut, and we were all standing awestruck and gawking at the fermented cabbage drip and plop off the ceiling, it became funny!

The next day, I asked young Jessy what she thought might happen if I put an unopened can of sauerkraut in a very hot oven. She thought about it for a minute and said, "Would they explode with the heat?"

Not So Settled

By this time we had been operating for twenty-one years and some groups and couples or families had been fishing with us for over eighteen years. The lodge was like a private club in the summer. We held onto personal fishing gear from one year to the next for guests who would definitely be fishing with us again the following year.

One particular group always came in September. They would arrive with thousands of dollars' worth of wine and whiskey and plenty of cigars for their guests. At the end of their stay, we would store the extra liquor in our locked office until the next season. That winter we hired an elderly commercial fisherman from Port Hardy as our caretaker. He lived mostly on his fishboat but he could also use our old retired guest cabin to spread out his belongings and entertain company if anyone visited.

When we returned in the late spring, he had left just before our flight landed. I can imagine that you know where this is headed. You are right. Our little old commercial fisherman had drunk his way through

Guests savouring dinner. The lodge was like a private club in the summer. In the top right of the photo is a granddaddy of Rivers Inlet, a 105-pound chinook.

five thousand dollars' worth of lovely wines, and the classiest bottles of scotch and port with not even an empty bottle left behind to show that they had ever existed. It's a good thing that we had listed all the liquor before we left in the fall. Insurance is a lovely thing.

At least the fisherman had lasted through the winter. One year, we hired Dan, an ex-RCMP officer, who had just retired after twenty years with the force. He was looking for something to do, and thought that being a caretaker would be a nice change from such a busy job. He arrived at the lodge a week before we were scheduled to leave. It was the end of the fishing season and George and I, as well as the kids, were running in all directions at once, washing and tidying everything before putting all the equipment away for the off-season. It's no good putting salty gear away because it will draw moisture to it all winter.

Dan set himself up in our caretaker cabin and came out once in a while to chat with us. He loved being there and was excited to tag along with George any time he headed out in a boat. We introduced him to the neighbours and made sure that he knew how to order groceries and how to run a boat. We finished the cleanup and finally got around to packing our bags. The closer we got to the day of departure, the more time Dan spent with us. He followed George and often stopped Casey for a chat. He even sat on the porch and had tea with Jessy. Finally the plane arrived and we left him with lots of instructions and supplies and numbers to call if he ever needed help. A few days after we arrived in town, George headed off to California to start working with a friend on an advertising plan for the lodge. And a few days after that, I received a call from Dan. He was in Port Hardy. The quiet had "gotten" to him. He couldn't take it for "one more minute," and called the airline to come and pick him up. He hadn't lasted a week on his own! George called our friends, the Coopers, who checked on the lodge every other day, and I put a help-wanted ad in the paper. We were finally able to hire a couple who also lived on their commercial fishboat, but who proved to be honest and trustworthy and stayed until George returned to the lodge the following May.

The next summer was once again an interesting season for motors breaking down. This time it was a tiny part on the fifty-horse-power engines that had once been made out of metal. Someone

George pointing out the best fishing spots to guests. George and then Casey always talked with the guests at the dinner table to go over the plan for the next day's fishing.

in manufacturing had made the ridiculous decision to replace the one-dollar metal part with a two-cent plastic part, and of course the plastic part kept splitting. We had to tow several boats into the lodge, and placate several guests, before George figured out what the problem was. Once he saw what was happening, he replaced the part with a little zap strap. Then for the next several days he zipped around our guest boats with a pocket full of zap straps. The zap straps held for the rest of the summer.

The engine company had several reps in the inlet at the time, and they had a couple of mechanics with them. One engine had blown the bottom end when guests hit an immoveable rock. They had been on their way back into the lodge in the evening when they called for help. George towed them in and pushed the speedboat into the boathouse to be worked on later. Casey took one of the mechanics over to look at the engine. Casey asked the mechanic to help lift the engine off the boat using our overhead winch. The fellow told Casey that he didn't work at 10:30 PM. It's okay though, because I made the guy feel guilty in front of the others in his group for leaving fifteen-year-old Casey to work on

271

the engine by himself. The mechanic shuffled back to the boathouse and gave Casey a hand.

Casey and Jessy, who was now twelve, both worked for the lodge. Casey had been helping his dad throughout the winter and then helped the summer crew every fishing season. Jessy started helping crew when she was three. Her first job was to walk along the dock with a wagon to carry the thermoses and lunch boxes that she picked up from the boats, then she stacked them in a basket for the kitchen crew. Both kids loved being part of the team. They had both advanced to be real help for the dock crew, which in turn helped everyone on the staff.

Halfway through August, I overheard the staff dividing the tip money from the group of twenty-four guests who had just left. I went in and suggested that it would be really nice if they acknowledged Casey and Jessy's help by giving them a bit of the tip. Even two dollars from each crewmember after a group of guests left would be enough to show their appreciation for all the work that both kids did. Each crewmember would make hundreds of dollars of tips on a changeover day. Upon hearing my suggestion, our very well-known chef—the one who blew up the oven with his misplaced soufflés—who had worked for us for the past five years, slammed his hand on the table and said, "I quit!" I turned to him and said, "Pardon?" He clarified: "I will quit if you give Casey and Jessy tip money."

We had three weeks left in our fishing season. We had two groups of twenty-four guests per week—arriving on Monday and leaving on Friday or arriving on Friday and leaving on Monday. That meant six groups of fishermen times two dollars for a maximum possible total of twelve dollars per crewmember to pay toward a pot to be split between Casey and Jessy. Because of my suggestion that twelve dollars be subtracted from a potential tip total of $1,200 to $1,500 in our last three weeks, our Very Well-Known Chef—oops, did I just say that?—quit in a huff! "Fine," I said, "you can leave tomorrow." And I left him blithering behind me. He came to my house the next morning and said he had changed his mind, but the damage was done. "Thanks, but no thanks," I said. "I will finish cooking for the season." And just when things were going so smoothly for me, there I was—I would be cooking again for the next three weeks.

It's Not All About the Fish

In the spring of 1996, Rivers Inlet, along with other parts of the BC coast, had been hit by an unprecedented non-retention of chinook salmon. It lost us a lot of credibility with many people wanting to book a fishing trip. Fishermen pay for the expectation of catching and keeping their fish. George was a sport-fishing representative on the Sport Fishing Advisory Board working with the Department of Fisheries and Oceans (DFO). He and others in the sport-fishing industry strongly resisted non-retention of chinook salmon and put forward alternative conservation measures. The proposals were rejected by the DFO, and the impact on the sport-fishing community was devastating.

We had long known that our main source of income was sport-fishing guests. The ban was lifted for the following year, and we had charged ahead, promoting the fact that guests could once again keep their chinook. We were finally recovering from the ban, and we were again looking forward to a good fishing season.

In the fall of that year, we finally received our thirty-year foreshore lease, which was the only lease of its kind in Rivers Inlet. Patience pays off when working with the government.

We had lots of bookings for the fishing season in the following year. Things were looking positive again, and we were already planning our airplanes and bait orders and upgrading most of our engines. George was working with Monaro Marine in Vancouver designing a beautiful new twenty-seven-foot speedboat to his specifications. He had ordered it and paid the down payment when, in May of 1997, Minister of Fisheries and Oceans David Anderson announced that sport fishermen would not be able to catch or keep coho in the upcoming season. Newspaper headlines shouted that there was about to be a total collapse of salmon stocks along the West Coast.

This was the second blow of massive proportions to the sport-fishing industry. There were many disgruntled fishing guests who cancelled their bookings with resorts up and down the coast. Lodges and businesses that service those lodges including hotels, airlines, food companies, tackle companies, as well as the number of staff hired at the lodges took a complete nosedive.

If conservation was the first consideration, the much more valuable sport-caught fish amounted to a small percentage of the total of fish caught by commercial boats. It just didn't make economic or conservation sense. We felt strongly that we should be able to catch and retain coho. There were so many coho that summer in Rivers Inlet, they were practically jumping into our guest's boats.

George and I, along with many groups who were protesting the decision, worked tirelessly to bring about change. All the meetings, all the flow charts and all the data pointed to the fact that sport-caught fish was much more valuable to our economy, and the act of catching them was much less invasive. George went to every meeting, he pointed out the economics of the decision and he argued that our Rivers Inlet North Coast Salmon Enhancement Association (RINCSEA) had started our own hatchery for chinook salmon at the head of the inlet in the early eighties just so something like this would never happen. We ran a fishing derby and sold tickets to guests for various prizes to be won for the biggest coho and the largest chinook caught. Over the years our association contributed over 2.6 million dollars to salmon enhancement in Rivers Inlet from the hatchery, in man-hours, and in Derby sales. Our hatchery had also put three million chinook smolts back into the ocean. Our association also helped cover the cost of many Fisheries operations that they could no longer fund themselves due to government cutbacks.

We managed to limp through that summer season, and George and I got back into fighting mode. At least he was able to do it in style in his beautiful and well-deserved very fast diesel-powered Monaro speedboat, our latest in a line of *Sportspages*. Our local association was strong, with many lodge owners involved. We kept emphasizing the worth of the sport-caught fish and worked toward getting priority for our industry. We finally succeeded. The DFO established the official catching priority for chinook and coho: the first priority would be conservation, then First Nations food fishing, then sport fishing and then, in years of high abundance, commercial fishing. There were several other types of

Sportspage, George's favourite very fast, diesel-fuelled boat (middle); Casey's well-used fishmaster's boat (background) and one of our custom-designed guest boats with sides high enough so guests would not topple out when netting that really big fish (foreground).

salmon—sockeye, chum and pink—that the commercial boats could catch until we were back to high abundance of coho and chinook.

Our fighting days were not over though. One of George's worst nightmares was that the islands that surrounded us would be clear-cut. Individuals and small companies had selectively handlogged in the Rivers Inlet area for many years, and the hills were still covered with trees. But if a larger company were to clear-cut, build roads and create huge log dumps in a small area like Rivers Inlet, which was the proposal at the time, it would take many decades to recover the beautiful wilderness feeling.

It was a chance comment by one of the nearby residents that got George really worried about the hills around us. He checked with the provincial Ministry of Forests office and, sure enough, a logging company had been given the go-ahead to log and build roads on the very island, Walbran, we were tied to and sheltered by. We called a meeting and invited everyone involved to come to the lodge one afternoon that summer. In attendance were people from the Ministry of Forests, local residents, the logging company, union reps for fallers and helicopter loggers, First Nations from the head of the inlet and other lodge owners.

Some people say that it's no use fighting against big business, but after a whole afternoon of listening to everyone's arguments, we were hopeful that BC Forests would make a new decision. Our stand was not to stop logging, as some union workers thought. We listened, and understood, as these workers told stories about needing to put food on the table for their children. We were solely against clear-cutting. The hills here were blanketed with lush green trees, and when clear-cutting is used, all that is left is ravaged rocky slopes covered with carcasses of unwanted fallen trees, grey and bleak. Helicopter logging is more selective and doesn't destroy the look of an area. We hoped the area could be helicopter-logged, which wouldn't require roads and would leave the stunning viewscape intact for guests, enhancing their wilderness experience.

Manfred Schauenburg, owner of Big Spring Sports Fishing Resort, was also in attendance at this meeting. Manfred loved coming to our lodge. He was amazed by all the planters full of flowers and, even though he was a lodge owner himself, he said that Rivers Lodge was the most beautiful lodge in the inlet. "You even have a babbling brook coming through the middle of your resort!" he said, speaking about the flowers that spilled down onto the float logs and continued to grow and spread there with salt water flowing between the separate floats.

He said he would take his guests in a line of boats through Magee Channel and get them to turn off their engines so they could just drift and breathe in the beauty. He said this area was simply, "magical." If it were to be clear-cut, it would never recover the magic in my lifetime or my children's.

Some of the First Nations people from the village at the head of the inlet made a formal proposal that our association could start a logging operation for them and clear-cut two hundred-acre blocks in one of the most beautiful, pristine side inlets between Magee Channel and Geetla Inlet off of Rivers Inlet. The logging company had paid the Ministry of

Forests, Lands & Natural Resources for the rights to log the timber. The First Nations people were given the two hundred acres by the logging company in question in order for the First Nations to make money from clear-cutting the timber and therefore not interfere by staging protests against the company's own logging. Our association, with no real background in logging, didn't start the operation and the beautiful little inlet is still untouched tranquility.

We listed the number of businesses that relied on our guests and also listed the number of staff we hire in the summer. We had put food on a lot of people's tables over the past twenty-three years. We put hundreds of kids who worked for us through university. There were doctors, architects, nurses, pharmacists, bankers, artists, psychologists and more whose schooling we helped pay for.

Forestry is the largest industry in BC, but sport fishing is also a huge industry. After several hours, the BC Forests personnel had listened to everyone's comments and the meeting was adjourned. Later that week, the ministry announced that logging in the area would go ahead with helicopters, and we all breathed a sigh of relief. Sometimes it is worth fighting big business.

Walbran Island was later selectively logged by helicopters, and when approaching Rivers Lodge in an airplane, you can't see that the island has been logged. For now, this piece of wilderness is preserved for the future.

A Day in the Life of George

It was 1999 and we were getting ready for our first guests of another season. Our Vancouver charter company had told us ahead of time they would no longer be flying long-haul trips into Rivers Lodge. They were sending their Twin Otters to Antarctica to fly tourists there. We found another company with various airplanes that we could charter: a Short 360 that could carry up to thirty-two passengers from Vancouver to Port Hardy, and three amphibious Goose planes that would then carry them to Rivers Lodge. There would be lots of room on the planes for twenty-four guests as well as for our food and any other freight bound for the lodge. There would also be room for the guests' loads of fish on their return trip to Vancouver.

George had spent the better part of a day fixing the on-demand propane water heater in the lodge. We had a thousand-pound propane tank as well as a three-hundred-pound tank that we hooked onto when the big tank needed to be disconnected and pushed out to the main bay for fuelling. We used a lot of propane. This meant that we didn't have to run the diesel generator twenty-four hours a day for electricity and could have a quiet night after the generator was shut down. We used propane for stoves, water and drying-room heaters. The swim hot tub also sucked up propane at an alarming rate. George fixed the water heater and moved on to the burners on the stove in the kitchen. Three pilot lights were out and needed cleaning, and the fourth one was two inches high.

Then he headed over to the boats that were getting waxed, washed inside and out and the bottoms painted. He spent several hours on his back rewiring a couple of the boats until I called him to relight the pilot lights on the stove. He cleaned them again and then they worked beautifully. He was back on his head in the boats until I had a dishwasher

I love gardening, so we always kept the flower boxes full. The various freight-boat skippers got used to delivering—and watering en route—pallets full of annual plants to fill the outdoor wooden planters, and dozens of beautiful ferns to grace the high shelf dividing the lodge dining room from the lounge area.

emergency. Over to the lodge again and he was able to poke and prod the machine to work once again.

There was a call for George to be interviewed by CBC Radio about the helicopter-logging decision. On his way back, he turned off the generator so he could fuel the big tank shortly. Still on his way back to the boats, he walked through the lodge to see what our computer helper was doing and found that he had somehow messed up its battery. This would have to wait because George left to fix the wiring in the boats. Once again on his way, he saw a crack in the windshield on Casey's bait-run boat and told him he had to remove it so it could be repaired before it got worse. Then George asked Jessy how she was doing in the tackle shop. Were there enough knives? Pliers? Apparently Casey had a stash of knives so we wouldn't run out. It's amazing how many got dropped overboard.

The pilot light in a guesthouse water heater was out, so George lit it. It went out again, so he cleaned it and relit it. It stayed on. The hot tub was leaking so he drained it to just past where the connection is and left it to dry so he could fix it later. Back on his head in the boats with the wiring. He then heard a call on the VHF saying there were orcas outside our bay. He jumped up and called for anyone who wanted to see them to climb into *Sportspage*. Our electrician went with them and when he came back said, "Well, now I can go home happy."

George headed over to the hot-tub float and spent some time gluing the pipe connections that he thought were leaking. This required him to climb under the pool deck and spend fifteen minutes hunched over with one leg over a truss and the other knee bent over the top of a log— his shoe dipping into the salt water beneath him. When he could finally stand up, all of his joints creaked and groaned.

And ... George was back on his head in the boats while everyone else had dinner. We all discussed ways to keep tabs on him during the day. He was the only one who didn't come running when the dinner horn was blasted. So much time was spent looking for him because he went from one job to the next, back and forth, and up and down, and there was always someone with a question for him which they brought to me eventually because I was easier to find. I was either in the kitchen or at the computer. The lodge was laid out in a long line so you could cover many miles in a day just trying to find him.

Bonus: After we had dinner, I headed back to the lodge and found that the dryer that had been out of service was actually working now. Somewhere in the mix of the rest of his tasks, George had managed to fix the dryer as well. The generator was going again but things settled down for the rest of the crew after dinner, and a lovely peace settled around the docks.

The crew and the kids would sometimes play badminton after dinner, or board games. Some went fishing or would exercise, read a book, take a paddleboat out or write letters. We hired crew based on their attitude and looked for people who could entertain themselves and not rely on big-city entertainments. Also, ever since our experience of having hired an alcoholic couple, we have had a strict non-drinking and non-smoking policy for our crew. Over the years, this has saved us a lot of trouble. Most of the lodges in the inlet followed our lead and the industry is much better and safer for it.

I would do paperwork or possibly write menus and consolidate the fridge and pantry. Then I'd organize grocery orders, check on the

A guest stands inside the lodge watching as other guests return from fishing. One of our dock crew waits outside to help tie up the boats.

laundry, water the greenhouse and check on the progress the crew had made that day in the guestrooms. Then, because I would feel so organized, I could take the time to sit and read a book. George would continue working until I told him I was going to shut the generator off in ten minutes. Usually between 11 PM and midnight. Then with the generator off, we would stand at the front of our house and enjoy the evening, watch the myriad stars, while our minds stretched in an effort to even mildly comprehend their numbers—a gauzy net of brilliant light cast out over the sea of darkness. We could sense the bats flitting past, and listen to the little mysterious splashes in the bay that created ripples through the moon's reflection on the water. It was comforting and exhilarating all at once. This was the only time in the summer that we could enjoy just being together before all hell broke loose. This was our own quiet communion with each other and this infinite universe.

What's Going On?

In the fall of 2000, George and I had travelled through Ireland as a twenty-fifth wedding anniversary present to ourselves. We cracked up laughing at every turn while George dealt with the backwards gearshift and the rearview mirror on the "wrong" side of the car. Our adventures all the way around the south end of the country were epic but I missed half the road signs because I was drowning behind an enormous upside-down road map. We became stuck in a dead end while George fought with the gears, and my head would spin when confronted with multiple street signs with arrows pointing in a dozen directions with unpronounceable names, each written with at least twenty-six letters. We drove through breathtaking country, met wonderful people, drank gallons of beer and knocked back many a whiskey. Every night there was fabulous music in every pub we visited. I love that country and the people who live there! It was such a happy time. We didn't want to leave.

Now, we were back at the lodge and into another summer fishing season. We had a group of friends and family fishing with us. The weather was good, the fish were biting and everyone was pleased to be there.

Almost all the boats came back in for lunch. One stayed out, and George was concerned because they were not answering him on the radio. By 1 PM they were still not back, so George started getting ropes and an extra lunch in the boat and told Casey to get a full day-tank of boat-gas into *Sportspage,* and to be ready to jump in when he started the engine.

George had this work of art made for our twenty-fifth wedding anniversary. It somewhat resembles a photo taken of us on our wedding day.

There were three people in the errant boat. The husband of one of them hadn't gone out with them. He jumped into *Sportspage* with George and Casey—it's always good to have an extra pair of eyes when searching. Just as George was about to pull away from the dock, there was a call from the people at Dawsons Landing. They had received a call from one of the airlines that there were three people on the beach on the west side of Calvert Island and they had spelled out a message with logs that read, "help rivers lodge." Now George knew where to head.

No one fished on the west side of Calvert Island. You can immediately see how rough the weather gets when you round the south end of the island and suddenly the trees become stubby and gnarled and are bent sharply away from the prevailing winds. George would lead our boats over to the south end of Calvert in the fog, but they always turned around if they started to stray toward the west side, which is open to the ocean and where the swells heave higher and higher and block out the view around them. How could our stray guests possibly not have noticed and then not turned back to find their bearings?

Talking, that's how. The three of them had not been together for a long time and they could not stop talking. They talked while they trolled from an area on the other side of the inlet known as "The Wall." They talked while they trolled across Fitz Hugh Sound. They talked while they rounded the south end of Calvert, and they were still talking as they drove up the west side and ran out of gas, luckily right in front of a patch of sandy beach.

They paddled the boat close to shore, ever minding the potential wrath of George if he caught them taking the boat onto the beach. After realizing that no one could hear them on the radio, they decided that it was best if they stayed where they were instead of trying to paddle back to where they had passed the south side of Calvert, which they now realized they had done. They anchored the boat quite close to the shore, jumped into the shallow water and slogged to the beach. Then they took stock of their supplies.

They had eaten their morning snack hours ago and emptied their coffee thermoses. There was drinking water on the boat but none on the beach. One of the ladies had two hard candies, so they tried to figure out how to divide them into three pieces. That wasn't going to ease their hunger.

I must interject here and tell you that these were friends of ours, Barb and Des Bell and Erica Harris, who had been at the lodge many times over the years and did know their way around, but sometimes chatting overrides common sense.

They could hear airplanes flying over the island but none of them flew above their heads. Our enterprising friend Erica decided they needed to make a sign in case a plane flew above them. They spent an hour dragging logs of varying lengths to create the message that eventually made its way, anonymously, to George. Thankfully, a plane passed over and noticed the sign, flew around in a circle, then tipped its wings to let them know that help would soon be on its way!

Other people in the inlet had heard that there were boaters stranded on the west side of Calvert. One report said that there was a boat overturned and three people were in the water. A fellow from another resort, who was fishing near Calvert, pulled in his fishing lines and bravely headed around to the outside of the island. When he found the people stranded on the beach, he called out to them from his rocking boat that he was there to save them. Des called back that they couldn't leave George's boat. The fellow insisted that they leave the boat and climb into his. All three of them called back to let him know that under no circumstances were they going anywhere without George's boat!

The poor would-be rescuer floated around in the bay hoping someone else would soon arrive, until George, Casey and Nigel arrived an hour later, discharging the kind man from his rescue duty. They helped the stranded folk onto *Sportspage*, swapped gas day-tanks in the speedboat, and George slowly drove home through the rising swells, with Casey driving the guest's speedboat behind them. The other brave boater who had come to save the trio was right behind him. In all the excitement of the rescue, no one thought to dismantle the help sign. George and Casey had to brave the swell two days later to pull the sign apart to stop other pilots reporting lost and stranded people.

A few days later, a new group of twenty-four guests arrived at our airplane dock. George was always there to greet new arrivals and usher them into his boat for the short drive to the lodge. As he was putting his hand out to help a guest into *Sportspage*, he introduced himself by saying, "Hi, I'm Jack!" There was a pause as he realized his mistake and said, "Wait a minute, no I'm not, I'm George!" All weekend, our guests who had been with us for many, many summers enjoyed calling him Jack. Late in the summer, George's head would be swimming with guests' names and mine would be swimming with the amount of food they would eat.

In 2002, we had a very, very dry summer. The driest we had ever experienced. We had a float with a couple of thousand-gallon emergency tanks that we filled with fresh water in early July when there was a good water supply. Once the tanks were filled, George towed the heavy float around the corner and tied it to shore, out of sight. We were saving a lot of fresh water because we had changed all of the toilets to flush with salt water, with two high-pressure tanks that pushed the salt water into the waste system. Late in August, our creek was just barely dripping water into our holding tanks. We encouraged staff to "shower" overboard and conserve laundry where they could. George towed the freshwater float back to the lodge, and pumped half of one container into our system up the hill. Then the next day—another half, then another half. By the fourth day, with only half a tank of emergency water left, and just as we were beginning to wring our hands nervously, rain started to fall and lasted just long enough to fill our reservoir.

It would be many years before those emergency tanks had to be filled a second time in the summer because of low rainfall. Just in case, there was a plan to tow the float with the tanks about a mile and a half away to a river that flowed from a large lake then hook up pipes to fill the tanks there and slowly and gently tow them home.

We were involved in another rescue later that summer. A couple had anchored their large pleasure boat in a bay near our fishing grounds. The woman went exploring in a kayak, and the man took their small inflatable boat over to The Wall. When he decided to head back, he turned the same way that our friends had turned, and accidentally headed over to Calvert Island. He got to a land mass and thought he needed to continue up the west side thinking he was just on the other side of the inlet. He had a GPS with him but without his reading glasses, he could barely read it. After driving for another thirty minutes, he stopped and made more of an effort to read the GPS and couldn't believe when it said he was on the west side of Calvert. He disregarded the information.

Then he too ran out of gas. After another quick look at the GPS, he decided that it was telling him the truth, and he started paddling hard. He paddled for five hours and finally could make out the light at Clarke Point on the south end of Calvert Island. He was worn to a frazzle, it was pitch black, and there were no boats to be seen as he pulled his dingy ashore and prepared for a very uncomfortable and long night.

Back in the inlet, after a mayday call to the Coast Guard from the woman who'd been kayaking, George, Casey and quite a few other lodge owners were on the water searching. George suggested to the fellows on the small Coast Guard boat that the man could be on the southern tip of Calvert Island just like our guests had ended up. It was too late for George or Casey to head over because it was now dark, but the Coast Guard boat could do it. They disagreed with George and said the lost man could not be that far away. After many hours of searching, everyone was told to stop until it was light again in the morning. They didn't want other boats running into trouble.

The following day, three of our guest boats arrived for the early morning bite at the south end of Calvert and they saw the missing man, frantically waving to them! They passed him several bottles of water and their container of snacks and radioed back to the lodge. The two-hundred-foot Coast Guard ship *Tanu* arrived shortly after and scooped the man and his boat onto their deck. He had spent the night sitting on a rock exposed to the elements with his dinghy tied to his waist. The ship's doctor checked him out and the *Tanu* delivered him back to his frantic wife. When they arrived at the Port Hardy dock in their sailboat a few days later, a commercial fisherman said to them, "In times of trouble, the whole coast comes together."

It was the middle of September of 2002 and George and I were finally able to sit down together with a coffee and a muffin. We were talking about not retiring. We thought it might be fun to eventually get to the point where we catered to only eight fishing guests at a time. We couldn't think of anything else we would rather be doing, but we thought we'd prefer doing it on a smaller scale. As we chatted, I noticed that George was having trouble swallowing. "What's going on?" I said. "Why are you having trouble swallowing your muffin crumbs?" He sloughed it off and said he didn't know why. I told him to phone our doctor in West Vancouver immediately, which he did, and made an appointment for the middle of October. I sent him back to the phone to make an appointment for the day after he would arrive back in town, two weeks hence.

I was wary of strange symptoms. My sister June was diagnosed with ovarian cancer after she thought she had a simple case of stomach flu.

When he finally got in to see the doctor, George was told that he probably had a hiatal hernia and that he could buy over-the-counter tablets to settle any acid reflux and make it easier for him to swallow. He took those for a month and went back to the doctor when the symptoms did not subside. He got a prescription for stronger medicine, still to help with the hiatal hernia. After a month of taking those pills, George's shoulder started to hurt, and it hurt more and more every day. Like a chainsaw-was-cutting-his-arm-off kind of hurt. I finally parked myself on our doctor's doorstep, and he sent us to meet a specialist that same morning in the emergency room of Lions Gate Hospital.

Then and only then did the ball get rolling. After tests and scans, we heard the dreaded word "cancer." Esophageal cancer. *Oh no you don't!* George was the most positive person I have ever known. He was always happy. We lived such a healthy life. *No, this cannot be.* More tests. I wheeled him around the hospital from one test to another; there were no orderlies to be found. Confirmation. Chemo started that day. Pain medication. Nausea medication. More pain medication. It was growing very fast. I did Christmas shopping at London Drugs waiting for prescriptions to be filled.

The next several months are a fog. Our sport-fishing association RINCSEA sent us to the Wickaninnish Inn for a relaxing long weekend at the end of March. The chemo treatments had been brutal, and we truly appreciated this bit of respite. My sister June and brother-in-law Sandy were supposed to join us there, but my sister's health had taken a bad turn with her own cancer treatments. We tried to enjoy the spectacular beach and the beautiful facilities, but George was noticeably weaker and could not walk far or savour the fine food.

We headed back to Vancouver for another round of chemo. Suddenly, my days were spent organizing drugs, blood tests, doctor appointments, chemo dates, slow walks by the ocean, and more drugs and chemo dates, and making special food that wasn't hard to swallow and would keep weight on George. I barely had time to answer the office phone. I would only work on the lodge when George was sleeping. People were booking themselves. I tried to keep up. An endoscopy had been scheduled. A scope would be inserted into George's throat to see what was happening now. We arrived for the test and the nurse, after consulting her paperwork, asked George to remove his trousers for the procedure. George, never one to lose his sense of humour, asked, "Isn't that a long way to go for this test?" The nurse checked her information again and backed red-faced out of the room.

Casey graduated high school in 2000. By now, it was 2003 and Jessy would graduate. I was no help. I was floundering. The phone would ring and I could see that it was my friend. I didn't pick it up. I couldn't talk. When it rang again immediately, I took the receiver into the bedroom closet and closed the door so George couldn't hear me talking/crying. My friends insisted on supporting me. I don't know what I would have done without them.

Our friend Nigel brought a barber to the house, and after George had his hair and beard trimmed, he slowly and carefully dressed in his best outfit to attend Jessy's graduation ceremony at the Orpheum Theatre. I rented a wheelchair. We wheeled in and proudly watched our dear Jess cross the stage. I was amazed that she was able to do the required work. Our kids were so strong.

Just a few days later we had yet another appointment with the oncologist.

Organizing the Lodge

It was early June 2003 and George was organizing the lodge and crew from a lounge chair on our deck in town. We figured that he would do the same at the lodge over the summer. We had just returned from the hospital. The doctor had shown us the scan of George's liver and how the cancer had spread there and bluntly, savagely, said, "You won't be going back up to your little cabin in the woods again." We reeled out of the oncologist's office and stumbled to the car. I turned to George and said, "Fuck the doctor, you will go back to the lodge!" I booked flights for us both, and we flew to Rivers Inlet two days later.

Our caretaker, Robin Cooper, Richard and Sheila's son, and his family were still at the lodge. Normally they would have left by now because George was usually there in the late spring, working on new projects and getting water lines running and equipment ready for the summer. Nothing had been normal this year.

The weather was warm in the day and cool in the evening. I had brought two books with me to read aloud to George: *Full Catastrophe Living* by Jon Kabat-Zinn and *The Power of Now* by Eckhart Tolle. The title of Kabat-Zinn's book was inspired by a line from *Zorba the Greek*, in which the title character explains that to live "the full catastrophe" is to live life to the fullest, whether it is good or bad—embrace all of it. George's attention span was not long, so I would read short passages from the books several times a day. We also listened to a meditation tape that came with the *Full Catastrophe* book. It led listeners through a body scan and would bring your whole being down to your breath and was completely relaxing. Something we both needed.

I helped George walk all over and around the lodge floats as he touched all of the things that we had created with such love and care: the house we had moved from one float to another, the planter boxes, the beautiful lodge building. We walked to the hot tub where our kids had played for hours in the sun, the rain and, at times, the snow. We walked to the tackle shop where most of the fishing gear was put away for the winter, then all the way to the boathouse where his woodworking shop was. We walked past the greenhouse, the big freezer, the woodshed, guestrooms and crew rooms. We went into the new generator shed and touched both generators and admired the ingenious fuel system he had designed, then into the metalworking shop to pick up and feel the motor parts and pipe fittings. George always loved to wander around the lodge when he first returned after spending the winter in town.

I set up a lounge chair in the shade at the side of the greenhouse so he could have a rest and hear our creek tumbling and splashing down the hill fifty feet away—the creek that he had tamed with pipes and pumps and huge holding tanks to ensure a steady supply of water over the summer. Our creek-and-water system was one of the most reliable in the inlet.

We went out in the boat the next afternoon. I drove into the middle of Klaquaek Channel, shut the engine off and we drifted and bobbed along with the sound of the water slap-slapping the sides of the boat as we gently rocked. The sky was a deep sea-blue with not a cloud in sight. We were in a cocoon of blue and green and the fresh salt air filled us with love and harmony. We floated along, just listening to the water and the seagulls. The tide started to push us a little too close to a rocky islet, so I had to break the peace and start the engine. George was getting tired as we headed back to the lodge, trolling slowly all the way. We could see Calvert Island with our beautiful snow-capped Mount Buxton towering over the surrounding miles of ocean and forest, and in the other direction we could see the snow-covered mountains toward the head of the inlet. George knew every rock, every sweeper, every tree and every craggy bay that we passed.

Later, we were sitting side by side on the porch chairs watching the kingfisher dive, the hummingbirds zoom and an eagle glide up above. I had just asked for information. I choked on the words and broke down gasping for breath unable to continue. I'm a terrible person. How can I ask this of him?

"Please," I cried. "Please help me understand how all the equipment works. I have a recording device. Please, I'm scared. What if you are sleeping and something breaks down?"

I was positive that George would be directing the guests, equipment and crew from a lounge chair, but I was still feeling panic clawing its way up my throat.

I had the recorder in my hand. We both looked at it, the size of it, the weight of it, the agony of it. George slowly reached for the recorder, took it out of my hand, stood up and, slowly and carefully, walked toward the generator shed.

The float plane arrived the next day to take us back to town. The pilot and I helped George into the plane. As we taxied across the water, we were both in a place of peace, following each breath in and feeling it spread throughout our bodies. This was a place that I would have to go to many times over the next many months, just to keep my head from exploding into a million tiny pieces.

PART THREE

Dear George

What Just Happened?

Dear George:

Well, that took us all by surprise. Especially me. I believed in you and was so sure that you would beat this thing called cancer. Last night Casey and I tried but couldn't keep you from falling as we walked together down the hall at home in West Vancouver. Then there was no way that we could lift you without hurting you. In panic, I ran to the phone and called Dr. Wilson. He said to call 911 and that he would be right over. He would help the ambulance attendants assess the situation, and help us make a decision whether we should just get help lifting you into bed or if it would be better for you to go to the hospital, where they could make you comfortable for the night.

The ambulance and the doctor arrived at the same time and before they lifted you, one of the fellows asked you to smile. You said, "Say something funny first." The tension that was crushing me turned to dust and drifted away. You would be all right. We just needed to get you up and moving again. The medics moved you into bed and our doctor spoke gently to you in a low murmur. Then he turned to me and said he thought he could make you more comfortable tonight at the hospital. My main concern at this moment was that you should be helped by someone who could do just that. That's what they do at hospitals right? They make you comfortable, and they ease your pain.

We drove behind you in various cars. Jessy went with you in the ambulance and later told me of how the two of you were there in the hallway of Lions Gate Hospital, you on a stretcher, her clutching your hand. She was overwhelmed and scared and told you, "Please don't leave me." You, never being one to think of yourself but always thinking of the comfort of others, patted her hand and calmly said, "Don't worry, I'm right here, I'm not going anywhere." It was only later that Jessy realized that *you* were worried about *her*. You were thinking that she was worried that your stretcher was going to be wheeled off, leaving her alone and scared in the hallway before the others arrived. You wanted to assure her that you wouldn't let them take you away without her. You were so firmly planted in the moment and stoically trying to shield her and put her at ease, and not thinking of yourself at all.

I didn't drive with you in the ambulance because of some perverse reasoning in my addled brain that if I didn't acknowledge the ambulance, it couldn't possibly be such an emergency.

Dr. Wilson reached the hospital before we did and already had a bed waiting for you. They hooked you up to a drip, morphine I think, and a heart monitor. Jessy and Casey, Gery, Erica and I gathered around your bed chatting about little things trying to keep the atmosphere light, but it wasn't working. You answered our questions some of the time, and at one point, you looked around and said, "I am surrounded by so much love!"

Then Casey said he wanted to read to his dad, and at the same time, he noticed that your feet were cold. Erica raced home and brought back the *Life of Pi* and a pair of warm socks, and we settled in for a long night. We took turns phoning your sister Marilyn. Marilyn and Phil just happened to be in town for the night and were out for dinner and not answering their phone.

Casey and a friend had left from Thunderbird Marina in West Vancouver that morning in *Sportspage*, heading up to the lodge to get started on un-winterizing. Thirty minutes after he left, he called and asked me to find a rescue boat to come out and tow *Sportspage* back to the dock. He had hit a large, mostly submerged log so hard that it had sheared the engine leg right off the back of the boat. One of many such coincidences in the days that followed, or you might call them serendipitous moments of the universe conspiring to make sure that Casey was there with us at the hospital and not stuck up at the lodge frantically trying to get back.

Nurses came by now and again to check your monitor and the drip line. You seemed to be sleeping but then you started talking. You said, "I need my binoculars and my boat and where's my fishing rod?" Casey held you and softly whispered in your ear. The rest of us sat quietly hoping not to disturb you. But the background beat of the heart monitor started beeping slower. And slower. Abruptly, the alarm signal went off and there was instant chaos as a chair crashed to the floor, a doctor came running, suddenly there were nurses everywhere, and we were tripping and desperately trying to get out of the way while holding onto your hands. The monitor continued its high-pitched buzz, and I stared at it in disbelief. What the hell? This couldn't happen. You wouldn't leave me! How could you be snatched away from us?! I entered another dimension as a force field bloomed and surrounded my heart then squeezed it shut. The doctor asked me questions and I answered them as if I were in his office. I hugged you and kissed you goodbye. You were no longer there. Your energy was already gone. Where did you go? What just happened? What?!

Dr. Wilson gently walked us out of the hospital, and said he would come by our house in the morning. Someone had finally reached Marilyn and Phil, and they were on their way. We drove home and silently walked into the house. Erica made tea, and we all sat in the living room trying to understand what just happened. You are our rock. You are Mr. Positive Energy. How could this have happened to you of all people? As we sat morosely staring at each other, my frog lamp—my wonderful tiffany shade, held up by two long slim frogs that you and Jessy bought for me in New York—blinked off and on. Conversation stopped as we all turned to stare at the lamp. We looked at each other, trying to read each other's thoughts. After a few moments, someone started talking again and once again the lamp blinked off and on and then off and on again. This time, I was sure that it was you letting us know that you were still with us. The lamp had never blinked before and has never blinked since.

The next morning, Gery and Marilyn went to tell your mom. She also entered an alternate universe when she heard the news. She was eighty-eight years old and did not believe that she could outlive her darling boy. It just didn't seem possible. She had been awake most of the night, and knew something was terribly wrong when both of your sisters arrived at her door. Your mom is so amazing. She has been so refined and dignified through this terrible time. People still comment on how lovely she is—even though she was dying inside. The two of us made a real pair. No one was going to get through our protective shields.

June phoned this morning. She wasn't surprised to hear that you had "passed on to your next assignment." She said that you visited her in the night and told her that everything would be all right, that she should not be afraid. Sandy was surprised when she got up this morning and made coffee and toast for him for the first time in many weeks. She was feeling really happy and content for the first time in many months. I understand we need to be open, to listen and enjoy the synchronicity.

In the meantime, the office phone keeps ringing. I can't possibly answer it. I just let it go to the machine. Casey checks for messages and writes them all down. He has also been contacting some of our old-time guests to let them know about you. We have bookings that I haven't recorded. People want to know when they can pay. When will we be sending an invoice. I had been using all of my time just to be with you, sometimes at the beach watching the boats or reading to you from our favourite books. I had no time to look after the lodge. But people still want to come fishing this summer. I'm still having trouble focusing on business. There are other things to think about.

Things like how will I get up in the morning? How will I keep breathing and walking? How will I ever fall asleep again without your shoulder to fall asleep on? And …? One step at a time is all I can do right now. People ask me how I'm doing. My only answer is, "In a backwards world, I'm doing fine," which sounds very positive to people I don't really know. Friends keep dropping off food. The house is full of wonderful people, but I don't know how to talk. I try to be polite.

Gery and Graham took me to the crematorium. Decisions need to be made. We went into the coffin room. I felt ants crawling all around inside my skin. We walked around looking at their wares, lots of different-shaped urns and small wooden boxes for the ashes. The deferential man walked us over and showed us the deluxe, highly polished and brass-decorated coffins. Aren't they going to get burned to ash along with your body? In one corner there was a rack with waxed cardboard boxes. They looked like very large versions of the fish boxes we had used for years. Suddenly, I was bent double, wracked with laughter and a deep ache that then dissolved into jagged sobs and weeping then swelled back into snorts and more demented laughter. Gery and Graham stood back and let me go on. The little man disappeared. I finally choked out that you would've loved the irony of the biggest fish box being yours. I hope you approve.

I had help organizing the funeral. So many writers in the family. So many organizers. I drifted from one task to the next: visited the minister, planned the food, received flowers, watched the kids being surrounded by their young friends who somehow knew what to do. At the end of the days, Casey, Jessy and I all piled in our bed and slept when we could. We all needed that connection. You really surprised us. Caught us making plans and went in a different direction. The lodge without you? Preposterous!

But the lodge was bigger than the four of us. It seemed like people were going to go there to fish whether we were there or not. Nothing is going to stop a fisherman from fishing, especially the ones who have fished with us for over twenty-five years. Casey and Jess organized the crew. I'm so glad that you had already talked to Marc, who agreed to cook for us even though he and his wife had been planning to move back to Quebec. Almost all of our staff from the previous summer was returning. The waitress was our only new crewmember. We just had to get them there. They knew what to do. The kids did an amazing job of ordering supplies, and having things delivered to the freight boat. Casey ordered fuel for the boats and generators, fuel filters, water filters, building supplies, fishing tackle, bait and boat parts and new engines. Jessy was keeping everything organized as well as packing all the items we would be sending to the lodge and making trips out to the freight boat with her truck loaded with "stuff."

I was worrying about my darling sister June who seemed to be getting sicker by the minute. I finally stopped packing for the lodge—which actually just amounted to me throwing clothes and shoes and, at times, a shoe, into a big box—and packed a bag to go and help her.

Chef Marc was a lovely man who was with us for five summers, including the awful summer of 2003 after George died. Following that summer, he and his wife moved back east.

I flew to Edmonton four days after your funeral, and Casey and Jessy flew to the lodge. June was not feeling well. A year and a half of ovarian cancer had taken its toll. We went for short walks in her neighbourhood. She tried to make me feel better, and I tried to make her feel better. The best we could do was to just be with one another. I walked over and picked up lattes in the afternoons. Sandy brought us dinners. None of us were up to cooking.

I had your phone ringing in one pocket and my phone ringing in the other. I wore out a notepad trying to keep track, trying to keep all the balls in the air. There were a lot of people I had to talk to—guests who had been coming to the lodge for so many years. I didn't call everyone back. I couldn't. I tried to talk to them from a place that was just above my head, but sometimes I found myself talking from a place deep inside my chest, a place that had become hard and hot and made swallowing difficult.

I started to feel an elastic band pulling me back to Vancouver to look after flights and payment details for the lodge. I told June that I would just go home for the weekend and would be back in three days. I flew to Vancouver, walked in the house and began booking flights for guests and sending out invoices. I worked all night and into the next day. I organized a huge grocery order, paid bills and checked in with the kids at the lodge. Then I stuffed my things back into my bag to head out to the airport for my return trip to Edmonton.

I was locking the door behind me when the office phone started to ring. I hesitated for three seconds and then ran back down the hall to the office. The man on the other end of the line wanted to rent rooms at the lodge for the following week. I explained that the lodge wasn't open yet, that crew had just arrived and had only just started to un-winterize everything. He said that they just needed rooms and meals and would not be fishing. They were with a telephone company and would be checking equipment in the area. They wanted to stay with us because of our helicopter pad. I apologized and said sorry, but we would not be able to look after them and I hung up.

I walked out of the house, locked the door, unlocked the door and then walked back in. I headed to the office, pressed the call-history button and dialled the number that had just phoned me. When the fellow answered, I asked him if we could make a trade. I would let the group stay and eat at the lodge, in exchange for the use of their helicopter and pilot for an hour or two. He asked what I wanted to use it for. I told him that I had your ashes and that you had always wanted to climb to the top of Mount Buxton, that you and Casey had planned to climb it together in the fall of the previous year but that you were just starting to feel unwell and didn't feel strong enough at that time. The man recognized your name, had heard about you for years, and agreed to do the trade. I hung up the phone and headed to the airport.

Sandy picked me up and told me that June had just been admitted to Edmonton's Cross Cancer Institute, and we headed straight there. She had a private room that was always full of visitors. Their daughter, Marnie, and I spent most nights with her, one sleeping on the extra bed and the other on a cot. I went back to their house one night and with the help of my *Full Catastrophe* body-scan audio tape, I slept all night long. I have become addicted to it.

When June became too weak for the Cross to be able to help her, we all moved to the palliative care unit at Edmonton's general hospital. Out-of-town relatives started arriving. At times it was like an old-time hootenanny, with people quietly singing in beautiful harmony, and other times June's son, Jordan, was just noodling on a guitar. Everyone chatting, always upbeat. I was along for the ride. People picked up beer and pizza. June enjoyed drinking a tall cold one. For her, it was like manna from heaven. A few nights later we were all together when the nurse came to speak to Sandy. She said June's heart is so strong, we will be here for a while. But twenty minutes later, June also had "passed on to her next assignment." I am positive that you were there to greet her, and make her feel at home.

Two days later, Casey and Jessy arrived. They had left a long-time friend and staff member, Steve, in charge of the lodge with a list of projects and gallons of paint for the crew, and were confident that things would get done. June and Sandy's house was full of people, full of food and full of flowers. I was there. I show up in some of the photos.

My beloved husband and my beloved sister. The weight on my soul was just too much, and only silence helped me carry it.

I love you and miss you so much my Darling,

Pat

Mount Buxton

Dear George:

I flew to the lodge, and Casey and Jess both came out to pick me up from the airplane float. We slowly trolled into the bay and I could see a huge WELCOME HOME banner across the front of the lodge and the whole crew waiting to tie up our boat.

Within minutes I was talking to the fellow from the phone company about their helicopter picking us up shortly to fly to Mount Buxton.

Casey headed out to a meeting with other lodge owners and representatives of the Wuikinuxv Nation from the head of the inlet. The First Nations group has requested that the area's lodge owners pay them money for every guest that we have here this summer.

We have to do a creel report for your guide licence. What does "creel report" mean? Paperwork for the Salmon Sport Head Recovery Program.

The accounting program on my computer needs upgrading, and I have to do TD1s for crew, figure out wages and get info to the accountant.

There's a letter from a different First Nations group asking for money for their elders to have a holiday.

Grocery orders.

Pay bills.

I feel hands clutching at me from all directions.

Tons of mail.

No file folders here.

Liquor stacked in the living room.

Sad. Sad. Sad.

Call back re: helicopter

The helicopter picked us up at 2:30 PM and flew Jessy, Casey and me on an incredible tour of Calvert Island, along the beaches, up over the mountains, across meadows and lakes, then up, up, up Mount Buxton. We landed near the top of the mountain on a flat bit of rock with a sheer drop off of 1,200 feet on one side and 150 feet on the other sides.

"Take your time," the pilot said.

Mount Buxton at sunset. We scattered George's ashes on the peak.

We climbed and stood on the very tippy-top of the mountain. I opened the box of ashes and let them swirl away on the dancing wind as we sang, "Spread your wings and fly away, up into the wind, above the trees you glide with ease, and round back again." Your favourite song by Ken Tobias, "Dream #2." We held hands and watched as the ashes rose and swooped with the gusts. "I drew a picture of a pair of wings, because I want to fly. He said that fewer people were trying, but the art of really flying is dying." The view was endless in all directions with tiny boats chugging up Fitz Hugh Sound three thousand feet below and Japan in the other direction. You are forever part of Mount Buxton and we felt you watching over us all summer.

The telephone company never did come to the lodge to use our facilities. I think they left us alone as a mark of respect to you.

We arrived back at the lodge and I was back on my head ...

Answering e-mails.

Searching for addresses of people who haven't yet paid.

There is a postal strike set for tonight.

There is so much stuff everywhere it is overwhelming me.

Unpacking, there is no room for my things.

There is laundry piled to the ceiling in Jessy's room.

A lodge owner called me on the boat-to-boat radio channel. He seemed to be talking in code. He finally phoned me to say that the liquor inspectors were in the inlet and they were going to all the lodges, harassing them with their new rules, but thanks to him, they will not be coming here.

Wine—have to order now.

Need an evacuation and safety check for the crew for Workers Compensation.

Order pop.

Grocery orders ... hurry!

Have to phone grocery orders in as I can't seem to e-mail them.

It's like going back more than ten years, having to phone grocery orders in.

Have to phone in an airplane manifest.

It is so hard to walk around here. Everything has your name on it. And there is so much of everything. It is swamping me. I am going to bed.

This is the end of my first day back in the inlet without you, my darling. How can this be? I can't grasp the idea that you won't ever be here again. I am crushed and I don't know if I'll be able to get up again.

Lotsa love my Sweet Georgie,

Pat

Are You Smiling?

Dear George:

I have to keep working on paperwork—e-mails, bills, wages, the rest of the grocery orders. I'm casting around for addresses. You and I had very different ways of organizing things. Casey, Jessy and Steve have the crew painting the red buildings and white trim, and power washing the decks everywhere. I received an e-mail back from the accountant so I can now pay the staff. I'm sure they will be happy to have a paycheque. I am spinning my wheels, having trouble getting things done because there is something else to be done everywhere I turn. I talked to your mom, sisters and Graham. I am barely holding myself together. Rescue Remedy under my tongue helps a little.

Another resort owner picked me up and drove me around the corner to see where the old beachcombers' string of boom sticks is being used by an American who has bought some bits and pieces of fishing resort from the lodge owner. The new American owner seems to be adding more floats. Hopefully his doesn't turn into a full-blown resort right next to us. I know you would hate that.

Guests arrive and drape themselves over my shoulders in abject grief over your passing. This happens all summer, and my arms feel like rebar reinforcing the concrete wall that is growing higher around me. I pat people on the back to console them, then gently push them away. A lock has clamped down on my heart, and the key slipped out of my hand and dropped overboard. When the last of the guests have been greeted I head over to our house and, once the door is closed, I gasp for breath. Then I grit my teeth and try to pull the knife out that has been twisting in my soul. *Breathe, just breathe—and another breath.*

The next morning, the vacuum packer packed it in. It was supposedly overhauled during the winter at a cost of five hundred dollars. Casey tried

We had twelve crew for twenty-four guests.

calling the company but they were closed for the weekend. He looked the machine over again and fixed it for the time being. Then the espresso machine had a broken heater. It too, had been overhauled in town, in this case for only three hundred dollars. Then Marc told me that the switch was broken on the meat slicer. I lay down to listen to my relaxation CD.

We didn't have crab for the last dinner for our group of guests. I think this is the first last-night's dinner in twenty-nine years where we didn't serve crab. Remember how one of our guest's favourite afternoon trips was to drop crab traps and then return the next day with you to pull them? It was just one too many things to try to organize. But still, all the guests are happy. There are so many fish, and the weather is wonderful. The food is great and the crew are all working so well together. Steve even organized smoking the salmon, and Casey and Steve keep the smoker going all day Sunday. Jessy is fantastic with the crew and has a way of keeping everyone busy, yet happy.

The Fisheries biologists came in again today to leave brochures about whale-watching and a poster to tack up by the cleaning table about the tagged salmon head recovery program. Steve talked to them. Casey and Steve are making sure that the bait runs are covered, as well as the lunch runs for people who want to continue fishing through lunch. I'm still

Jessy and another staff member cutting, vacuum packing and flash freezing salmon. Twenty-four guests can catch a lot of fish.

having trouble sending e-mails. I finally found out that I have to change the settings for the outgoing mail, but I have no idea how to.

We had our first big changeover day with people coming in and going out. Our long-time guest Mark had been at another lodge in the Queen Charlotte Islands a month earlier and told the owner, "Nope, you're still not as good as Rivers Lodge!"

Crew were working so well and the guests have been impressed. The guests love to watch as the crew rush the heavy fish boxes out to the waiting boats to deliver them to the airport when we hear the airplanes flying over. Still a well-oiled machine, thanks to Casey and Jessy and our amazing crew.

The outgoing guests told all the incoming guests that the fishing is fantastic and that they had a wonderful time. So now all the new guests arrive already happy. At 5 PM your mom called and asked, "Are you smiling? You have to smile for the guests." So that's what I'm doing—I just kept smiling and smiling. I don't want to scare everyone off the floats never to be seen again. Next season depends a lot on how good my performance is.

Love always,

Pat

One Step at a Time

Dear George:
    The new group is in and very pleased. I ran around with wine and liquor orders, placing bottles in electric coolers in each guest's room. The BC Liquor Distribution Branch has changed the rules and I can no longer offer liquor to guests, unless I get a liquor licence, and I'm not going to do that. The document with liquor rules is an inch thick and I don't think it's worth the trouble. We have always put liquor on the bar, beer outside in the beer fridge, and wine on the tables with dinner for guests to help themselves to, but we can't do that any longer. But we can be part of the delivery service as long as guests order and pay for the liquor. More people sitting in windowless rooms thinking up ridiculous rules, so now the beer fridge is called the bottled-water fridge.

Casey visits the guests at the dinner tables every evening to talk about the next day's plan. Big shoes to fill since you had always done that. Steve stays up late and shuts the generator off, so I am able to crawl into bed and not sleep. I run through things that need to be done and finally start to practise simply breathing in and breathing out.

I worked on the computer again. I had filed all of your letters in Netscape and then found out that I needed to be in Outlook, so I spent another three hours re-filing all the letters. Then I spent some time answering letters from people who had written to us in the spring. I was close to panicking and took some more Rescue Remedy drops. Any little thing sets me off and I feel like I'm going to freak out. The Rescue Remedy seems to smooth out the activity that gets rocketing around in my chest.

So far, we are doing all right with the water supply. I wasn't sure if the recent heli-logging in the hills behind us would mean more or less fresh water this season. It's still coming down the hill well enough, especially after last night's hard rain. The first rain since I got back. The air smells so fresh. I can't enjoy it.

I've had my dear Erica and my dear Bonnie here to stay with me at different times. They are helping me keep the top of my head on, as well as helping clean and do laundry and visit with me over coffee. What would I have done without their presence? They have been amazing and really buoyed up Casey and Jessy, who are also working so hard at keeping me from exploding or imploding or maybe just slipping off the side of the dock and sinking quietly with the weight of my sadness.

I had to call the airline. They pulled a dirty trick and sent a different plane than my regular chartered plane and loaded other people and freight on it, without giving us a discount. Our friend Al McDonald is still sending off our charters from Vancouver and meeting them on their return, and he will keep track of the people and freight on the rest of our flights.

As Bonnie was climbing onto the plane to return to town, she said, "You have to feel the pain." But I really can't go there—it might just tear me apart. There are so many things to do: advertising, licences, bookings, food orders, goddamn liquor, GST, bank, wages, airplanes, marketing, lodge upkeep. Also, I see new things that need doing, like the woodshed roof has a crappy old tarp where it was leaking, and one of the guest-house roofs has rust on it. The flowers are not as good this year—I just didn't get to them. Good thing Erica and Bonnie helped. Now I have to take pictures of some of the guests with their fish to go on our website ... shit, shit, shit!

How is it possible that I have been left with this place? This is your thing not mine. I finally found your guide licence. Casey needs it so he can fill in last year's creel report to make the licence valid. Robin Cooper, who works for DFO in the summer, came in to pick up the fish-tally sheet and let me know that he and his family will be the caretakers for the lodge again this

Erica, one of my dear friends, came to the lodge to stay with me to help ease the pain of losing two members of my family.

winter. What a relief. They will be here to stay by the end of September.

Casey and Steve tried to hike to the lake by going around the bottom of the hill that's on the other side of the bay, instead of going over it. They used flagging tape to mark the way, but they overshot the lake and ended up in the lagoon. Then on their way back, they ended up at our water system instead of where they left the boat. So much for flagging tape, I thought. Jessy had to row over and rescue them. Yay Jessy!

Again the guests are leaving happy, but there is so much sadness from the new guests that I find that I cannot carry theirs too, despite them heaping it on my shoulders when I stand at the front to greet them.

The hot-tub heater is leaking again. Salt water feels so good, like an effervescent bath, but it wrecks everything in the pool. There are pinholes in the heater, so water is spraying all over the place. Marc and Casey are able to kind of fix it. So far the boat motors have all been good. One day at a time. One foot in front of the other.

We took Marc out in the boat one evening to watch a humpback whale that was lazily rolling at the surface right in front of our bay. Jessy had grabbed her Yorkshire terrier, Salty, and sat him on the wide engine cover at the back of the boat. Casey stopped the boat and shut off the engine as we drifted along with the tide, surrounded by a sunset-painted sky and damp evening air. Jess's little 14-pound dog suddenly noticed the massive bulk of the whale as it rolled again. Salty started vainly barking a ferocious warning to the behemoth to stay away from the boat and his girl Jess. I thought we should rename the dog David!

One of the resort owners came by and said his wife thought I might like a trip to the beach with her one day. I could feel myself start to panic at the thought. I think I'm afraid that I might lose the tenuous hold I have on my emotions if I were to do something relaxing. Late afternoon is a bad time. There is some internal clock that starts to wind up, and I can feel things going wild in my chest, zinging in all directions at once. I know you should be here by now for us to have our coffee and chat. And it's been far too long since I talked to my darling June on the phone.

The manual that your Marilyn transcribed from your voice memos and printed out for us has been invaluable. Even though Casey and Jessy worked with you all their lives, there were still some details that were in your head only. Well, a lot of details. With some jobs and repairs that we managed throughout the summer it felt like we were working in Braille, always just barely able to figure out what to do next, and then next, and next again. But the manual was very helpful, so thank you for doing that, I know it wasn't easy. And thank you for looking over our shoulders and helping push us in the right direction.

I spent hours on the computer bringing our accounting up to date. What a job! I have to have it done for the GST report, which is a few weeks late, but that can't be helped. I haven't done any computer accounting for way too long. I need to get new price lists printed for next year, but the US rate is so volatile that I'm afraid to do it too early—or too late.

My big brother, Jimmy, arrived today! Such a wonderful bear hug. He needs a place to live after escaping a bad relationship and is also mourning our dear sister June, so I'm happy to provide a place for him to rest and rejuvenate.

We start warning the crew that there may be a shortage of water if we don't get some rain soon, so staff showers are overboard now. We have had one night of rain in the last five weeks. Marc came over and told me the hot-tub heater is leaking again. I finally ordered a new one and it will be here on the Monday flight.

It rained in the afternoon for ten minutes, which was enough to get our bottom tank to overflow again. We will last a little longer. It has been pouring rain in Vancouver every day and we got ten minutes' worth.

Marc came over again and said the big outside fridge wasn't working, so Casey went over to see why. He looked at the on-off switch, flipped it back on and the fridge is working again. He's just so smart!

Jimmy has kept us amused with beautifully written stories of his adventures since he arrived here. Including his flight to the lodge in the "bucket of bolts" Goose airplane, his trip with Casey in *Sportspage* looking for guests in the fog, and dumping himself out of a canoe, just as the Goose arrived to bring in new guests.

More family and friends here. Even though our guests are happy and familiar, it's still nice to have my private friends to talk to. I can relax with them a little. Not a lot, because there are still guests around to look after, crew to keep hopping and a very fragile mind to keep hold of.

It started raining in the middle of the night and it was socked in and rainy all of the following day. Three of our group of guests had been stuck in Detroit because of bad weather, but they finally landed on a scheduled flight, in our bay at about 3 PM. The pilot had told them that he was heading straight back to Port Hardy with the rest of the people on board who had been hoping to fly in to Dawsons Landing. He said, "This is the last stop I'm making today. I can't see a thing out there!"

More happy guests leaving, more guests arriving. The problem is that so many people arrive so full of sadness that I end up clenching my teeth and digging my fingernails into my hands wishing a skyhook would come and whisk me away. No, what I really want is for you to come and rescue me. You always have before.

We have a group of German- and Spanish-speaking people here. I could hear some yelling that I didn't understand, but got the gist of it:

a boat was broken down and drifting near the rocks. Casey was out on his sailboat and Steve was up in the bush. Those two are essential to the smooth running of the lodge. Big mistake letting them go out at the same time! Just as I was heading out, Casey came around the corner and took my place in his bait-run boat and sped off. He is amazing when something needs to be done. I sent Jessy out in another boat to swap for the one that wasn't working, and Casey came back with Jessy and was towing the broken boat. The hub of the propeller had spun out because of fishing line around it. The guests thought they had such a big fish on their line and the whole time it was just the line wrapping around the prop. Casey changed the propeller and the boat was good again. So much less hassle than what was in my imagination. But from now on, both Casey and Steve will not both be away from the docks, unreachable, at the same time.

The vacuum packer stopped working altogether. Casey worked most of the day trying to figure out what was wrong. He talked to the man on-call for the company who happened to be driving down the freeway into New York City. Then Casey took photos of the machine and e-mailed them to him. The end diagnosis: the machine was toast. First thing Monday morning I called the company in Vancouver, and they put a loaner machine on that day's flight to the lodge. There were only a few fish that didn't get vacuum packed but they were flash frozen in plastic bags. They would still be an amazing product to take home since it's the flash freezing not the bag that makes a superior frozen fish fillet.

We had a group of people arrive to film an episode of TV's *Get Out! With Shelley & Courtney* about fishing at Rivers Lodge. It was exciting to have them here, but Casey was run off his feet tending to all their needs over and above everything he was already doing. They got some excellent shots of our guests catching fish and of Casey telling tall tales, so I think the episode will be a winner.

Our waitress suddenly quit with six dinners still to look after. Well, six lunches and six dinners for our last two groups of salmon-fishing guests. She had no real reason, other than I think she probably knew, before she even started to work for us, that she was going to leave early to have the long weekend in town. I don't understand some people. Jessy stepped in and added waitressing to her dock-manager duties, and of course she did a great job.

After our last group left, we spent a couple of days working feverishly with several of the crew who would also leave shortly, to go back to school or to their regular jobs. Jessy headed to town very much alone, for her first year of university. Only Casey, Jimmy and Bunny, our beloved breakfast cook, and I were left to look after the river-fishing guests who came in for the September fishing up the Chuckwalla River at the head of the inlet. Ah, this is what the creel report is for—guiding freshwater fishermen.

The guests took turns fishing in the river with Casey—since he could only take three at a time—and fishing on the ocean out where we usually fish. Casey was again run off his feet because he was up early with the guests, then running them up rivers all day, cleaning fish and gassing boats at night and sorting out fishing tackle and repairing fishing rods. On top of all that, the freight boat came in at 2 AM, and Casey spent two hours dealing with it. He was enjoying the river-running though and took lots of beautiful pictures to share with me.

Bunny made breakfast and cleaned the guests' rooms, then started closing down the rooms that were empty. Between us, we made lunch and washed all the rain gear and the tons of laundry left from stripping all the extra beds. I made dinner, paid the bills, filled out the forms for the fishing licences and derby tickets for our hatchery and collected and packed my office files, my pantry goods and my own gear and put heaps of belongings away.

Bunny and I went to the island to pick flowers for the table. We stood admiring the beautiful lodge from this perspective across the bay. She turned to me and asked, "Where would you even start to build something like this?" *Where indeed*, I was thinking. One day I'll tell you the story.

Jimmy has been washing fishing tackle and putting it away for the winter. Walking, walking and walking because, of course, all the storage rooms are so far apart. He also helped when Casey came back and helped when the ocean fishers came back in. One day he tried to take lunch out to the guests who were fishing on the ocean but was freaked out by the huge waves near Fitz Hugh. He came back to the lodge, so I hopped in the boat and delivered the lunch.

June's family flew in on the flight that took the last guests and Bunny out. The lodge was one of their favourite places to be, and we have had a lot of fun together here over the years. We had a little ceremony and sprinkled some of June's ashes on my garden island. They spent most of the time out fishing, but one afternoon Casey drove them all to the store for provisions. It was the first time I had been completely alone in four months, and I stood outside the lodge and screamed and screamed at the world and the injustice of life. Then, with no one there to hear me, I cried and cried and sobbed and howled. It had been locked up inside me for far too long, and once I let it go I had trouble reeling it back in. Then I finished packing up twelve boxes of office work, my clothes and gear that Jessy had left behind. I drove the boxes over to our airplane float to wait for the next freight boat.

There was still so much to do to finish closing down the lodge. Casey worked on the fridges, freezers and plumbing, while Jimmy and I washed and dried everything that was left to put away, clean and dry. Jimmy had been sitting or sleeping a lot over the summer, and was a little disconcerted by the work that we suddenly had him doing. He started calling me Boss Ratchets, after the head nurse in *One Flew Over the Cuckoo's Nest*.

I am so full of wonder that we made it through a whole summer without you here, but I do believe that you were with us in a different way. You were helping where you could, and that's why we were able to muddle along with no major catastrophes. Thank you to our friends and family who pushed and pulled and held on to us throughout that summer.

But most of all, thank you for sticking with us when we needed you so badly.

Bottomless love and thanks Dear,

Pat

No Break for Me

Dear George:

Casey, Jimmy and I drove *Sportspage* to West Vancouver past all the familiar bad-weather landmarks: Grief Bay, Cape Caution and the Storm Islands. We made it in record time and shuffled up the dock to the street like our heads were stuffed with cotton batting. Cars zoomed past in all directions at once while we stood transfixed. I felt like I had just returned from the moon.

I was anxious to meet with friends for coffee. On my way there, I stopped at the doctor to see why I was having trouble swallowing. Did I now have esophageal cancer? She assured me that I had simply cramped the muscles in my throat, in an effort to stave off my heartache. There was a lump down there that I couldn't get past. Two blocks from the doctor's, I pulled to the side of the road and cried for twenty minutes while the cramp eased a little. I mopped my face and then continued on to meet my friends. Best decision. And I can tell you, there is nothing more important to me than seeing my family and friends. I will drop everything to meet with them.

The freight arrived in town not long after, and I started unpacking office work and dove right in to get myself organized. I had always taken a break when we got back from the lodge and would visit with my sisters or just relax while you continued with correspondence, but now I'm doing it all. I'm not as good at contacting guests as you have been. I set up a letter and had price lists printed and started sending out the letter and brochure to stir up more interest in bookings for next year.

I lost quite a bit of money over the next several years because you always wanted the price lists printed in Canadian dollars for Canadians and US dollars for the US customers. The US dollar has fluctuated a lot lately, and I didn't trust what was happening with it. I finally decided that they would just have to learn what our dollar is worth and eventually only printed our prices in Canadian dollars. We are in Canada after all.

I took your place on the DFO's Sport Fishing Advisory Board. You always believed that we had to stay involved with the politics of West

Coast fishing so we wouldn't be blindsided again by sudden regulation changes. The ban on chinook fishing in 1996 had protected fifty-seven female chinook on the west coast of Vancouver Island and cost the sport-fishing industry 130 million dollars. There were better ways of protecting the salmon for the future of the industry.

I have had several groups get in touch with me to see if I want to sell the lodge. Beyond the fact that I can't think about that now, I also don't want to make a decision like this so soon. It's Casey and Jessy's favourite place in the whole world. I would have to think long and hard about selling. And I don't want people to think that they can offer me peanuts just because it will be a huge job to carry on without you. So I told them all that, no, I wasn't selling right now but might think about it tomorrow.

I joined a singing group in North Vancouver with my friends. The power of music and singing has a healing effect on my soul, and it also gave me a focus beyond the lodge and how sad I was. Singing made me breathe better, too, and I found myself standing up straighter to facilitate my breath. The camaraderie of the group felt like a warm blanket wrapped around my shoulders.

I love you, Dear,

Pat

A Big Break for Me

Dear George:

Our dearest chef Marc moved back to Quebec after cooking for us for five years, so the following year I interviewed and hired a lovely local fellow. He was with us for two years before he decided that he had to work full-time in town. Many of our staff continued to work with us over the next several years.

I sometimes take guests out for tours in the afternoon. The country is so beautiful and not just where the trophy fish are. When the tide is almost halfway to low, I show our new guests that, when the water is very still, you can see faces where the reflection of the water meets the shore. I tell them about the totem pole–like images, just like you would. I tell them they have to turn sideways to see the monkeys with big noses, scary masks, and—what do you know—someone I used to know. We wait for the bubbles to subside from the small school of fish that are trying to get away from a bigger fish, and lots of pictures are taken. We have some of these images hanging in our guestrooms. I don't drive through the narrow channels fast like you did though. I do what I can.

That summer, I turned over in my sleep and my shoulder dislocated. Yes, it had happened before but never in the busy summer with guests at the lodge that I had to take care of. We tried everything to pop it back in. I had put it back in place twice before, once in the middle of the night and once as

When the water is very still, you can see "faces" where the reflection of the water meets the shore. When turned vertical they resemble totem poles. We instructed many guests over the years to look for this when the water was flat and calm.

I was sliding swiftly down Whistler Mountain in a slippery onesie. But nothing worked this time. Too bad I didn't have a stash of Ativan that I could pop to help relax the muscles. I ended up flying to Port Hardy the next day to get it fixed. At that point, they had to give me enough drugs to knock out a horse to get my muscles to relax enough so that they could get my shoulder back into place. I spent the last week or so of the summer with my arm in a sling, feeling glad I wasn't cooking this year.

One of the dock crew that summer was a little off. Thinking back to my interview with him, I remember that he was wearing a cross on a chain around his neck, and he mentioned his family in such a kind way. I had called one reference, who said he was a good worker, so I hired him. And we were very sorry I did. He scared the crew when I wasn't around, and was caught throwing apples trying to hit our beloved great blue herons. I had already warned him once and then given him written notice to change his attitude. Any time he was in the tackle shop and saw me walking toward it, the crew said that he would continuously stab the wooden countertop with a hunting knife with a vengeful look on his face. No one wanted to work near him. I had just been warned about him again, when I walked outside and heard him yelling and swearing at Jessy in front of the lodge and in front of several guests. I caught up to him on the back walkway and told him to pack his bags. There was a plane in the area heading back to Port Hardy and he was gone from the lodge in less than an hour. We all breathed a sigh of relief.

You know that for me, the chef has always been the toughest staff member to hire. Chefs need to have a lot of experience, be creative, not mind living in the wilderness and be able to live away from home for three months. A very tall order for an older, responsible and skilled person.

We had started preparations for the upcoming 2006 fishing season. I hired a chef who had run his own restaurant and had lots of experience in both cooking and living away from large cities. Partway through the summer, we brought his wife up to stay with him for a week, and I cooked several meals so he could have time off while she was there. After

Casey bringing in supplies from the freight boat. The freight boats over the years were never able to make deliveries right at the lodge. We met the freight boats in Darby Channel or at our float outside the bay. Morning, noon and middle of the night, Casey was always ready to spring into action at the lodge. People all over the inlet called on Casey in an emergency.

she left, he seemed to deflate. He tried to take shortcuts with meals, but I was always watchful and called him on a few things. The final straw for him was when I told him that frozen peas were not an appropriate vegetable on our guests' dinner plates. He slammed a tea towel into the counter and stalked off.

I headed back to the house where I had to step over the doggy gate that I had put up to keep my new puppy on the porch. Minutes later I headed out the door and step-tripped over the gate and went flying down the front steps, landing with my left arm twisted under my side. I was filled with immediate, exquisite pain as my wrist bones blew apart into many pieces. Jessy came running with a frozen bag of peas—ha ha, much better use for them—and Casey leaped into action with a board and bandaged my arm into a cast.

As Casey was cautiously wrapping my arm, the hot-headed chef arrived at my door, walked in and, while he watched the casting process, with me keeled over barely able to breathe through the pain, told me that he was leaving. That meant he was leaving me with a broken wing to cook for twenty-four guests and twelve staff for three more weeks. The next group of twenty-four people were arriving from South Africa, Chile, Costa Rica and Australia in about four hours.

Both kids tried to talk me into flying to Port Hardy and going to the hospital to have a real cast put on. But I couldn't do that—not yet. I had to say goodbye to the group that was leaving that day and greet the new group. I had to make sure the kitchen was organized. I had to call the accountant to have them calculate the amount to pay the pathetic cook who was leaving. Mr. Chef, I still wonder what you told your wife!

I organized the kitchen and flew to the hospital the next day. The X-ray showed pieces of shattered wrist, no surprise there. The doctor wrapped my arm in a real cast that was not as comfortable as the one Casey had put on. I flew back to the lodge and took over the kitchen again.

While I was gone, Jessy added chef duties to her dock-managing duties. She hadn't left the kitchen for hours—I get that!—when Bunny walked in and shouted, "Oh God! What's burning!" The crew's dinner roast was an absolutely blackened lump of coal that had been welded to the pan. The whole shrivelled mess had to be tossed. Shortly after that, Jessy accidentally added baking soda instead of cornstarch to her meticulously sliced strawberry compote, and the whole pot of stewing gorgeous strawberries exploded like Mount Vesuvius all over the stove, walls and floor. After a major cleanup, and more help from Bunny, Jessy finally got dinner organized again.

One of the dock crew who had kitchen experience helped me a lot, and the crew always passed the hall at the end of the kitchen to see if I—because of my broken arm—needed anything heavy moved. A guest brought me the milt (you know, the sperm-filled reproductive gland that has a creamy texture) from a male salmon that he had caught that morning. He thought the other guests would love having a taste of it if it were lightly fried in butter. I tried to convince him that I was pretty sure no one else would want any, but I agreed to quickly sauté it as an added "treat" for lunch. He happily passed the plate around the tables and was awfully disappointed when the plate came back to him with not one piece taken. Aside from that failure, we managed to finish the season with the same wonderful four-course dinners that Rivers Lodge built its reputation on.

That fall I headed to France to meet up with friends. We drove to all the markets, bought gorgeous linens, ate delicious French food, drank lots of wine and saw amazing little towns and hillsides covered in vines, and little tractors pulling wagons full of grapes. While she was back at home, our darling Jessy was in over her head in a relationship with an older man who, I understand now, could see her vulnerability and took advantage. I felt that it was an emergency to get home to try to avert a disaster. A friend of the family offered to kneecap him. I was so very close to agreeing. There was a lot of tension at home, and we spent an excruciatingly bad Christmas season with none of our usual happy celebrations, but thankfully, our family won out in the end, and Jessy came back to her senses and back to us.

I feel like I'm wearing out, but I love you, Darling,

Pat

Edgy Stock Market, Edgy Crew

Dear George:

I heard from three different groups of our guests that the new American resort owner near us is trying to undercut our success by telling people at sport shows in the US that Rivers Lodge is going bankrupt and so not to book with us. This, after Casey endlessly helped them with bits and parts, propane tanks and expertise as they were trying to pull a fishing resort together. It was like a knife in the back. Then another resort sent a fast boat around where other lodge guests were fishing, with a huge sign on the side of the boat saying that they will send fishermen a free photo of their fish that they just caught. A blatantly underhanded way of collecting everyone's address for their own contact list. Oh George, you would not be happy about the way the inlet feels these days.

Thanks to the instability of the 2007 stock market, some large companies cancelled their fishing trips. Once again, as in the mid eighties, the perception of the owners and top clients of a company going on an expensive fishing trip is not what people want to see, when the people who work for these guys are losing their jobs and losing their homes. There are still people with enough money to come fishing though, and for some people—the people whose eyes glow when they talk fishing stories—it would be the last thing they would give up.

I hired a young woman to work at the lodge who had sent her excellent resumé from where she lived in Halifax. She wanted to move to the West Coast. She had studied in Europe for several years and now was fluent in German and Spanish, which would be a great asset because some of our large groups were from Germany and South America. Even without meeting her in person, I thought she would be a great addition to our team that summer.

When she arrived at the lodge, the raven-haired beauty immediately caught Casey's eye. The two of them soon became inseparable. We had always shied away from having couples at the lodge but Casey assured me that everything would be fine. Things weren't fine, though—the woman became a major problem. She spread vicious rumours about the kitchen crew and created angst amongst the dock crew, then would head into the kitchen and spread vicious rumours about the dock crew and create angst among the kitchen crew. Before long they were all looking over their shoulders—no one trusted anyone. Jessy tried her utmost to keep the atmosphere from spiralling out of control, but it was exhausting her. We had never had this problem before. This young woman ordered the other crew around, wasn't doing her own work and went swanning out to climb in the boat whenever Casey did the bait run. This broke a firm rule that we always followed: *no extra people riding along on a bait run*, as it should only be about business and helping our guests.

The turning point came one night, as I sat working at my computer. This person came in and started haranguing me. I had given bonuses to a few of the crew for going above and beyond and, as she noted, she hadn't received one. I had embarrassed her. She, who had barely lifted a finger unless it was to stab someone in the back. *Blah, blah, blah, her life is so hard*, she yelled. *No one understands her. No one likes her.* Casey came in and listened for ten whole excruciating minutes. Then they both left, and I could hear heavy objects crashing against the walls next door like there was a moose trying to get out. I sat stunned. What was that? Casey came back into the house and told me that he and this young woman were going to leave the lodge the next day.

Now this has been no easy thing, George, running the lodge after you died. I knew that the lodge was Casey and Jessy's favourite place in the world to be. I struggled these past five years, running the lodge to keep the kids happy. This was your thing and their thing. Many times I had checked in with them both to make sure they still wanted to manage the lodge. I asked that they let me know, with lots of time, if they ever wanted to move on to a different career. As I sat there hearing the threat, my breath caught, my heart seized and I knew that I would sell the lodge.

For the time being though, Casey didn't leave, so I kept a low profile and stayed away from the woman, until she finally left with the rest of the crew in early September. I used Jessy as a go-between with Casey to keep things running smoothly, and we crawled and clawed our way to the end of the season.

We finished winterizing everything and waved goodbye to the last of the crew as they climbed on a Goose and headed to town. Just Casey, Jessy and I stayed on to tidy up any loose ends, and for some tentative family time as we all tiptoed around the girlfriend issue. One night Jessy and I were waiting for Casey to come over and watch a movie with us, when suddenly there was a glass-shattering, high-pitched shriek that lifted me off the couch. I flew across the room for the door. At the same time as the shriek, the door slammed on Casey's cabin. As I raced around the house, I had visions of a cougar on Casey's back and prepared myself to have to haul it off with hand-to-claw combat. What else could make that sound? Casey, however, was standing outside his cabin staring awestruck toward the main bay fifty feet from his dock. A humpback whale had come right up out of the water with its mouth wide open, scooping up the pilchards that were swarming in the bay in the hundreds of thousands. That was the sound of the humpback whale shrieking out of the water. He was telegraphing his friends that tonight's banquet had started. It was unusual to see so many pilchards in Rivers Inlet, and I wondered if their large numbers helped feed all the humpback whales that we had been seeing in recent years. It was the first time we had ever seen a humpback whale in our main bay.

The next morning I woke up to the sound of water falling all around. I had never heard such a sound coming from the front of our house, so I crept near a window to see what was happening. I had a vision of the humpback whale being stuck in the bay by the falling tide, and I was afraid that it might come crashing down on top of the house in its panic. Seems that my imagination is often working overtime. What I saw was sudden rushes of pilchards rising together, a foot out of the water then pouring back in. Thousands upon thousands of them lifting out of the water in an effort to get away from the eight hungry seals that were feasting on them. The constant action sounded like a waterfall. The poor pilchards didn't have a chance. I was starting to get an inkling of how that feels.

I made a pot of coffee, poured it into a thermos and carried it on a tray with three cups to sit undercover and out of the rain in front of the lodge. Shortly, Casey arrived. Then Jessy arrived, and we sat drinking our steaming coffee and quietly watched the mesmerizing feeding frenzy. I felt our hearts beat as one and knew that we would win our Casey back into the family.

The next morning the caretakers arrived, Casey left for Vancouver in *Sportspage*, and a few hours later, Jessy and I flew to town.

I have made a decision, but I still love you,

Pat

Living Every Man's Dream

Dear George:

Jess and I pulled together through another winter and both worked toward organizing the lodge for another fishing season. The paperwork is pretty well sorted out finally, and I have interviewed quite a few potential chefs but have not found one that I believe will be a good fit. I finally decided that I would do the cooking this summer, which seemed easier to me than finding the appropriate chef with the appropriate attitude. I re-hired a breakfast cook/baker who had worked for us for five years, thirty years ago. She was a wonderful girl, and even though I hadn't seen her in the past twenty-five years, I was looking forward to working with her again.

Here I am, continuing to live "every man's dream." The funny part about that is that it had never really been my dream. I was enjoying the country, the adventures and the perks of the lodge, but as the man said to you one day, "you are living every man's dream," he was really only talking to you. And this summer was more about living through my nightmares than living my dreams.

I told Casey that I will not hire his girlfriend again. I said that she could come for a visit, but I would not hire her. No, never hire her again. A few people advised me to cast Casey out of our family. This I would *never* do. No matter what happened, I would deal with it and welcome him home with all my heart.

Jess and I flew into the lodge around the end of June. Normally you, or in the past many years, Casey, would fly into the lodge first. You would open up our house and un-winterize it by getting the freshwater pipes connected, the saltwater pump going for the flush toilet and propane connected for hot water and the little two-burner stove. The caretakers were still here, ready to leave for their summer adventures, and our long-time friend Dave Stafford had arrived a few days ahead of us and had started the water lines and propane. He still loves being at the lodge and helping out at the beginning of each summer. Casey is conspicuous by his absence. He only shows up sporadically.

It's so peaceful at the lodge when we first arrive. The first cup of coffee is always a pleasant surprise. With the water coming off the hill, filtering through cedar peat, it makes such delicious coffee, tea, rice and porridge. It's the same thing that colours a good glass of scotch. So many people have asked for my recipe for my plain old oatmeal porridge, but there's no trick to it, it's just the extra flavour in the water that makes it taste so good.

Jess, Dave, the caretakers and I all sat and drank coffee for most of the afternoon, comparing stories about the winter at the lodge and winter in town. Then I did a walkabout and checked how everything had managed to make it through a rather cold and snowy winter. Just like in town, a lot of my plants suffered from the extreme cold and heavy snow load. The bay leaf trees and a few other herbs were severely frostbitten. Some of the herbs were only just starting to poke fresh green leaves out of the soil in the wooden plant boxes. I'll send for more herb plants.

I had the grocery orders and liquor orders organized. I had the staff hired and airplanes lined up and had shipped the office boxes and plants to the lodge. Jess and I had timed our arrival to be there shortly after the freight boat had arrived so we could handle the supplies. After our coffee party, we got to work. The new walk-in freezer that I had built behind the kitchen is a godsend. The fishing has been so good in the past few years that there was barely enough room left for my freezer goods in our other big freezer. Now it's so much easier to organize the kitchen food and any baking that can be done ahead of time.

It's a good thing too, because the baker didn't show up on the flight today. I finally tracked down her sister and hear that my breakfast cook is now a drug addict and won't be making it up to work any time soon. Now I am baking bread as well as making breakfast, lunch and dinner and

Jessy and Casey in the lodge kitchen having fun with guests, who dressed them up for the picture.

morning snacks and afternoon snacks for the guests in the boats. I know I have said this before, but it is a little overwhelming! I have very little time to breathe between baking, cooking, wrapping, chopping, sautéing, ordering, paying, billing, checking and putting away. It's pretty hard to find another breakfast cook from here. How can I trust a letter or even a telephone interview? But I do. The new breakfast cook I hire is related to someone in the inlet and has apparently even been to the inlet, so I think this person will be all right with the wilderness. Not so much. She worked here for less than two weeks and decided to leave, so I'm back on my head. My saving grace has been my ability, learned through necessity, to sleep for ten minutes sitting up in the blue chair in the living room. I wake refreshed and ready to go again.

I had a visit from a little man who arrived in a Fishery boat. He said he was an inspector for Environment Canada. He threatened me with a $200,000-per-day fine if I didn't put in a septic system. I'm sure the gun on his hip made him feel very important. I'm also sure he wanted to make a name for himself, because I understand he threatened all the small lodges in Rivers Inlet without so much as testing the water. While cities like Victoria were dumping between 82 million and 129 million litres of sewage a day, this little man came after me for several hundred pounds per year—which is less than the amount that the sea lions poop in a twenty-four-hour period on Stevens Rocks just outside of our bay. Our winter caretakers have video of eighty to ninety, even a hundred sea lions on Stevens Rocks.

Researching and letter writing consumes a lot of my energy these days. Okay, I'll give you the end result here and now. I eventually found a fantastic, not-too-expensive composting toilet that flushes into a holding container at the back of each building that could be retrofit into our lodge and guestrooms. Afterward, the little man was moved away from his post and away from dealing with the public, which was not his strong suit. But by now, some of the lodges had spent between $250,000 and $500,000 trying to comply with equipment that would never work in the long run because of the short fishing season. The septic systems that were available rely on continuity for the bacteria to work their magic but by the time the bacteria could start to work, the lodges would be closed for the season leaving a tank full of effluent. Ours, meanwhile, turns out a nice little package of compost material.

Casey was here some of the time and helped with the heavy equipment, machinery, plumbing and boats. There was no girlfriend to cause problems "at the lodge," but I still felt her heavy presence. He did arrive later than usual and left during the busiest time, but he was here for the rest of the summer. Just as it was for you, Rivers Inlet is in his blood, something that I am banking on to bring him back into the fold.

One night while our guests were enjoying dessert, I walked around the tables chatting with our satiated and now sleepy diners. There was a gentle, salty sweet breeze wafting in the open front doors when suddenly a bat flew in, followed by the cat hot on its trail. The bat was frantically zipping this way and that, just barely missing the heads of people who were shocked into stillness while the cat dove across tables and flipped through the air in a heroic effort to catch its favourite snack. I ran and grabbed a tea towel, darted up the stairs to the mezzanine and opened all the windows there, then stood ready to flap the towel to help send the traumatized bat back out into the night sky. Jessy saw the commotion and quickly grabbed a little herring net and ran into the lodge. Alexander, one of our Chilean guests, who happened to be a world-class lacrosse player, shouted to Jess to throw the net to him. He stood up at the table and, on the bat's second pass over his head, scooped the frantic creature into the net, gave a professional twist of his wrist to close the top and elegantly handed it over to Jessy who then let the poor wee thing go outside. Our guests, now very much wide awake, stayed up a little longer to laugh about the incident over a nightcap.

We had a man book into the lodge to stay and fish on his own. He went out fishing by himself in the mornings and again in the afternoons and evenings. One afternoon, there was a cryptic call on the radio from the fellow. He said, "I've had a bit of an accident."

Bit of an accident? My ass! He had driven full speed onto the shore, wedging the front of the boat fifteen feet up on the rocks, completely destroying the boat in the process. The heavy fibreglass hull was smashed and mangled from the impact, with the rocky shore breaking through and shoving the passenger seat into the air. He was lucky he wasn't dead. There was a long sweeper that had smashed through the windshield and jammed itself into the driver's seat. When questioned about what on earth he was doing to ram into the shore so dramatically, he said, "I was doing some little task." *Some little task* that we never did figure out. He certainly wasn't in the driver's seat. It was some little task to completely rebuild the boat in town that winter. Months of repair, rebuilding the whole hull, fibreglassing the entire shell, replacing the hardware, the windshield and the smashed seats as well as the engine leg and smashed housing. Still not worth the cost of insurance for our boats all these years.

One of the engines wasn't working right, and I heard that there was a mechanic living temporarily in the inlet. I was finally able to track him down and he agreed to come to the lodge to work on the boat. He was a very old but sprightly little fellow with a long craggy face and wild untamed masses of yellow hair that stuck out as if he'd been electrified! His clothes were ragged and threadbare, and his shoes were grimy and worn with a hole for his big toe to poke out of. He had a grubby unkempt beard that hung down to his chest and was stained from a century of smoking. All in all, he had the appearance of a savage Icelandic troll, but he was a kind man and a very good mechanic. Unfortunately for Jess, he was also the embodiment of her recurring nightmare about "wild and terrifying people who come sneaking down from the back hills in the dark." She nearly fainted when she saw him on the back walkway and had nightmares again for a week after he left. Her wild imagination often got the better of her too.

Mornings for me were the worst. After four hours of sleep I would head into the kitchen to start filling coffee thermoses. One morning I heard the freight boat calling us to say that they would be at the lodge in thirty minutes with freight and propane. Propane! We needed lots of propane and the thousand-pound tank was tied to the end guest cabin in the corner of the bay. I got the generator going so I had some light to see by outside, then woke one of the dock crew and told him to turn the valve on the big tank so he could switch to the three-hundred-pound tank while the big one was out being filled. I rushed back and jumped into the work skiff. Oh, did I mention that Casey had gone to town?

I got the engine going, and headed into the back of the bay to start working the propane float out from between logs and floats. By now, Jessy and a member of the dock crew had arrived and were helping push on the floats with pike poles. It was pouring rain and pitch black, and it was an emergency to get the tank out. And of course the float was caught underwater on a log. It took my years of boating expertise to manoeuvre in and out and in and out inch by inch. When I finally had it disentangled from everything, I hooked the line on the towing post and pulled it out to the front of the lodge, stepped off the work skiff onto the dock, and left it for one of the crew to easily tow the rest of the way out to the barge.

Quite a few guests were up and about by now, so I quickly headed into the kitchen to continue breakfast prep, but all the pilot lights were out on the propane stove, including both ovens. I muttered, "He didn't switch the valve," as I ran back to turn on the three-hundred-pound tank, and raced back to light the pilots. So there I was, lying on the kitchen floor and reaching in at a ridiculously awkward angle before I could push the red button down and hold it for several seconds while I got a propane torch going and lit the flame. I know, you have been there many times, but I haven't. Burners going, ovens going, I grabbed a serving thermos of coffee and went out to greet the guests. I was dripping with great droplets of rain as I went. Meanwhile, Jessy walked around the guest cabins and re-lit the pilot lights in the hot-water tanks that had also gone out.

I was working so fast and furiously that one night I made five courses for dinner instead of four. I saw the waitress read the menu just before dinner was to be served. The tables were already set, but she ran into the kitchen, saw what I had bubbling away on the stove and started to collect soup spoons. I also had the menu in front of where I work and wondered what the fuss was about. "I didn't know there was going to be soup too!" she said. I started to laugh so hard that I had to rush to the hall away from where the guests could see me. The waitress joined me and we had five hysterical minutes of uncontrollable, almost-silent snickering. Tears were pouring down my cheeks. Jessy walked in the back door and stared quizzically at me, but I could not form words to explain what was going on while I leaned on the wall for support, soup dripping from the ladle still clutched in my hand.

Shortly after that, I made one too many trays of boat-snack treats. As you know, George, when I'm cooking, I spend a lot of time counting. Counting people, counting eggs, counting cookies, counting slices, counting steaks. I miscounted again and made a huge batch of chocolate-crisp bars—two massively gigantic trays that had no real purpose. I still can't think about those bars without laughter gurgling up my throat. We wouldn't need them, but there they were cooling on the baker's rack. I lost it every time I walked past the rack.

Love you,

Pat

First Annual Art Workshop Retreat

Dear George:
It's now the fall of 2009. Jessy has not only been working hard for the lodge this summer, she's also been studying to finish a couple of courses for her art history degree from UBC in the midst of all the fishing. She wrote her last two exams at Dawsons Landing with the postmaster

as invigilator in the middle of August. And now she is in her last few weeks of studying for her prerequisite math courses for going to the UBC nursing program.

Casey left for town after winterizing motors, equipment, fridges, freezers and plumbing, and Jessy and I stayed on our own for our First Annual Art Workshop Retreat. Aside from studying, Jessy has painted and rowed while I've read and written. Just to have the time and the space to spread out and paint to her heart's content has been very special. This extra time at the lodge has provided very real "stolen moments" for us both. We've also sat in the sun, watched movies at night, eaten whatever we wanted, whenever we wanted and then blissfully started it all over again the next day. It had been such a crazy busy summer that we've really needed this time to unwind.

It has been one week since Casey left us on our own. We had such a stormy day yesterday, with the wind blowing the rain sideways and pounding at the windows, and there were waves rushing across the normally flat calm bay. The floats shifted and bumped as the wind swirled around. We both stayed inside most of the day, only going out when it was necessary to start the generator or collect firewood. We are running

Jessy, me and Casey.

the generator about eight hours a day for the fridges and freezers and cozy movies at night. What oil does the generator take? Why didn't you write it on the generator? Can I add oil? Is there anything I should be careful about, like what happens if I add too much oil? Does the small generator use different oil than the big generator? What's in the oil can outside of the generator shed and why is it sitting there? Luckily, I find out that Jessy knows how to change the oil. It would be so easy to run the generator all day but we both love the quiet with no engine thumping away in the background. The winter caretakers will be here in about ten days.

We haven't had groceries delivered since the charter came to pick up our last guests twenty days ago, but I've had a lot of experience after all these years of managing produce over a long period of time. We even have lettuce that is still quite fresh. Iceberg lettuce lasts the longest. We've had a few people drop by for a visit, and have handed out containers of yogurt and cartons of eggs, as well as a dozen or so of the fern plants that grace the high shelf in the lodge living room all summer.

Jessy went to fill the kettle for tea and there was no water coming out of the tap. I checked the valves everywhere and found that the one at the front of the finger float, coming from the big white tank up the hill, had been knocked open. It drained the tank when the floats were bumping into each other. Now the pipe would have an airlock in it, and it would be tough to get the water moving through it again. I managed to figure out which valves to turn to get the water over to the house from the lower green tank instead. While I was wrangling hoses and valves to hook on to the lower green tank, Jessy walked around the floats to check on the stiff legs. She found that the one that connected one end of the buildings to shore had broken free. The stiff leg and the perpendicular connector log had swung wildly in the night and had left our floats to fend for themselves. No wonder there was so much bumping in the night and this would be why the freshwater valve had been nudged open.

Jess went to the shop, put on a pair of your gigantic old cork boots, collected a pike pole, a couple of heavy staples and a sledgehammer, and then she clumped around in the boots to scrounge up an extra boom chain. She then went out onto the back walkway closest to the miscreant stiff leg and hauled it into place with the pike pole. By now, it had begun to rain so hard that the huge drops ricocheted noisily off the water at least a foot back toward where they had come from. Drenched but determined, Jessy tied a buoyant rope with a small loop in it to one end of the chain, dropped it down through the hole in the end of the stiff-leg log and then caught the loop underwater with the pike pole, dragged it under the hole in a stationary float log, then hauled the chain up inch by inch and around the stiff-leg log in order to fasten it with the staples and many swings of the heavy sledgehammer. The slack in the chain allowed the stiff leg to have a bit of give for tide changes, while remaining very much locked in place. She appeared in the house midway through the job, dripping and shivering with cold, to fetch a life jacket. The old cork boots were digging in and providing trustworthy grip, but the damn boots were so big and heavy on her feet that she kept toppling out of them and nearly ended up in the frigid water several times.

Why is there blank flagging tape on equipment and water lines, valves and hoses? What does the flagging tape mean? Write on it! And

Jessy fixing one of the the stiff legs after the big storm. "I am woman, hear me roar!" I'm so proud of my chip-off-the-old-block daughter.

now, neither of the toilets work, and I can't figure out how to get water to them. There's probably an airlock in that line too. Not the biggest problem though, we have lots of buckets for scooping sea water to flush the toilets.

Then three days later the propane tank for my room heater and hot-water heater at the back of the house ran out of fuel. No hot water in my bathroom sink, and even on the warm days, it was nice to have the other two pilot lights going to keep the dampness out of the back of the house. This means that the hundred-pound propane tank is empty. Why is there duct tape on one of the propane tanks by the workshop? Why doesn't anyone write notes?! We have extra tanks but I wouldn't be able to get a new tank into position to change them. I'll amend that to say: it would be a lot of trouble for me and Jessy to wrangle another tank from where the full ones are, down the back walkway, and then across the foot and a half of water to the little platform behind the back of the house. Not impossible, but a lot of trouble. This is not the biggest problem either, since we could have used the hot water in the kitchen sink to wash our hands.

Then the next day, the kitchen sink clogged for the first time in thirty-five years. I tried using a plumbing snake outside the house at the outlet pipe, but the coil wasn't long enough. I had pictured a pilchard wriggling its way up the pipe because the bay is full of them, and the outlet from the sink is just slightly underwater. We had to take the pipes apart under the sink and jam the snake down the pipe about ten feet. We finally broke through whatever it was that stopped the drain, and then I flushed it out with two kettles of boiling water.

But the biggest problem was when the last of the water in the green tank stopped running in the taps! I went to the woodshed and brought a case of bottled water back to the house to make coffee in the morning. We had a leisurely breakfast with tea, coffee and cinnamon buns, and finally worked up the enthusiasm to find out why the water in the green tank ran out. Jessy rowed the little boat to shore where the tank is and climbed up beside the creek that was tumbling happily down the rocks. The water was just dribbling into the green tank, so she climbed a little farther to the natural pond that collects our water. The pipe coming out of the pond was clogged, so very little water was coming out of it.

She unclogged the pipe, and right away there was a steady stream of water going into the green tank. Next, we undid the filter on the water line behind the house. There was lots of water coming out of the hose at that point. Jessy did that one up and we undid the filter on the line going into the kitchen. Lots of water coming out there as well. All the taps were open in the house but the only tap that water was coming out of was in the bathtub. No water in the bathroom sinks, and no water in the kitchen tap. Yes, this is the biggest problem. It's really hard to get along without fresh water running into the house. While we were trying to sort this out, it suddenly started raining hard and I ran and quickly put containers under the eaves to catch as much rainwater as I could.

We tried hooking up a hose to the valve behind the kitchen stove and sucking on it to pull the airlock through. You used an air pump somehow, but I couldn't even begin to figure out where it might be. Jessy sat on the bottom step of the porch and just about turned her face inside out trying so hard to pull the airlock out. Then I got a ladder and climbed up with a jug of water and poured it into the hose. Maybe if we backfilled the hose, then dropped it down low it would draw the water and airlock out at the same time. Nope, that didn't work either. And of course I was working under the eaves, up the ladder as far as the hose would reach, with the water running off the roof in sheets. We decided to take a break at that point and have lunch. We would try to get rid of the airlock at around 10 PM when it was low tide. There might be a better chance with better gravity behind the water flow.

As I was writing that last little bit, I could hear water start burbling into the kitchen sink. It's a start, and maybe when the tide goes out for four more hours there will be more than a trickle.

Two hours before low tide, water and air started spitting and burping out of the kitchen tap. Jessy and I cheered it on and, over the next couple of minutes, all of the air blew itself out of the line and water started pouring out! We are back in business.

We had Casey's kitten with us. Kitty was too young to stay at the lodge over the winter, even with caretakers. She needed to be looked after. She and my dog ran circles around each other, playing all day long. The kitten would come back to town with us.

Somewhere along the line the kitten had knocked one of the wires off one of the six-volt batteries that were hooked up together to make the twelve volts needed to make Casey's inverter work. The inverter works when the generator is off so I can then use small 120-volt electrical appliances, or in this case, the internet and telephone or TV. One day, the internet wasn't working so we looked at the mass of wires going in all directions at once to modems, routers, batteries, phone jacks, power bars and a few other electrical bits that I don't know anything about. I noticed a wire disconnected from a battery terminal. I had no idea how long the wire had been disconnected but the battery hadn't been charging for a while to be completely out of power. The connection had been tenuous at best. It looked like a wad of green gum where there should have been metal, and because we had been using the inverter for days for the TV, DVD player, my computer and printer, and the phone, the power had drained out of the batteries. The kitten was very lucky that she didn't knock the open positive wire from one battery into the negative terminal on the other battery, which could have made for a quick and explosive exit from this world into the next.

I thought I might know how to fix it. I poked around in the mechanical shop to find tools to remove the messy end of the wire and could only find needle-nose pliers and some kind of cutting tool with weirdly shaped scissors. Then I looked around for the little part that gets pushed over the end of the bare copper wires, gets crimped on, then sits over the terminal and the butterfly nut gets tightened on top. There were dozens of these things that were too small, as I searched drawer after drawer, shelf after shelf in the office and various workshops until I finally found the one and only terminal connector in the entire lodge that would fit the bundle of copper. You would have gone straight to it!

I used the scissor thing and sort of cut and twisted the wire apart from the ruined end. Then I stripped the plastic wire coating back an inch from the end and rolled the copper wires as tight as I could to fit them into the little connector. I crimped the plastic part and wrapped the connection with electrician's tape. Then I lifted the connecting bar from the terminal on the positive side of the second battery and lowered the connector on, replaced the bar and screwed down the nut. There was a little life left in the batteries because there was a bit of a spark when I first attached the wire. But it didn't explode so I figured that I had done it properly.

We finally arrived back in town and were looking forward to the winter ski season. The 2010 Winter Olympics would be in Vancouver and Whistler in February. It was going to be so exciting. Then just before Christmas I got a call that Casey had been taken by ambulance to the hospital. He had fallen through a roof he was working on here in Vancouver, and had broken his back. He had moved into our garage just a few weeks before, right after—thank the Lord—permanently leaving his contentious and combative girlfriend behind. We moved him into the basement rec room so I could dance attendance on him, and he started on the long road to recovery. Workers Compensation was amazing with rehab help once the bones were healed enough.

Love, love, love,

Pat

I Give the Lodge Up to the Universe

Dear George:

While Casey was recuperating and not able to ski or work, he reconnected with a friend, Lindsay, whom he had competed with for the Whistler Ski Team, in ski races when they were younger. She was now the gold-medal-winning guide for visually impaired Paralympian Viviane Forest, racing down the mountain at seventy-five miles an hour while turning around at each curve or corner to make sure her skier was also making the turns. Watching the Paralympic downhill racing was some of the most exciting skiing I have ever watched. Casey was able to keep Lindsay and Viviane well nourished with homemade soups and lots of hot chocolate.

I cross-country skied every morning at Whistler and then in the afternoon I joined in on the Olympic fun in the village. One day when I was skiing, I stopped at Lost Lake, where there was an opening in the trees. The sky was a deep cobalt blue with a few pure white puffs of clouds. I became anchored to the spot. I flung my arms out wide and,

The lodge at night.

in that moment, gave the lodge up to the universe. I gave thanks for still being able to look after it, but suggested that it was time to sell and move on to my next adventure.

That night, I woke myself up with a huge guffaw of laughter, sat bolt upright and rejoiced in the freedom and lightness of being that I suddenly felt. The laughter bubbled up again and again, and I knew I had made the right decision.

Casey is with us all summer, from the time he was released from his intensive rehab to build up the muscles on his broken back. He is a joy to have around, plus he knows the equipment like the back of his hand—just like his dad. And once again, just like his dad, he jogs from one job to the next and is always ready with a smile. Jess and I are so blessed to have him back with us.

I told my brother Kenny about some of the trials and tribulations I have been going through for the past few years. He was really mad at me for not calling him and asking for help. He was self-employed in Vernon at the time, and summer wasn't his busy season. He is an awesome chef and has joined our team as the breakfast cook. His wife, Hope, has amazing organizational skills and is looking after the guestrooms. Of course Jessy is here full-time this summer. What a relief!

We did it again. It's the end of the summer of 2010. We had lots of happy fishermen, lots of beautiful fish in the freezer. Thank you for sticking around and making sure that we kept everyone safe and happy. Well, I guess the exception was that fellow and his two grandsons. They just weren't paying attention and ended up driving all the way to the head of the inlet. They didn't notice that they were still driving after three hours when they should have made it back to the lodge in twenty minutes. It happens. There were lots of other lodge owners and staff all over the inlet helping to look for them. I was coordinating the many searchers with a huge chart that I drew lines across when someone radioed that a bay had been checked. No one looked promptly at the head of the inlet because no one believed someone could make that mistake. Toward the head of the inlet, the hills turn into three-thousand-foot mountains, the channels narrow and the water becomes a milky fairy-tale green—you remember. Reason enough to turn around. They turned around only when they came to the head and could drive no farther. They were finally found when they ran out of gas after they turned back toward Dawsons Landing. They were holding on to a long branch that hung out over the water. Once they were found, Casey and Jessy rescued them and towed them back home by moonlight.

Near the end of the summer, I drove *Sportspage* to the airplane dock with eight men on board. I made a perfect two-point docking, casually stepped out and tied up both ends while all the men stood amazed. I wonder at all these people who still haven't figured out that I'm not just another pretty face!

Jess and I had our Second Annual Art Workshop Retreat, this time staying till just after Thanksgiving.

The caretakers are taking a little longer to arrive than we thought because they have had to wait out some bad weather. Casey did an oil change on the generator the day before he left, but we should only put about two hundred hours on it before it needs another oil change, and I have never done one. Something else to put on my "must learn how to"

Jessy and I during one of our annual art workshop retreats. We stayed on at the lodge after the fishing season to enjoy the solitude of our beautiful Rivers Inlet.

list. Also on that list: how to check the power level in a battery and how and where to add water to a battery. The list is getting longer every day. Once again, I'm glad that Jessy knows how to change the generator oil.

Love and hugs,

Pat

Cue the Grizzlies for a Fond Farewell

Dear George:

This ninth fishing season is going to be my last season owning and operating Rivers Lodge without you. I have made up my mind. This is it. I know that there are people out there who want to buy the lodge. We just need to connect. I have done my part. I have honoured your memory for as long as I am willing to. Now is the time for someone to come forward. Someone … anyone?!

Casey, Jessy, Kenny and Hope are part of the crew all summer. What a relief! It's so much more fun to have family here! And I can get more than four hours of sleep a night now. Things have been going so smoothly. Until ...

Judas has started to hijack my chartered planes. After the financial crash of 2008, it made sense for me to share some of the space on my charters with another lodge. We both benefited from the arrangement until ... we didn't. I had been chartering the same planes for years and suddenly found out that this fellow from the other lodge had insisted that, if there were ever an overage in weight for a plane load, the airline should carry his passengers and his luggage and his fish boxes *first*, before my passengers, luggage and fish boxes. It stinks and I felt another knife twist into my back, and right through to my heart with this one. Yes, it's time to leave the inlet.

One morning as I sat having tea with one of the crew, there was a blood-curdling scream, "*MOM!*" Again, I leaped off the couch and, like the roadrunner, felt my legs spinning around a hundred miles an hour. I zipped out the sliding door at the front of the lodge and turned to where the scream had come from. There were four grizzly bears in front of the end cabin! I could just see Jessy's head poking out of the second guest-house door. The four faces looked right at her with big yellow eyes, mere feet away. She yelled again, then quickly ducked back in and slammed the door. I grabbed my dog, who wanted to run toward the danger, and I threw her through the doors, slammed them shut, then ran off to get Casey, who was having a nap several buildings away. I was shrieking his name as I ran, so by the time I got to the cabin he knew something was terribly wrong. I hollered that there were grizzlies on the third guest-cabin float, then turned and ran back, grabbing a foghorn out of a paddleboat on my way and blasted it as I ran. I'll run toward danger for our kids anytime.

Casey, always so quick in an emergency, arrived at the lodge at the same time as I did. He was holding a rifle and two bear bangers. He shot the rifle in the air and waited. The mother didn't flinch. She was intent on pulling up the planks that were nailed down with nine-inch spikes. The very large three-year-old cubs snuffled around her. Casey shot the rifle again. Then he set off a bear banger. The huge *kaboom* made me want to run away! It was best to build a wall of noise between them and us.

Our guests were out fishing, so all I had to worry about was our kids and the crew.

The mama tossed one ten-foot plank aside and yanked another up and tossed that one too. Then she leaned down and grabbed a dead animal in her mouth—the remains of something like an otter or a young seal—then turned and marched off and around the end of the cabin with the cubs scrambling after her. They swam back to shore and we could hear them bashing around in the heavy bushes, snarling and growling as they tore their prized rotten carcass apart.

Jessy peeked out of the door to make doubly sure it was safe to come out. She had been cleaning rooms when she heard some loud splashing behind the end cabin. Assuming it was merely a pesky seal up on the float, she lurched around the cabin clapping her hands to chase it off, but instead came, literally, face to face with bears, bumping the nose of the first of the four grizzlies. She was able to retrace her steps backwards around the building and then dove for a door while the mama was still distracted shaking the water out of her fur.

We were all shell-shocked! Grizzly bears have always been around, but never in thirty-seven years had they climbed onto our floats. We didn't have much time to process what had happened because our fishing guests were coming in shortly and we had to get ready for them. Casey and Jessy used the fire pump on the area where the bear found her food, and generously sprayed dish soap around to clear up the oily scum that was on the water between the logs. A grizzly can smell dead meat up to eighteen miles away, whereas we had smelled nothing. After the bears left, there was a lot of noisy activity around the lodge: crew cleaning everything, boats coming in full of chatty guests excited over the beautiful fish they caught, the fuel barge fuelling our tanks and planes arriving to whisk our guests back to town. After all that had been going on, I was confident that the bears wouldn't be back. We had a new box of bear bangers and a few bear-spray canisters arrive on the plane, just in case.

No guests were scheduled to come in that day, so we relaxed a little thinking the grizzlies would be miles away by now. Several of the crew jumped overboard for a cooling swim. I stood at the side of the dock joking with the swimmers while keeping an eye peeled for bears. "So

Chase, how do you like swimming with the grizzlies?" Ha ha! The kids climbed out of the water and headed for the hot tub. Within seconds, I heard a bear-banger blast and turned to see Casey heading over to me. He shouted that there was a bear swimming just twenty feet from the float where I was standing, where the kids had just seconds before climbed out. Casey set off a couple more bear bangers then jumped in the boat and started then gunned the engine in an effort to scare the bear into turning away. When he didn't, a dripping-wet Jessy jumped in behind him, and Casey positioned the boat to stop the grizzly from getting closer to the lodge. With Casey driving and Jessy poking at the bear's giant rump with a paddle, the grizzly grumbled and turned to eye them, then snapped at the paddle. But they were able to herd the bear out of the bay and over to the far shore.

Later, we all had dinner in the lodge and discussed where the safest place was to be for the night. We came to the conclusion that there was really no safe place to be. Maybe up the ladder in Casey's old attic bedroom. A grizzly wouldn't be very good on a ladder, but it could certainly make its way up any of the sets of stairs or through any door or window. The conservation officer that Casey had spoken to in the afternoon said to be extra vigilant since the mama had found a reward. "They will be back," the officer said. I finished dinner and opened the sliding glass door to head over to my house. Remembering to be extra vigilant, I looked both ways and there in the evening mist were the four grizzlies, fifty feet away, snuffling around looking for more tidbits. I had to do a double take, not believing my eyes. This time, we all stayed in the lodge while Casey went out and shot a few more bear bangers off. If nothing else, we were too noisy to be good neighbours, and the bears finally left. The next day, the Fisheries officer brought Casey a box of rubber bullets, designed to hurt like hell but not damage the bear. If the noise didn't get them to leave, this was the next step in deterrents.

The bears showed themselves along the shore for another day and a half and then finally moved on. They didn't come back that summer, but I never stopped looking over my shoulder—just in case. They seem to be too accustomed to humans, and they really weren't bothered by us at all. My dog is on lockdown, we're now shutting doors behind us, and the new bear spray canisters are located all around the docks within easy reach. It feels like our tranquil Rivers Lodge is under siege.

Whenever I spoke with guests, I mentioned that this was going to be my last summer at the lodge. I have decided not to run it any longer. I have put the lodge out to the universe and am confident that the right people will come along and put in an offer. Near the end of the summer, I was chatting with a group of avid fishermen on the last day of their stay. Before I knew it, I was shaking hands with one of the fellows over the price of the lodge. These men are the new group who now own the lodge. They are the type of fishermen whose eyes shine when they talk about their fishing experiences.

I love you, Dear,

Pat

No More

Dear George:

I will miss the country. But wait! First I will tell you what I won't miss. These are the things I'm looking forward to saying goodbye to:

- No more twenty-hour workdays.
- No more cooking, cooking, cooking.
- No more extreme fears about guest safety.
- No more hassle of changing offices, moving paperwork back and forth from the lodge to town and trying to remember how to set everything up again.
- No more waking up at 3 AM to check to make sure the breakfast cook is in the kitchen. Sometimes she wasn't, then I would have to scramble to wake her and help with breakfast. Of course, sometimes it was just me! Nope. Not one more time.
- No gardening in my life because I haven't had time in the past nine years.
- No more being responsible to repair boats that have broken down.
- No more being responsible for forty people at a time all summer.
- No more staff creating hell on water.

- No more worrying about the floats sinking.
- No more arranging and managing caretakers.
- No more Fisheries', halibut quota, salmon, licences.
- No more little inspectors who want to make a name for themselves.
- No more assholes trying to take advantage of me.
- No more Canada Revenue Agency.
- No more HST and GST.
- No more Workers Compensation—paperwork, timing, safety rules overkill, getting crew to wear life jackets while working on the floats!
- No more end-of-year paperwork—*tons* of paperwork.
- No more Transport Canada regulations—boat rules, boat licences, boat registration, boat-*driving* licences.
- No more Land Management—increasing taxes times twenty in one fell swoop.
- No more foreshore lease rules, water rights.
- No more health inspector—demanding no towels, no hand soap, must use paper towels, no-touch soap dispensers, so no more pretty shellfish hand soaps, testing water we have been drinking for the past thirty-seven years, testing everything.
- No more Liquor Distribution Branch.
- No sanitation levies and inspections, no more incinerator rules.
- No more cooking, cooking, cooking. Even though I have always produced gorgeous food with pride.
- No more eight-thousand-dollar gas bills—in one single bill!
- No more otters pooping on stored furniture over the winter.
- No more ridiculous, expensive insurance.
- No more accounting all year long.
- Did I mention cooking? No more.
- Too many distressing, panic-filled boat trips. No more.
- Too many edge-of-my-seat flights in small planes, in fog, in high winds, wondering will we make it before dark? Nope.
- No more missing my friends all summer.
- No more smiling at people when I actually feel like crying.
- No more having to make decisions with no "you" to help me.

I will sorely miss the country. The wilderness. The mountains and the wildlife. I will miss the quiet of the fall, winter and spring, and the sound of an eagle skimming over my head. I will miss my inlet friends. And I will miss showing new people the spectacular scenery. I will miss so many of our guests, many of whom became like family. And long-time crewmembers who are still like family. I will miss the seals, otters and herons in my backyard. The grizzly bears … not so much. I will miss the Milky Way and the Big Dipper, which I communed with every night when I turned off the generator.

I will miss the whales. We watched whales from the shore of the lighthouse. We watched them from boats. We had both orcas and humpback whales appear at our wedding. We watched them from the front of our house float in our tiny bay. I will miss their graceful and smooth yet massive shapes as they glide out of the water, blow a fishy mist and then slide gently back in. I will miss the orcas always travelling in a group, often with little ones that somehow manage to keep up. I will miss the humpbacks, usually travelling alone, or travelling in twos.

There is something so magical in the way whales surface and take a look around. They have caught up to us before and swum beside our boat, surfacing and looking right at us as we stand holding our breath, holding the camera close instead of taking pictures. Not wanting to lose the moment by looking through a viewfinder. We have sat rocking in the flybridge at the top of *Sportspage*, watching an incredible dance of orcas slapping their tails, floating on the surface and hitting the water with their side fins then leaping right out of the water to twist and fall back down again with an enormous white wave that rocked our boat again and again. We have watched mother humpbacks teaching their young how to jump— its mammoth form surging high out of the water only to be followed by a smaller form triumphantly pushing its head out of the water and flopping sideways. Not quite the same show of power and strength but fun to watch.

I will miss the exhilaration of catching my own fish and digging clams and pulling a trap heavy with Dungeness crabs. I will miss reaching into the ocean and plucking out dinner: mussels and clams, seaweed and kelp, abalone, rock scallops, prawns, salmon, halibut and cod! And sea cucumbers! Yes, they are gross looking but quite tasty. Oh, what feasts we have had over the years. With little more than garlic butter, a fresh loaf of bread and a few greens. Still the best meals of all. Here in town we have to mortgage the farm to buy crab, scallops or halibut. And they are *never* as fresh.

I will miss the feeling of pride in our accomplishments, how the lodge had a life of its own. Pride in how we kept thousands of people happy and safe over all these years. How we kept staff secure and happy through some very trying times. I will miss our bay, which is as healthy after thirty-seven years as it was the day we moved into it. I feel richer for the experience of living in the wilderness and, yes, even thankful for having had the close encounter with the grizzly bears.

But most of all, I will miss you. Love of my life, funniest, most caring, eccentric and adventurous father of our darling children. I miss seeing you walk into a room, breaking into a huge grin when you see me there. I miss hearing you call out that you are home. I miss our chats over coffee any time of day. I miss falling asleep on your shoulder. I miss your spirit and capacity to try new things. I miss bouncing new ideas off of you and feeding you new recipes. I miss having you bring me coffee in bed on your early-rising ski days ... only to wake up an hour later and wonder why you brought me cold coffee ... again. I miss your surprises. You, who love surprises! I miss you every day. I carry you close in my heart and thank you again for helping us through these past many years.

I'll love you forever,

Pat

Epilogue—*Il Dolce Far Niente*

I did it! I sold the lodge. And now I am staying in town for the summer. *Il dolce far niente* is my favourite phrase from this summer. It means, "the sweetness of doing nothing." I have excelled at doing nothing. Just sitting in the beautiful garden, watching the vegetables grow in the deluxe raised garden boxes that I built in early July to match my fence. This is the first summer in thirty-seven years where I have sat outside just to enjoy being outside. By the time the weather was warm enough to want to sit outside at the lodge, there would be a dozen crewmembers running around in all directions at once, and I could not make myself sit still when everyone else was busy.

Casey and Lindsay on their wedding day.

Jessy is now a nurse.

People have asked me again and again over the summer, "What are you doing now? What are you going to do?" My first answers were along the lines of "Wait a minute, give me some time to breathe." This eventually turned into being able to proudly say, "Nothing, I'm just watching my vegetables grow." No guilt, no apologies, no explanations. I have sat in my Adirondack chair, which I also built at the beginning of the summer, and read stacks of books. When my eyes get tired of the close-up work, I turn them to look at the vegetables and the flowers and the apples in the tree above me. Such sweetness of doing nothing! I am grateful and I am happy.

Me, happy at home with champagne and berries.